The Early Childhood Graduate Practitioner Competencies

The Early Childhood Graduate Practitioner Competencies

A Guide for Professional Practice

Editor
Carolyn Silberfeld

Contributing Authors:
Gayle Blackburn, Sigrid Brogaard-Clausen, Lindey Cookson, Michelle Cottle,
Carol Fenton, Janice Grinstead, Diana Harris, Jill Harrison, Eunice Lumsden,
Bruce Marjoribanks, Helen Perkins, Tanya Richardson, Julie Sealy,
Helen Simmons, Emma Twigg & Helen Haygarth

Los Angeles | London | New Delhi
Singapore | Washington DC | Melbourne

Los Angeles | London | New Delhi
Singapore | Washington DC | Melbourne

SAGE Publications Ltd
1 Oliver's Yard
55 City Road
London EC1Y 1SP

SAGE Publications Inc.
2455 Teller Road
Thousand Oaks, California 91320

SAGE Publications India Pvt Ltd
B 1/I 1 Mohan Cooperative Industrial Area
Mathura Road
New Delhi 110 044

SAGE Publications Asia-Pacific Pte Ltd
3 Church Street
#10-04 Samsung Hub
Singapore 049483

Acquisitions editor: Delayna Spencer
Production editor: Zoheb Khan
Copyeditor: Sarah Bury
Proofreader: Brian McDowell
Indexer: Cathryn Pritchard
Marketing manager: Lorna Patkai
Cover design: Wendy Scott
Typeset by: KnowledgeWorks Global Ltd.
Printed in the UK

Library of Congress Control Number: 2022931371

British Library Cataloguing in Publication data

A catalogue record for this book is available from the British Library.

ISBN 978-1-5297-6011-8
ISBN 978-1-5297-6010-1 (pbk)

This book is dedicated to all those
who have helped to make this seminal text a reality.

CONTENTS

ABOUT THE EDITOR

Carolyn Silberfeld is Chair Emerita of the Early Childhood Studies Degrees Network (ECSDN). She spent 26 years developing and leading Early Childhood Studies degrees contributing to all aspects of their development, including development of the QAA ECS Benchmark statements, and practitioners' options. Developing the Early Childhood Graduate Practitioner competencies has been the culmination of all the work she has done to enable Early Childhood Studies graduates to practise at graduate level. Carolyn has a professional background in health (children's nursing, midwifery, health visiting), social sciences (BSc), teaching (PGCEA, Surrey), education (MEd, Cambridge) and practitioner research (MEd, Institute of Education), and has worked in many different settings, cultures and contexts. Carolyn has taught in HE since 1988 and her research interests include children's learning and development, national and international child health and wellbeing, reflective learning in higher education and the influence of studying abroad. Carolyn coordinated several international projects, including student exchanges to Europe, Africa, Australia and North America. This has all contributed to her pedagogic approach, which views childhood as being contextual and holistic. During the last two years, she has very much enjoyed being part of the Early Years Coalition, leading the Child Development section of Birth to Five Matters, and participating in the CPD working group.

ABOUT THE CONTRIBUTORS

Gayle Blackburn qualified as a Primary teacher with a specialism in Early Years in 2000. The Early Years has always been of interest to her. Gaye has worked in education for over 20 years in Primary settings, Further Education and Higher Education. Her career has always involved supporting students in childhood settings and enabling them to meet the needs of children and improving their outcomes. Gayle's current role as a Senior Lecturer in Childhood Studies at the University of Sunderland involves leading on the Early Childhood Graduate Practitioner Competencies and encouraging students to be proactive in developing their skills in a range of settings and promoting their reflective skills. Her PhD research is based on attachments and the importance of attachments in the Early Years and how these impact on development and outcomes for children. Gayle is also a Senior Fellow of the Higher Education Academy.

Sigrid Brogaard-Clausen's education as a Danish Social Pedagogue forms the platform for her work in Early Childhood Studies, influencing her role as both a lecturer/tutor and researcher. Her research focus is on young children's wellbeing, and democratic principles and practice in early childhood. Her research has included young children's engagement, wellbeing and assessment, professional and parental understandings of young children's wellbeing, as well as the identity formation of the Early Childhood professional, and comparative curricula policy studies, especially with knowledge of English and Danish Early Childhood systems and pedagogies. Empowering Early Childhood students and professionals with democratic and holistic approaches to working with young children, forming collegial and democratic professionalism, is her aim as an academic tutor, researcher and member of the Early Childhood Studies Degree Network (ECSDN). As a member of the ECSDN Executive Group, she has contributed to consultation and development of professionalism, such as in the Early Childhood Graduate Practitioner Competencies 2018, the Standard Occupational Qualifications 2020, Birth to Five Matters (Early Years Coalition 2020), Early Childhood Studies Benchmark Advisory Group 2021.

Lindey Cookson is a Principal Lecturer for Childhood Studies at the University of Sunderland. Lindey began her professional career as a Nursery Nurse and worked in a range of Early Years settings before graduating in Social Policy and moving into post-16/adult education and training roles. Lindey has developed and led Early Years and Childhood Studies programmes in Higher Education since 2005, with her research and teaching interests focused specifically around child development, social justice and inclusion, Early Childhood policy and leadership. Lindey is also a Senior Fellow of the Higher Education Academy and has many years of experience as an External Examiner for Early Years and Childhood Studies at other universities.

Michelle Cottle is a Senior Lecturer in Early Childhood Studies at the University of Roehampton. She originally trained as a primary teacher and taught in international schools for ten years. Since moving into higher education, her research and teaching has focused on policy and practice within Early Years settings and primary schools, specifically exploring understandings of quality and creativity in the context of neoliberal policymaking and the wellbeing of children and professionals connected to this. She is also interested in issues relating to the professionalisation of the Early Childhood workforce and the development of the Early Childhood Graduate Practitioner Competencies, professional identity, leadership, advocacy, curriculum and assessment. Michelle is committed to social justice and participatory research and is keen to explore the ways that theory can be used to challenge and counter performativity and inequality within educational institutions and to develop reflexivity and inclusive pedagogies.

Carol Fenton is a Senior Lecturer on the BA (Hons) Early Childhood Studies and a Fellow of the Higher Education Academy. Prior to joining the University of Derby, Carol worked as a primary school teacher and Head of Mathematics in a middle management role before acquiring a post as a primary school headteacher. She also taught vocational Early Years courses at a Further Education College in Nottingham. Carol has undertaken research into colour vision deficiency and the effects on social and emotional development in children, and the importance of continuing professional development in developing quality education in Higher Education. She lectures across the undergraduate programme, teaching modules on Leadership in the Early Years and Early Research.

Jan Grinstead is a retired Senior Lecturer for Childhood Studies at the University of Sunderland. Her research interests are centred around young children's learning and development and professionals who work with young children. She is also a Senior Fellow of the Higher Education Academy.

Diana Harris describes her professional career as a 'meandering pathway through education', working as a teacher, lecturer, mentor, facilitator and professional leader across nursery classes and infant schools, primary and secondary settings, Further Education and Higher Education. Individualism, freedom of choice, empowerment and pedagogical practice are her central principles and interests, alongside her passion for children's literature. Professional and personal values are interwoven. Diana strives to spend equal amounts of time reading in the library as weeding in her garden, interspersed with exploration of culture and spaces through travel. She remains a child at heart, which is probably why she initially trained as a qualified nursery infant teacher!

Jill Harrison is the academic portfolio lead for Early Years and link tutor for SEGI Colleges Malaysia. She has worked in Early Years for many years as an Early Years practitioner, working her way through the ranks to become a coordinator of a work-based nursery, and then a manager of a children's centre, which was part of a research project to introduce High/Scope to the sector. More recently, she has been a college lecturer before moving to the University of Greenwich. She now has a research focus on leadership and mentoring in the Early Years and is near completion of her research on 'Maids or Masters: A study reviewing the concepts of leadership in Early Years provision in Malaysia and England. She is an advocate for developing professionalism and raising standards across Early Years.

Helen Haygarth is a passionate Early Years advocate with 30 years' experience in a range of settings. Having successfully led provision for two-year olds she fully recognises that nurture and high-quality early years provision is key to transforming life opportunities for children. Helen has a firm belief in the holistic approach to education and care and currently works in Early Help where she specialises in early years and use of creative tools to gather the voice of the child. Helen is committed to empowering positive outcomes for children and their families. Helen also works for the University of Sunderland as an Academic Tutor supporting Childhood Studies students on several modules focusing on theory into practice, observations and assessments and supporting Early Childhood Graduate Practitioner Competency students in placement. Helen believes in creating a graduate workforce within early years and was the first student in the University of Sunderland to gain the Early Childhood Graduate Practitioner Competencies. Helen is continuing her studies studying part time for her MA in Childhood and Youth Studies.

Eunice Lumsden is the Subject Leader for Childhood, Youth and Families and an Associate Professor at the University of Northampton. She is also a Route Panel Member for the Institute of Apprenticeships and Technical Education, Fellow of the Royal Society of Arts, Senior Fellow of the Higher Education Academy, and a registered Social Worker. She has extensive experience working with children and families and her research interests include the professionalisation of the ECEC (Early Childhood Education and Care) workforce, child maltreatment, social justice, poverty and adoption. Her book on child protection (Lumsden, 2018) was shortlisted as the best professional book of the year in 2018. She has also received awards for her 'Changemaking' work, her contribution to improving child welfare, her contribution to equality, diversity and inclusion, and her research in the Early Years. Nationally, she has been a member of several external expert groups advising the Government on Early Years qualifications, the Health Inequalities Review and led the development of the Early Childhood Graduate Competencies for the Early Childhood Studies Network. She has also advised on workforce development internationally, including the inclusion of Early Childhood on the Sustainable Development Goals.

Bruce Marjoribanks has worked internationally in the UK, North America and Asia. Bruce is currently programme leader for the MA Childhood and Youth Studies at the University of Sunderland. His interests lie in multiculturalism and social justice, class, religions, race, gender, sexuality, and fair education – including the assessment and evaluation of community-based education programmes. Bruce has taught on the wide range of diversity issues reflected above, as well as on issues that are related to diverse communities, and is also a Senior Fellow of the Higher Education Academy.

Helen Perkins started teaching in the Foundation Stage in 1986. She then moved in to further and higher education 2002, beginning her academic career in FE first as a tutor, then as Head of School for Early Childhood Studies at Solihull College. Following six years at The University of Wolverhampton, as Programme lead for Early Childhood Studies, Helen is now an Associate Lecturer at the Open University and an Honorary Research Fellow at the University of Wolverhampton. Helen received her Doctorate in 2017 from the University of Sheffield. She is an executive member of the Early Childhood Studies Degrees Network (ECSDN) with responsibility for the Research and Knowledge Exchange portfolio. Helen's research interests are the professionalisation of the Early Childhood Workforce and the Role of Men in Childcare.

Dr Tanya Richardson is a Senior Lecturer in Early Years at the University of Northampton and is Programme Leader for the Early Childhood Studies programmes. She has previously managed and led her own 'outstanding' day nursery and out-of-school club. The nursery setting was fortunate enough to have a forest school as part of its ethos and Tanya became very interested in the impact that this environment had on children's speech and language development. She is therefore lucky enough to have the practice wisdom that she is able to apply to the academic studies and her PhD researched the impact that different learning and play environments have on young children's speech and language development. She is also particularly interested in the student experience for those studying Early Childhood Studies and researches aspects with the aim to enhance this experience and produce professionals who will be excellent advocates for children and their families.

Julie Sealy is a Senior Lecturer in the Early Years Department of the Faculty of Education and has led the Early Childhood Studies programme at Edge Hill University for the past five years. Dr Sealy has worked for over 25 years in Early Years practice in the Caribbean, working predominantly with families and children with developmental challenges. She is the former founding director of an early intervention centre in Barbados that provides essential services for at-risk children and disadvantaged families.

Helen Simmons is a Senior Lecturer in Education (Childhood, Youth and Families) in the Faculty of Health, Education and Society at the University of Northampton, UK. Helen has worked in Higher Education since 2008 and, prior to this, she was a practitioner in early years settings, worked as a private nanny and taught vocational early years courses at Further Education and Sixth Form Colleges. Helen has undertaken research and publication relating to leadership in early childhood and early childhood policy. Her doctoral research and subsequent monograph '*Surveillance of Modern Motherhood*' provided a feminist post-structuralist analysis of experiences of new mothers who have attended universal parenting courses. Helen is Vice Chair for the Early Childhood Studies Degrees Network (ECSDN): Policy, Lobbying and Advocacy (National and International) and is a Senior Fellow of the Higher Education Academy. Her research interests include the sociology of childhood, modern parenting, children's workforce development and critically reflective practice.

Emma Twigg is the Programme Leader and Senior Lecturer on the BA (Hons) Early Childhood Studies degree at the University of Derby and a Fellow of the Higher Education Academy. Her background is within the Early Years, qualifying as an NNEB nursery nurse and working as a nursery assistant and manager of a couple of day nurseries. While working as a Childcare Improvement Officer for the local authority, Emma completed her BA (Hons) Early Childhood Studies degree and later started teaching at the university. Her published research and interests focus on play and creativity, childcare law, safeguarding and child protection. Emma has recently started a PhD focusing on the experiences of children exposed to domestic abuse.

PREFACE AND INTRODUCTION

Carolyn Silberfeld

This seminal text introduces students, lecturers, teachers, mentors, professionals and practitioners to Early Childhood Graduate Practitioner Competencies, which can be completed as part of an Early Childhood Studies Degree. Graduate practitioners will be competent to practise at Level 6 in Early Childhood settings, within health, social care, education and care settings.

It has been written by those who have been involved in the writing of the competencies and those who have pioneered the competencies by embedding them in their Early Childhood Studies degrees. The authors come from seven of the eight universities which pioneered the competencies in September 2018. The first graduates, who had the competencies integrated into the third year of their degree, achieved the competencies the following year. Those whose competencies were integrated into the second year of their degree achieved them in June 2020. The majority of students undertaking the competencies undertook them throughout the three years of their degree and should achieve them in June 2021.

Although each author was responsible for a particular chapter, they are familiar with all the competencies. This means that they could all be critical friends for other chapters within the book. Meetings relating to the book were attended by all the authors, if available, and all the authors have read and commented on all of the chapters. In addition, students, graduates, practitioners and colleagues have been consulted as to the 'fit for purpose' nature of the chapters in relation to the competencies.

We are extremely proud of all those students, graduates, staff and colleagues who have so wholeheartedly embraced the Early Childhood Graduate Practitioner Competencies. I, personally, feel enormous pride to have been involved at the start of the journey, to have evaluated all eight pioneering programmes in April/May 2019, and to have proposed the book to Delayna Spencer at SAGE, who has provided magnificent support for the project, advising, encouraging and supporting us all so well.

The structure of this book is based on the nine competencies which graduate practitioners will have met through assessed placement tasks, observations of practice and academic assignments (Early Childhood Studies Degrees Network (ECSDN), 2019). There has been an attempt to give the chapters consistency by using similar features of reflective questions and first-hand accounts from professionals, practitioners and students. We were guided in this by Jill Harrison and Diana Harris, who wrote the initial draft chapter (Chapter 2), which was used as a template for the other competency chapters.

Chapter 1, comprising the introduction to the book, has been written by the pioneer of the early childhood graduate practitioner competencies, Eunice Lumsden. Eunice has inspired others to 'dive' into the unknown and has helped develop the competencies into what they have become today. Eunice charts her own journey as well as the rationale and development of Early Childhood Studies (ECS) degrees in all their complexities. She explains why it is important for ECS graduates to be competent graduate practitioners who can work with young children in a broad spectrum of settings and organisations.

Chapter 2 was the first draft chapter to be written. Its focus is on *Competency 1 – Advocating for Young Children's Rights and Participation.* Key to the chapter is the importance of how practitioners listen and take seriously the voice of the child in their daily practice. It considers how a graduate-level professional should lead practice within an Early Childhood context and have the skills and strategies to advocate for children and families. Jill and Diana have included a fascinating interview with Alison Clark, who developed the listening tools of the Mosaic Approach to gain deeper understanding of children's perspectives and improve Early Childhood provision.

Child development underpins our knowledge and understanding of young children. Chapter 3, focusing on *Competency 2 – Promote Holistic Child Development,* has been written by Tanya Richardson, who supported the first Early Childhood Graduate Practitioner Competencies graduate. This is not a typical chapter on child development as its focus is on how practitioners can promote and support young children's holistic development, rather than the characteristics of how children develop. Tanya's interview with parents shows how the context of a child's life can impact on their development. Using interviews in this way helps practitioners develop their own knowledge of child development and enhances their practical application of that knowledge.

In Chapter 4, Helen Simmons and Carol Fenton focus on *Competency 3 – Work Directly with Young Children, Families and Colleagues to Promote Health, Wellbeing, Safety and Nurturing Care.* It considers the importance of these skills and how practitioners can demonstrate their knowledge and understanding of these skills when leading practice in an Early Childhood context. Although Early Childhood health and safety policies contextualise this chapter, readers are signposted to relevant policy rather than a detailed interrogation of different policies, which are covered in more depth in Chapter 6.

Chapter 5 focuses on *Competency 4 – Observe, Listen and Plan for Young Children to Support their Wellbeing, Early Learning, Progression and Transitions.* Gayle Blackburn and Jan Grinstead emphasise the need for practitioners to examine their own pedagogy and values when observing and listening to children, to focus on what children are doing and the importance of including parents and carers in this process. Leuven's scale of wellbeing and involvement is used as an example of how practitioners can assess children's emotional wellbeing to inform their planning of activities and experiences, which are underpinned by child-centred play.

Drawing on her background in Social Work, Eunice Lumsden focuses on *Competency 5 – Safeguarding and Child Protection* in Chapter 6, written with Emma Twigg. It will help students to understand the complexities involved in safeguarding children and the challenges faced when working with other practitioners and professionals who may hold different perspectives.

Inclusive practice is the focus of Competency 6 and Chapter 7, written by Bruce Marjoribanks Lindey Cookson and Helen Haygarth. It encourages practitioners to consider how they can lead practice within the Early Childhood context using knowledge, skills and strategies to include all children and families. As well as offering an operational definition of inclusion and inclusive practice, this chapter uses Bronfenbrenner's Ecological Systems theory to show the complexities of children's lives which need to be understood if practitioners are going to develop a pedagogy of inclusive practice.

In Chapter 8, Julie Sealy focuses on *Competency 7 – Partnership with Parents and Caregivers*. She also uses Bronfenbrenner's Ecological System's theory and leads on beautifully from the previous chapter. This chapter helps to develop practitioners' reflective practice and inclusivity in their communication and relationships with parents and carers, showing how practitioners can develop real partnerships with parents and carers, rather than the rhetoric we see so much in practice.

Helen Perkins' focus on *Competency 8 – Collaborating with Others* in Chapter 9 uses different voices in this interesting and engaging chapter, bringing it alive and making it contextual. It follows on extremely well from the previous chapter and continues to develop the notion of respectful relationship with colleagues and other professionals working with young children. It explores how professionals from multidisciplinary perspectives can work together successfully as a team.

Competency 9 – Professional Development and Professional Identity in Chapter 10, is the final set of competencies which graduate practitioners need to demonstrate their knowledge and understanding. Sigrid Brogaard-Clausen and Michelle Cottle use the voices of students and practitioners to question the concept of democratic leadership through professional reflection. They demonstrate the importance of reflective praxis in professional development to transform practice and challenge inequality.

The final chapter looks forward to the continued professionalisation and development of the Early Childhood Graduate Practitioner Competencies. It highlights some of the challenges for all those involved in the graduate competencies and the political awareness that is required for understanding what is happening within Higher Education and policy. It emphasises the importance of mentorship and mentorship training for all professionals and practitioners involved in the graduate competencies.

Lastly, we have provided a glossary of the terminology used in this book and some examples of the professional roles in which the graduates may be employed. We hope you will find the features of this seminal book useful and interesting.

On a personal note, editing this book, as well as contributing to it, has been, in many respects, the culmination of my 28-year involvement with Early Childhood Studies Degrees.

ACKNOWLEDGEMENTS

We would like to thank all the members of the ECSDN who contributed to the development of the Early Childhood Graduate Practitioner Competencies, most especially the authors who initially embedded the competencies into their ECS degrees and who developed much of the programme materials which are in use today. It could not have been written without the support of the students, early childhood settings and the authors' families and friends.

Special thanks and appreciation must go to Delayna Spencer who has guided and supported us all during the process.

Chapter 1

INTRODUCTION TO THE EARLY CHILDHOOD GRADUATE PRACTITIONER COMPETENCIES

Eunice Lumsden

Chapter Aims

This chapter introduces you to the Early Childhood Graduate Practitioner Competencies and the historical and contemporary context of Early Childhood Studies. By the end of the chapter, you should understand:

- the importance of engaging with policy
- the policy context from which the study of early childhood emerged
- the different terms used in early childhood
- the factors leading to the development of the Early Childhood Graduate Practitioner Competencies
- the cycle and importance of applying knowledge to practice

Introduction

When, as a social worker, I stumbled on the study of Early Childhood, I felt I had found a community where the rights of the child were at its heart, a place where I felt at home. I hope this introduction and the chapters that follow enable you to see yourself as a member of this community of practice, a community that is unapologetic in striving for excellence for all infants, children and their families. As Rumi, the Turkish philosopher, stated: 'what you seek is seeking you'.

It is therefore my privilege to introduce you to the academic study of Early Childhood and the Early Childhood Graduate Practitioner Competencies. These were written to ensure that students studying the degrees, where they are embedded, are equipped with graduate-level knowledge, higher-level skills and professional behaviours in applying this learning in work with children and families. The competencies are assessed throughout the degree, with a final assessment in year three (Level 6) or as part of post-graduate study. They are not a professional status akin to teaching, social work or nursing; rather, they are a vehicle for you to learn about the holistic development of children in the early childhood period in an ecological context. They will promote the development of higher-level skills in applying this knowledge to promoting young children's development, nurturing their identity and agency, and ensuring that their *voices are* heard in the systems they interact with, regardless of what career trajectory is pursued.

In the discussion that follows I want to return to the core of the Early Childhood Studies degree, which was introduced as an interdisciplinary programme of study. It is taught by academics who reflect the different disciplines and professions that occupy the early childhood space. It is an area of study located in the social sciences that has evolved to have its own Benchmark Statement (Quality Assurance Agency (QAA), 2022), which identifies the subject knowledge to be taught on the degree.

You will be introduced to the context from which the degree emerged and the contemporary context in which your studies are situated. Through engaging with the voices of those who were instrumental in developing the degree and the competencies, you will begin to understand the important place of this degree in developing the professionals of tomorrow. Former students tell us how important their studies have been in providing a foundation for what comes next in their personal and professional journeys.

The Importance of Understanding Policy

One rationale for the development of competencies was in response to the complex policy landscape in which the study of early childhood is nested (Bronfenbrenner, 2005; Fitzgerald and Maconochie, 2020; Winstone, 2020). However, students often commence an Early Childhood Studies degree with little knowledge or understanding about the socio-political and policy context of working with children and families. Anecdotally, many also report challenges in engaging and understanding the relevance of policy to their studies. However, students need to know, critique and develop skills in understanding and applying a range of policies to practice. They also need to engage with structural and health inequalities, racism and other oppressive behaviours that impact on early childhood and life chances (Marmot, 2020; Tedam, 2021; Thompson, 2021a).

Exploring these areas both theoretically and in practice provides rich learning opportunities which reinforce that legislation and policies are not something 'out there'; rather, they impact everything. You need to understand it, interact with and use your learning to shape professional practice.

For those of you new to policy, it is best understood as 'a process, something ongoing, interactional and unstable' (Ball, 2017: 10). It helps to consider it being located in two broad areas (Ball, 2017):

Policy with a big 'P' that emerges from legislation (the law). Health, education and social care, for example, all have legislation relevant to their specific area and the policy and procedures that stem from it. There is also legislation relevant to them all, such as Health and Safety and Data Protection.

Legislation may be static or amended over time through subsequent legislation. The Children Act 1989 (Legislation.gov.uk, 1989) is an example here. It is still the main legislative framework for public and private law concerning children. However, it has been added to or amended by, for example, the Adoption and Childcare Act 2002 (Legislation.gov.uk, 2002), the Children Act 2004 (Legislation.gov.uk, 2004) and the Children and Families Act 2014 (Legislation.gov.uk 2014).

The policy that emerges from the legislation is also not always static. It evolves, reflecting learning from practice, case law or changes in policy direction and/or the ideology of the political party in government. An example here is the *Statutory Framework for the Early Years Foundation Stage* (EYFS) in England, which covers children aged 0–5 in England (Department for Education (DfE), 2021). The legislation for the *Statutory Framework* can be found in the Childcare Act 2006 (Legislation.gov.uk, 2006). All settings need to follow it, but how it is operationalised depends on the setting and settings will have policies in place to support this. Bringing the EYFS alive is supported by *Development Matters Non-statutory Curriculum Guidance for the Early Years Foundation Stage* (DfE, 2020a).

Policy with a small 'p' emerges at a local level or is relevant to a specific organisation. For example, as a student, your Higher Education institution will have policies in relation to assessment processes that you have to abide by. In the workplace, there are policies for how you apply for annual leave and record sickness.

The holistic nature of early childhood means that, regardless of the country that you live in, it is an area influenced by legislation and policies from a range of areas. Some of these are influenced by the United Nations Convention on the Rights of Children (UNCRC) (UN General Assembly, 1989) and the Sustainable Development Goals (United Nations, 2015).

If we focus specifically on the Graduate Practitioner Competencies, the knowledge is derived from the QAA Early Childhood Studies Benchmark Statement (QAA, 2019), and the practice skills are based on those required to work with infants, young children and adults in different contexts, including those described by Thompson (2021b) as *people skills*. They are also connected to legislation and policy that address such things as child health, public health, early learning, family support, safeguarding and child protection.

In summary, understanding how Early Childhood is linked to legislation and policies is key. It is the only area of human development where so many theories, laws, policies, professionals and organisations interact together. This reinforces the importance of the interdisciplinary knowledge you will study and the skills you will develop to enable you to work in multi-professional contexts and with other agencies (inter-agency/multi-agency working).

Understanding the Study of Early Childhood

This section explores Early Childhood as an area of study, its relationship with more specialist areas and how the Graduate Competencies aim to provide the higher-level skills to apply the knowledge in different specialist areas. Those studying Early Childhood need to understand the range of terms used by the different disciplines and occupations inhabiting the Early Childhood space.

As a student of Early Childhood, you will access and develop language that is subject- or occupation-specific, or where the same terms are used by all but are nuanced or used and understood differently depending on the context. For example, Early Years practitioners, teachers, social workers, family workers and health practitioners, including midwives, health visitors and infant mental health workers, all have different roles and may use the same word but interpret it differently. The word 'transitions' is a useful example. In health, it may mean the transition from the midwife to the health visitor, or to different stages of an illness or disease. In social work, it may be for the children's family into foster care. In education, it could be the transition from a year group to the next, or in preschool provision, for one room to the another.

Before introducing some of the terminology and debates embedded within them, I would like you to complete Activity 1.1 *What does this mean to you?* Understanding how others see things is a crucial skill, but it is also important that you reflect on your understanding.

Activity 1.1

What does this mean to you?

One of the most important skills you need when working with children and families interdisciplinary and multi-professionally is the ability to ask questions that provide new insights. The question '*What does this mean for you?*' is one that you will use repeatedly in your career. It is important to ask this question constantly of yourself as well.

Part One

Write down what the following terms mean to you:

Early Childhood
Early Childhood Development
Early Years
Early Childhood Education and Care
Early Childhood Education
Early Childhood Services

Part Two

Ask a peer(s) what these terms mean to them.

Part Three

On your programme of study, reflect on how the challenges of terminology have been addressed.

By comparing your answers with those of your peer(s), you will begin to develop an understanding of the nuances and different views that emerge in Early Childhood Studies. This in turn, will enable you to critique and position yourself in the subject area you are studying – this is important.

The terms briefly addressed below aim to highlight the breadth of the subject area so that you can develop your understanding of the complex debates that operate in Early Childhood Studies. This understanding will enable you articulate to others what differentiates you as an Early Childhood Studies student and why the Graduate Practitioner Competencies are not just focused on practice in Early Childhood preschool settings, but are caught up in debates about graduate leaders in Early Childhood Education and Care (ECEC) (QAA, 2019).

Early Childhood is a specific period of childhood development, from conception and usually ending at the age of eight (Murray, Swadener and Smith, 2020). In some societies and cultures, this is different and the transition to middle childhood range from five to eight years (Berk, 2012).

The holistic nature of this period for all children is captured effectively by Britto, Engle and Super (2013). They use the term **Early Childhood Development** (ECD) to embrace conception to the age of eight, or when the transition into school is complete. They argue that the term captures:

> … a multifaceted concept from an ecological framework that focuses on the child's
> outcomes (development), which depends on characteristics of the child and the context,
> such as health, nutrition, protection, care and/or education. (Britto et al., 2013: 4)

It is important to note here that, globally, children start formal education at different ages. Many children do not have access to education and, even if they do, they face barriers accessing it (UNICEF, 2020). In England, school starts in the September of the year that children are five, so some children can still be four years old, sometimes up to a year younger than others in their class. In many European countries, the age at which children start school is around seven (World Bank, 2020), which is more aligned to the definition of the Early Childhood period as being to the age of eight (UN General Assembly, 1989).

It is this multifaceted approach in an ecological context that is embraced in the Early Childhood Studies degree. The *Early Childhood Studies Benchmark Statement* (QAA, 2022) recognises that Early Childhood begins at conception but does not include a higher age boundary. Students need to understand Early Childhood in the ecological context of families, communities and the services they engage with at a local, national and international level. It is this breadth that distinguishing students of Early Childhood from others and provides the foundation for you to become more expert in Early Childhood and/or pursue more specialist career areas in, for example, health, education or social care. This is no different from programmes that award a professional status where different specialist branches of the profession can be pursued post-qualification.

The breadth and depth of knowledge and understanding required in Early Childhood is has been recognised in the Sustainable Development Goals (SDGs) (United Nations, 2015). I had the privilege of being involved in the movement and consultation processes that led to Early Childhood being included in them. The debates were complex but crucial, as the inclusion of Early Childhood was a signal that ECD was important for the sustainable development of all societies. Commentators were concerned about whether its inclusion in the form it took, located in the broader education goal (SDG 4), was the right one. SDG 4.2 states that by 2030 all countries should: 'ensure that all girls and boys have access to quality early childhood development, care and pre-primary education so that they are ready for primary education' (United Nations, 2015). However, as the policy brief commissioned by the Department for International Affairs (DFID) in 2016 stated:

> ECD is about so much more than this single education target. Quality ECD is fundamental to achieving the SDGs related to poverty and inequality, gender and social inclusion, health, well-being and the promotion of sustainable futures for all. (Woodhead, 2016: 5)

This reinforces the importance of the ecological study of Early Childhood, differentiating it but also providing insights into the breadth of knowledge required. While the study of Early Childhood is not a profession in its own right, it does provide transferable knowledge and skills that can be developed in the different career directionsyou might follow.

It is this differentiation that people sometimes find difficult to fully appreciate. It is therefore helpful to think about the Early Childhood Studies degree in relation to generalist versus specialist debates. These debates are complex but, in short, the degree is generalist, enabling you to gain breadth and depth of knowledge of the ecological context of the multifaceted area of child development within a global context. What differentiates those with placements or with the Graduate Competencies embedded are the opportunities to develop key skills in the application of knowledge aligned to different occupational areas in Early Childhood (see Chapter 10).

Nested in the study of Early Childhood are a range of other terms that relate to the different occupations and specialist services:

Early Childhood Education and Care (ECEC) is used to embrace the importance of both 'care' and 'education', in the pre-statutory education period (often referred to as preschool), in different systems internationally. It is supplementary to the family, as it is the family who has primary and legal responsibility for the health, wellbeing and care of their children.

It is important to note that some countries and organisations prefer to use **Early Childhood Care and Education (ECCE)** instead, emphasising the importance of nurturing care. The United Nations Educational and Scientific and Cultural Organisation (UNESCO) originally used the term ECEC (UNESCO, 2006), which they defined as:

> Growth, development and learning-including health, nutrition and hygiene, and cognitive, social, physical and emotional development-from birth to entry to primary school in formal, informal and non-formal settings. (UNESCO, 2006: 3)

More recently, they have used the term ECCE, which they argue:

> …is more than preparation for primary school. It aims at the holistic development of a child's social, emotional, cognitive and physical needs in order to build a solid and broad foundation for lifelong learning and wellbeing. ECCE has the possibility to nurture caring, capable and responsible future citizens. (UNESCO, 2021: lines 7–11)

What is important here is the nuances in the two definitions that evidence the shift to consider investing in Early Childhood for economic return (Robert-Homes and Moss, 2021).

In the United Kingdom, the importance of 'care' and 'education' in provision outside the family has a long history (Male and Palaiologou, 2021). In England, the Childcare Act 2006 enshrined ECEC into law, placing equal weight on both in the Early Years Foundation Stage (EYFS) (Section 39), thus locating ECEC firmly as part of the education system. The EYFS covers the period from birth to five years old, therefore from non-statutory ECEC provision to the end of the reception year in the statutory education system.

Early Childhood Education (ECE) is used instead of ECEC, emphasising the focus on early education and learning. 'Care' is seen as implicit in this area of the education system (Cameron and Moss, 2020; Moss, 2013).

Early Years is a generic term in common usage in education, health and social care.

Early Childhood Services includes universal services in health, social care/welfare and education and specialist services, for example, perinatal mental health services. There are also services, such as children centres or family services that provide universal and specialist services in one place.

The Historical Context of Early Childhood Degrees

The previous section has illustrated some of the terms you will engage with in your studies. It has also touched on some complex ideological and socio-political debates at the core of Early Childhood. There is a plethora of literature charting the history of welfare, health and educational provision in England, Europe and internationally (Ball 2003; Chitty, 2004; Male and Palaiologou, 2021; Melhuish, 2004; Oberhuemer, 2011). For those studying and working in this area, it is crucial to understand that contemporary issues are deeply linked to politics, the historical context of motherhood, the positioning of women in society (aee Activity 1.2), as well as the different approaches globally to health, social care and education services. There are ongoing debates and discussions about the nature of early childhood provision; whether it is more care or education. These discussions also reflect the challenges of the twin-track and multifaceted nature of the 'education' and 'care' systems that have existed (and continue to) in England and elsewhere (Calder, 1999; Cameron and Moss, 2020; Miller and Hevey, 2012).

Turning to the Early Childhood Studies degree specifically, it was, and continues to be, pioneering in its endeavours to develop an academic field that embraces the multifaceted study of early childhood. It continues to strive for higher-level study opportunities that contribute to a graduate workforce that understands the importance of a holistic approach to early childhood and can integrate knowledge of the care and education of young children (Calder, 2019).

The conversations in the following case studies with Pam Calder, the founder of the Early Childhood Studies Network, and Carolyn Silberfeld, former Chair of the Network, provide their insights and reflections on their pioneering work.

Case Study

In conversation with Pam Calder (Founder of the Early Childhood Studies Network and Honorary President)

What led you to becoming involved in the Network?

Twenty years of my earlier activism culminated in my campaigning with others for the necessity of creating a new and different, degree-level education and training, for all nursery staff, in Early Childhood Studies. With some success, in getting such degrees established, it became clear to me we needed to become an organisation. In 1993/94, I became the convenor and Chair of those of us in Higher Education who were advocating for and had begun developing the first such degrees, and the Network was born.

The reasons for me were threefold and linked:

1   To advocate for women's freedom from oppression, including for mothers to have the opportunity to enjoy having children, while combining this with taking part in public life and pursuing a career.
2   For that to be possible, to advocate for the provision of new resources/places [called] 'children's centres' where children, from being babies, could, for part of the (168 hour) week, be looked after – loved? – have fun, in relationships with other children and other adults.
3   The early childhood workers'/pedagogues' attitudes, knowledge and experience would be crucial and to develop such knowledge and research in the praxis of Early Childhood we needed a new subject area of Early Childhood Studies in universities.

Freedom from oppression also meant that to avoid yet more exploitation of women, the pedagogues' work, too, should be valued in professional degree-level pay and conditions, and this should be part of a wider advocacy for the values of democracy, and for recognising and opposing power inequalities based on gender, race and poverty.

What has motivated you to keep advocating for Early Childhood?

The problems I have been trying to solve as a feminist psychologist continue to keep me advocating for the significance of Early Childhood.

From my perspective of a social relational developmental psychology, early childhood is a crucial time for both theoretical and applied research into how babies become persons, and adults, and to how the relations they develop with other people and other people with them (interactions) contribute to their enjoyment in the present and to their development in the future.

Early childhood is also a critical time when babies are not independent beings, and cannot look after themselves, but the current default position, that it is the mother's responsibility to do so, is one challenged by feminism.

Finding a way to reconcile women's desires to have and bring up children, and to have their children flourish, without being the default providers of their care, for 24 hours of every day, is at the heart of trying to build a better system of support. This includes developing 'good quality' nurseries that support children, their parents, and the staff/pedagogues who work there.

Developing the knowledge and praxis of Early Childhood Development, as it relates to research, education and training, is of continuing theoretical, applied and policy interest to me.

Case Study

In conversation with Carolyn Silberfeld (Chair of the Early Childhood Studies Degree Network, 2015–2020)

I became involved in the ECSDN originally because we were one of five HEIs [Higher Education institutions] delivering the new Early Childhood Studies (ECS) degrees. It was an exciting time, with new developments emerging at each meeting and fascinating people with which to have discussions. I was proud to lead the first full-time, specially-written holistic programme about children and childhood, and I loved developing the degree. I was fortunate enough to be at the forefront of all the developments within the ECSDN, including the QAA ECS Benchmark Statements, which were essential to give credibility to the degrees as well as the underpinning of all ECS programmes, and the ECS degrees with Practitioner Options, agreed by the Department for Education, when we recognised that graduates needed to have practical experience as well as their academic qualification. This development was a forerunner to the Early Childhood Graduate Practitioner Competencies.

Early Childhood Studies encompassed all I thought and felt about children, their families and the wider community. One cannot separate children's complex existences into compartments and disciplines. My professional background in children's (and adults) nursing, midwifery and health visiting underpinned my knowledge and understanding about children and families; my academic background in Social Sciences and Research gave depth and breadth to my understanding; and the years I spent working abroad (and in the UK) helped me to develop greater cultural awareness, the knowledge and understanding of which should underpin all ECS degrees. I have had the privilege of leading two ECS degrees and contributing to three others during my retirement! In the beginning it was a struggle to have ECS degrees recognised as being credible academic programmes, and I have had to overcome many almost insurmountable challenges to develop them into the holistic programmes which they

(Continued)

should be. During this time, the support and encouragement from the ECSDN was essential in my endeavours. I have spent 28 years championing ECS degrees with colleagues from other professional, governmental and non-governmental organisations and academic institutions. I have been overjoyed about many of the developments which have happened during my professional life, but I have also been bitterly disappointed that policy is often formed by those who know little about young children. This is what keeps me striving in my passion to advocate for children, and always will.

Reflection Point

What led you to choose this area of study?
What is your ambition for yourself?
What is the gift you want to give children?

Activity 1.2

Early Childhood as a gendered space

One of the characteristics of this area of study and work is a gendered space. Many roles in health, ECEC and social care that are focused on children and families are prominently occupied by women. Reflect on the following questions:

1   What is your gender and background?
2   Are there any barriers you have experienced because of your gender, cultural and religious background or ethnicity?
3   What led you to study Early Childhood?
4   What are your career aspirations and how do you think they will be impacted as a consequence of your gender and background?
5   If you are a male, what additional issues do you face that challenge your reasons for wanting to work with children, such as your sexuality and how your female students and colleagues react to you?

In answering these questions, you are starting to position yourself in the debates about the place of women in society. Historically, women were regarded (and arguably still are) as the nurturers and carers of young children, a situation that is compounded by the misinterpretation of Bowlby's (1949) theory of maternal deprivation. This reinforced the status of women as being primarily responsible for childcare. If women displayed reluctance to be carers, they were deemed to be unnatural women (Noddings, 2001). The positioning of care as an extension of mothering, and therefore 'women's work', is one of the contributing factors that fuels the low status, low pay, low qualification levels and poor employment conditions that prevail in ECEC (Calder, 1999; Moss, 2006, Robert-Holmes and Moss, 2021) and other areas of care services internationally.

The Early Childhood Graduate Competencies

The Early Childhood Graduate Practitioner Competencies are courageous, pioneering and challenge us all, students and tutors alike, to reflect on our motivations, knowledge and practice. They emerged in response to a range of factors that reflect the different perspectives in Early Childhood and the increased global focus on this area. They are aspirational in their drive to shape a new genre of practitioner with transferable knowledge and skills, assessed at Level 6 (graduate), with international applicability and transferability.

The competencies aim:

1   To remove the confusion in the sector about how ECS degrees are aligned to practice requirements in the four nations of the UK.
2   To address the inherent challenges of different types of Early Childhood degrees and study pathways, enabling the wider workforce to be clear about individual early career graduates' expected level of knowledge, skills and actual experience in practice.
3   To acknowledge the different pathways that lead learners to undertake the degrees, enhance their practice experience and enhance their employability skills.
4   To ensure that Higher Education academic routes are responsive to the changing needs and training routes in Early Years practice, education and the wider children's services workforce.
5   To make a significant contribution to strengthening a graduate-led Early Childhood workforce that is responsive to workforce needs and improves outcomes for children.
6   To afford students the placement opportunities in which to critically apply theory to practice in a range of Early Childhood settings and/or schools, social care and health settings. This will enable students to develop graduate skills in the application of the interdisciplinary Early Childhood knowledge base to enhance reflective practice.
7   To provide new opportunities for graduates who want to strengthen their practice in Early Childhood and/or progress to post-graduate academic programmes or professional training, including Early Years Teacher (0–5), Teacher (3–11), social work and health professions.
(Early Childhood Studies Degree Network, 2019: 6)

The pilot phase started in September 2018. It was included in the Department for Education's full and relevant criteria for England in 2019 (DfE, 2021) and incorporated into the Benchmark Statement for the degree in the same year (QAA, 2019). They have applicability across the four nations of the United Kingdom as well as internationally.

They facilitate the ecological study of Early Childhood in practice contexts. For example, this could be in an ECEC setting, a prison, a mother and baby psychiatric ward, in social work or a multi-agency safeguarding team (MASH). At their core is understanding the multifaceted nature of Early Childhood and the importance of ensuring the child in central to all we do, although this is not easy if we work in organisations that have their own cultures that must be adhered to. Furthermore, as evidenced in Child Safeguarding Reviews (formerly Serious Care Reviews), infants and young children are often invisible in the systems that are meant to protect them (see Chapter 6).

Professional conversations

I used the word 'courageous' in the opening sentence of the previous section purposefully. The introduction of the competencies has challenged us all to think about the degree programmes we provide, to explore student perspectives and to address some challenging issues. It is important to appreciate how healthy and important this is, especially in an area of study that embraces so many dimensions. It is through professional conversations and debates that we extend our knowledge and criticality, confirm or challenge our views and develop new ways of understanding that lead to change.

In all my professional roles, as a social worker, working in policy and in Higher Education, it is the respectful professional relationships and the conversations we have with people with different perspectives, including students and the children, young people and families, that have created environments for change. As Freire (1993 [1972]) argues, sustainable change requires a community to take action. In the case of competencies, it is the professional conversations that shape them to ensure they continue to reflect the ecological approach to the study of early childhood, in the context of the degree they are embedded into.

Ultimately it was professional relationships that recognised the need for change and provided the opportunities that led to the development of the Early Childhood Studies degree. It is the professional conversations that have happened through the Early Childhood Studies Degree Network have led to:

- Early Childhood becoming an academic field, with a Subject Benchmark Statement (QAA, 2022).
- Practitioner options being introduced into degrees in 2006. These were in response to the shifting landscape in ECEC, ensuring that those studying the ECSD with placements, who did not have a relevant qualification to work in the ECEC, could practise on graduation in England.
- The articulation of practice at Level 6 through the Early Childhood Graduate Practitioner (see the case studies below in conversation with Eunice Lumsden and Helen Perkins). These did not just happen; it was the professional conversations that took place that acknowledged differences and enabled a shared understanding and vision to emerge (see Table 1.1 The Early Childhood Graduate Practitioner).

In fact, a core part of your practice will be developing professional relationships with a range of practitioners, professionals, children and their families. The professional conversations you have will require you to develop skills in what Thompson (2021b) describes, under the umbrella term *personal effectiveness*, as:

- self-awareness
- being able to communicate effectively, verbally and non-verbally

Table 1.1   The Early Childhood Graduate Practitioner

Early Childhood Graduate Practitioners are advocates for young children's rights and participation who recognise that young children are active co-constructors of their own learning. They critically apply high-level academic knowledge of pedagogy and research evidence to the holistic development of infants and young children (0–8), in a practice context that is respectful of the child, their family and community.

Early Childhood Graduate Practitioners will have met nine competencies through assessed placement tasks, observations of practice and academic assignments. They will understand the importance of:

- Advocating for young children's rights and participation
- Promoting holistic child development
- Working directly with young children, families and colleagues to promote health, well-being, safety and nurturing care
- Observing, listening and planning for young children to support their well-being, early learning, progression and transitions
- Safeguarding and child protection
- Inclusive practice
- Partnership with parents and caregivers
- Collaborating with others
- Ongoing professional development.

(Early Childhood Studies Degree Network, 2019: 12)

- being able to listen
- being appropriately assertive
- having skills and techniques in managing stress
- time and information management.

Developing your professionalism and the importance of reflective practice will be explored further in Chapters 4, 6, 7, 9 and 10. However, it is important to appreciate that these skills are transferable in whatever direction your career takes you.

Case Study

In conversation with Eunice Lumsden

What was your role in developing the Early Childhood Graduate Competencies?

This is so difficult to answer because it takes a community to create something, but communities need people who see the need for change to take on different roles. In essence, I led on their development on behalf of the Early Childhood Studies Degree Network, writing to them, gaining feedback, as well as engaging students and stakeholders and bringing together the final documentation. But I could not have done it without the support of my colleagues. And,

(Continued)

we did it all over four months, March–July 2018. There was a huge commitment from everyone, although there were, and continue to be, some hearts and minds to be changed and some were still not convinced.

I can never thank everyone enough for their allyship and trust in making a vision a reality – it really takes a community of like-minded people.

I think it is important to say that the way their development was led was with purposeful, democratic leadership, enabling all to participate. My previous experience in workforce reform in Early Years, alongside my journey as a social worker and working in Higher Education, reinforced the importance that the development needed to be owned and developed by my peers at the Early Childhood Studies Degree Network. For me, this was key to ensuring that people would see them as valuable, something they understood, a development they would want for their programme and that they would be sustainable. It was also important to evidence how a sector working together could create change in a relatively short period of time.

In fact, what emerged were some very deep pedagogical conversations in teams across the country around the purpose of the degree, which, not surprisingly, evidenced the different backgrounds of those working in HEIs and, if there were placements, how they were embedded, observed an assessed, or not.

The impetus for them emerged over time. The work I was involved in and as well as numerous conversations with colleagues led to periods of deep reflection about the core purpose of studying Early Childhood, the variations emerging, the different types of practice opportunities and issues around graduate employability.

One conversation was with Helen Perkins (see the case study below in conversation with Helen Perkins). We had talked about developing our own standards and then a brief conversation between us at a tube station in London following a meeting with Save the Children was a pivotal moment and a catalyst for change.

What are the Competencies?

The development of the competencies was not a one-off event. They are deeply rooted in the history of Early Childhood and the aspirations of generations of women who have worked with children to ensure that the multifaceted area of 'childcare' receives the recognition it deserves. Personally, when I first started to engage with the richness of the degree, I really wished I had had the opportunity to study it before going into social work.

There were a number of interrelated drivers for their development, including:

- The inclusion of Early Childhood Development in the Sustainable Development Goals.
- The lack of a benchmark for assessing what practice in Early Childhood would look like nationally or internationally at Level 6.
- The development at a policy level of apprenticeships in childcare, education, health and social care and how these developments would sit alongside the academic study of Early Childhood.

- A lack of clarity about the different types of Early Childhood degrees that had emerged, and the knowledge and skill set of the graduating student. I often got asked 'Why can't your students change nappies?' Some people in the workforce didn't quite understand the nature of the degree.
- The need to strengthen Early Childhood Studies degrees that included placements. Some students joined the degree with a relevant Level 3 qualification, which meant they could practise in ECEC in England. For others, it was not clear whether the levels of practice and assessment processes provided the same rigour.
- The lack of graduate employment for those with an Early Childhood Studies degree,or a specific career pathway for students in Early Childhood.

The competencies had to capture the interdisciplinary nature of Early Childhood, as articulated in the QAA Benchmark and have the flexibility to be internationally applicable. They also had to have the flexibility for different programmes to explore what they meant in the context of their degree and the communities they served. They were originally designed for standard ECS degrees but very quickly their applicability for work-based programmes was recognised, leading them to be integrated into 'Top Up' degrees.

The final competencies resulted from several rounds of consultation. We were determined that the assessment would not become a tick-box exercise or a technical qualification. Achieving them would require students to demonstrate considerable skills in their ability to critically apply learning in practice in a way that evidenced the multifaceted nature of Early Childhood. They are not for all students, but they provide a foundation on which students can build on in their chosen careers.

What next?

I really want to stress that they are still primary focused on students studying ECS degrees to ensure we are equipping them appropriately for future careers. They are not intended for work-based programmes for those already embedded in ECEC. The fact that they reinforce the need for the development of a framework for assessing and developing practitioner practice at Level 6 in an ECEC, and that they are applicable in different contexts, was not the original intention.

It will take several years for this new genre of practitioner to take their place in the workforce and I hope over time it will evolve into a profession in its own right. Their unique contribution is in their holistic understanding of Early Childhood Development and their skills in drawing on interdisciplinary knowledge in a multi-professional context. But only time will tell. I think they have certainly fulfilled a purpose and re-energised some programmes and the teaching teams.

It is important that we keep the focus on the breadth of Early Childhood and that programmes ensure that students have access to the interdisciplinary teaching teams. We need to learn from how they are developing and ensure that supporting practice material is developed to strengthen the learning experience.

(Continued)

Case Study

In conversation with Helen Perkins

Why do you think the Early Childhood Graduate Competencies are important?

There are several reasons why they are important. Children deserve to have around them people who are knowledgeable about how they think, grow, learn and develop, and how they operate and their place within the world. And children need to be front and centre of everything that we do.

My thesis was all about why we need a qualified workforce. I was part of the Nutbrown Review (DfE, 2012), which emphasised the need for people to have qualifications. Not just any qualification, but the right qualification. In the ECEC sector, it's that old thing that you don't know what you don't know. When you've got a ECEC workforce that is 50% unqualified, 50% can be Level 2, with one Level 3, who may have learnt through a very technicist approach – not theoretical, not critical, definitely not involving policy – then how are they expected to give children what they deserve? They can't.

So when we started talking about it – and I think you (Eunice) were feeding back from the Apprenticeship – we were going, 'Oh no' and arguing about what should be in the Standards, I just said to you, 'Why don't we write our own?' And you said, 'Why don't we?'

The reason why they are the right nine competencies is because they're based on researched evidence; they are based on not just 10 and 20 years but hundreds of years of quality provision and research about children. That's what they are about, and they will not change when policy changes because, actually, they don't need to, because they contain what's important. They make all of the theory and all of that complex knowledge base make sense. They make students think holistically about children and practice, rather than compartmentalized in boxes. It really helps the students to have a greater connection to their Early Childhood Studies degrees at a graduate level. Higher Education, different to Further Education. In FE, you find you have one or two teachers and they are with you for two years of your Level 3. Within HE, you end up with lots of different lecturers because they've all got different specialisms. And actually, what the competencies do is bring all of that together. It connects it all and synthesises it all into this holistic entity that actually puts all of that knowledge into a useful and coherent space.

How have they been received by your students, though?

Those that do it are absolutely thrilled with themselves that they have managed to do something, because it is an enhancement, it's an extra to what they have to do, although part of it is embedded in their degree and so they are producing evidence anyway. But to pull it all together requires that special somebody, that somebody who is absolutely the person that you'd want looking after your children. That's the person who thinks this is important.

What's your vision for them? What would you like to happen with them?

There are two things, one is that they don't change because they are absolutely the pillars on which all good Early Years practice should stand. I don't want them to change. They'll evolve, but I don't want them to change their central tenets; their central pillars shouldn't change.

And then what I want them to be is to become the norm. I want them to be what you expect to be doing when you are engaging in working with children. And I want people to talk about them. And at that point I do think we should have thought of something shorter in terms of a name – maybe we should call them Graduate Practitioners.

Values and Ethics

The competencies are built around the three core values of *advocacy*, *democracy* and *participation* (see Chapter 10). These were chosen as they embrace how we should work alongside children and families, co-constructing our practice in partnership with them. It is important to appreciate that values and ethics go in hand in hand. For example, working in Early Childhood, I value the importance of participation. I therefore always endeavour to engage the voice of children in my work and enable them in advocating for themselves.

Whatever your future career trajectory is, working with children and families requires you to understand your personal and professional values, as well as ensuring you practise ethically. You also need to appreciate the world through their eyes, not yours. As Maya Angelou (1928–2014) stated: 'They may forget your name, but they will never forget how you made them feel.' Therefore, you need to understand social justice, anti-oppressive and anti-discriminatory practice and explore your assumptions – change starts from within. Through this learning process, you will be enabled to understand how oppression and discrimination is embedded in different societies. You will need to evidence how this learning is shaping you as a critically reflective practitioner who is focused on your ongoing professional development (Competency 9).

Social justice and anti-oppressive and anti-discriminatory practice are complex areas and subject to considerable scholarly attention (see suggested Further Reading at the end of the chapter and the Glossary). For example, social justice it a broad term and the principles underlying it are reflected differently in the disciplines that occupy the Early Childhood space. In social work, for example, it is a core value of the profession that must be evidenced as part of the professional standards (Social Work England, 2021). Tedam (2021: 60) states:

> Social justice is the fair, just and respectful treatment of all people, while recognising the unfairness, corruption and inequalities are the leading causes of war, conflict, inhumane treatment, suffering pain, exploitation and many other ills that confront our world today.

As Freire (1993) argues, some members of society are treated inhumanly (oppression). Anti-oppressive practice, which is closely aligned with anti-discriminatory practice, is about recognising the oppression individuals, groups and communities face and proactively addressing them.

We can do this by recognising the influence of power at an individual and societal level and then taking actions to address it through empowering practice. I find the following question helps me to continually reflect on my practice.

Reflection Point

How do I promote social justice in my work and ensure my practice is empowering and recognises that those I work with may have faced oppression and discrimination because of their age, gender, disability, ethnicity, religious affiliation or sexual orientation?

In summary, we know that our experiences throughout the Early Childhood period can have an empowering or disempowering impact across our life course. Therefore, professional relationships and the conversations we have are powerful, but for them to happen we need to constantly develop our knowledge and skills to enhance our professional practice. In the competencies, we have called this *the skilful application of knowledge to practise and practice to knowledge* to reflect the ongoing ecological cycle, where contextual knowledge is applied to practise and contextual practice is applied to knowledge, in Early Childhood (see Figure 1.1).

Summary

The Early Childhood Graduate Practitioner Competencies were developed to strengthen ECS degrees with placements, providing a benchmark for the multifaceted knowledge base and higher-level

Figure 1.1   The ecological cycle of applying knowledge to practise and practice to knowledge

practice skills required at Level 6. While they are not a professional status, the core knowledge, skills and professional behaviours embedded within them provide the foundations for a range of career trajectories in working with children and families. This is not unlike profession programmes like social work, nursing and teaching, where graduates build on their foundations once qualified or specialise in a branch of their profession. The importance of continual professional development in enabling the individual to move from novice to expert over their working lifetime is key.

The case study conversations included in this chapter have provided some personal insights into the historical and contemporary contexts from which the competencies have emerged. The competencies have built on our collective learning through research and practice wisdom. In this way, we have ensured they capture the study of Early Childhood, sitting outside policy changes or specific workforce development initiatives. They also provide the framework for deep pedagogical conversations among programme teams about their specific programme, the values underpinning it, the skills base of the teaching teams and the opportunities afforded to the students. The competencies are not right for all programmes, or all students, nor are they a tick-box exercise. They are much more complex. Students will require quality mentoring to develop the higher-level skills of professional effectiveness required. In short, to create a new genre of professional practice, investment is required by all: HEIs, programme teams, students and the communities they engage with. Through working together, we have and will continue to create a community of practice committed to the ecological study of Early Childhood with children's rights at its heart.

Key Points

This chapter has explored the historical and contemporary context of Early Childhood Studies and the Early Childhood Graduate Practitioner Competencies, which include:

- The development of Early Childhood Studies degrees
- The development of the Early Childhood Graduate Practitioner Competencies
- Definitions of the terminology used within Early Childhood
- The nature of policy in Early Childhood and how this relates to practice.

Further Reading

Fitzgerald, D. and Mconochie, H. (2020) *Early Childhood Studies: A Student's Guide*. London: Sage. This edited book comprises a range of chapters that covers the breadth of subjects pertinent to the study of Early Childhood. It provides an excellent foundation from which to develop your knowledge and practice.

Tedam, P. (2021) *Anti-oppressive social work practice*. London: Learning Matters/Sage.
This is an excellent introduction to understanding what is meant by anti-oppressive practice and how you embrace this in your practice. While written for a social work audience, it is pertinent to all who work with children and families.

Thompson, N. (2021a) *Anti-discriminatory practice* (7th edition). London: Red Globe Press.
This text introduces you to the importance of anti-discriminatory practice and how we embrace this in our practice.

Thompson, N. (2021b) *People skills* (5th edition). London: Red Globe Press.
This is an excellent book in supporting your professional development and skills in working with others.

Quality Assurance Agency (QAA) (2022) *Early Childhood Studies: Subject Benchmark Statement*. Available from: https://www.qaa.ac.uk/quality-code/subject-benchmark-statements/early-childhood-studies

Chapter 2

ADVOCATING FOR YOUNG CHILDREN'S RIGHTS AND PARTICIPATION

Jill Harrison and Diana Harris

Chapter Aims

This chapter will support your knowledge and understanding of how to listen to and empower children as part of high-quality provision and practice. By the end of the chapter, you will have had opportunities to reflect upon and extend understanding of how to:

- demonstrate how you listen to and work in collaboration with young children, individually and in groups (Graduate Competencies 1.1)
- observe, support and extend young children's participation in their learning through following their needs and interests (Graduate Competencies 1.2)
- support children to respect others by providing opportunities for their participation and decision-making (Graduate Competencies 1.3)

Introduction

This chapter focuses on the importance of how we listen to and take seriously the voice of the child in our daily practice. It will consider how a graduate-level professional should lead practice within the Early Childhood context and have the skills and strategies to advocate for children and families. This is not a new phenomenon, but will offer new perspectives and develop knowledge and skills to help you to reflect on your practice.

Not Just Sitting in a Circle, Chatting or Getting Bored

When we define *Listening to Children*, we believe that this requires patience and understanding, truly listening to their words or actions, taking children seriously, having honest conversations of mutual respect, outlining what can be achieved and giving opportunities for children to express themselves in many ways. This practice has developed over time within Early Years, gaining increasing prominence on the global stage through legislation, policy and curricular approaches.

Since the conception of the United Nations Convention for the Rights of the Child (UNCRC) (UN General Assembly, 1989), there has been a growing interest in understanding and empowering children, making the link between Early Childhood and social cultural perspectives more prominent (James and Prout, 1997). The UNCRC (1989) identifies the importance of respecting children's views and rights to self-expression in Articles 12 and 13. This advice has led to many misconceptions of what it means in day-to-day practice, with practitioners adopting laissez-faire attitudes (let them do as they like) (Lewin, 1946) or tokenistic ways of sharing power with children. It is not just including circle time, or giving children everything that they expect, nor asking them to take part in planning and discussions when plans are already preconceived and formulated. The child should be respected equally within team discussions, which need to be structured to be developmentally appropriate, so each child is an active participant. When listening and advocating for children we can learn from past theoretical approaches, experiences and develop new practices from focused research.

It is important that you take the child's social and cultural context into consideration when listening to children. Bronfenbrenner's Ecological Systems theory (1977) highlights the child in the context of the immediate family and provides a framework that considers the impact of the environment on the child and family's life and the influence that the child and family have on decisions and actions within the wider community. Listening, empowerment and advocacy are intertwined in this everyday practice.

Reflection Point

How do you listen to children and understand them?
Are their voices heard in your setting's policies?

Looking Back at Conceptions of Childhood

We acknowledge that around the world, depending on time and the social-political context of where children live their lives, their experiences will be very different but they all have the right to be who they are, free from political and domestic maltreatment, to have economic and emotional wellbeing.

Some of the key influences within the Early Childhood Community help practitioners to understand the concepts of childhood and promoting children's rights, enabling us to draw on their work to sustain and enhance inclusivity within our practice. Advocacy for children's lives can be seen through eminent Early Childhood thinkers. Solly (2017:38) reminds us that Froebel recognised 'the integrity of childhood in its own right. He saw the child's uniqueness and the importance of their unique development … recognized the child as part of a family and the community, the setting being an integral part of the community it serves, working in close partnership with parents and other skilled adults'. Pestalozzi (1746–1847) highlighted the importance of observation and reflection, and the power of individual communities. Steiner (1861–1925) felt the unique stage of childhood is incredibly important and raised the importance of respectful relationships between the child, practitioner and the family. He emphasised the importance of allowing children to express themselves freely. Montessori (1870–1952) believed in social justice and empowering all.

More contemporary influences impacting on practice include Vivian Gussin Paley (1929–2019), who strongly believed in listening to children's words and honouring what they said. Her practice and advocacy of children's storytelling was taken up worldwide as practitioners saw the benefits for social development and how it supported their understanding of children's interests and thought processes. Malaguzzi (1920–1994) believed in the competency of children and practitioners to co-construct learning through reciprocal relationships of mutual respect and effective listening without recourse to formulaic policy documents guiding this practice (Moss, 2016). Margaret Carr with Tilly and Tamati Reedy supported the development of, and were involved in the writing of, the Te Whariki curriculum in Aotearoa New Zealand (Ministry of Education, 1996). They have promoted that children should have opportunities to become 'competent and confident learners and communicators, healthy in mind, body and spirit, secure in their sense of belonging and in the knowledge that they make a valued contribution to society' (New Zealand Government, 2017).

The active learning approach of HighScope (Hohmann, Weikart, and Epstein, 2008) is focused on high-quality practices and theoretical approaches to develop a system of working with children and their families, promoting partnerships and enabling children to make choices. The High Scope approach encourages children to voice their feelings and thoughts in a variety of ways. The Plan–Do–Review daily routine (Hohmann et al., 2008) (see Figure 2.2 below) provides planned times for children to organise their day, reflect and discuss what happened, which develops their skills for planning and reflection, and helps them to see how their behaviour impacts on others. This cycle allows them to have control over their learning and the environment. Central to this approach is the importance of children making their own choices and being competent learners.

The approach Reggio Emilia have adopted in Northern Italy is child centred. It is based on the principles of respect and responsibility and has a strong sense of community. Maluguzzi (1920–1994) advocated for children to have control over the direction of their own learning, and that these experiences should be active, feeling, touching, sensing. Community support and parental involvement are key to this approach. Clark and Moss's (2001, 2011; Clark, 2017) research has been used to develop policy across the world, influencing practices and environments, as well as being a tool to engage children and practitioners in advocacy (see the case study interview later in the chapter). Clark and Moss (2001, 2011) developed The Mosaic Approach, which combines visual and verbal modes of communication to hear and empower different voices (see Further Reading at the end of this chapter).

Reflection Point

Thinking about the above perspectives, how does this link to wider policy and legislation?

How do your setting's policies reflect the above thinking?

What about your own practice? What do you believe is important and what influences you?

What is Listening? Frameworks and Tools to Support Professional Advocacy

Case Study

An interview with Alison Clark, September 2020

Introduction

Alison Clark is a contemporary and key influence in today's practice in supporting *Listening to Young Children* (Clark, 2017). Her initial work with Peter Moss has evolved, so The Mosaic Approach has become synonymous with listening to marginalised groups. The Mosaic Approach supports practitioners to listen, understand and advocate for young children, families and staff in an equitable way.

How did you become interested in the concepts of listening to children? What was your inspiration for this?

When I first started working on the Listening to Young Children Project with Peter Moss – this was in 1999 – my immediate background to that had been working with the National Children's Bureau on research around the guardian *ad litem* service, looking at how professionals work with children through the legal process. I think listening in that project became such an important thread. It built on my work as a primary school teacher in the 1980s. So when I saw the advert for the original job to work with Peter Moss on Listening to Young Children, I brought my experiences as a teacher but also as a mother and as an artist to thinking about what ways were there to tune into the important things in young children's lives.

The original project, out of which The Mosaic Approach grew, provided time to look more widely at how Early Childhood was being talked about and practised in different countries, so, I had a study visit to Norway and to Denmark. Part of those early discussions were around how adults were working in different environments with young children, and what ways there were to play to young children's strengths – that became quite a strong theme. So rather than having a deficit model of children that is about trying to work out what they didn't know or what they couldn't do, I was interested in starting from a position of a strength, a strength-based model.

The first stimulant came when I heard the phrase 'strength based' by Margaret Carr. There is the work in New Zealand on the curriculum – Te Whariki was one of the approaches that I was reading about – and also, for example, looking at the preschools in Reggio Emilia in Northern Italy. So, the Listening Project was trying to draw on the best global examples and to look at that in a very practical way, thinking about what we could learn from that in terms of day-to-day listening in the UK.

What do you see as good day-to-day practice for listening skills?

I think one of the important threads was to realise that young children communicate their points of view and experiences using many different languages, both in their bodies in terms of gesture, and in terms of drawings and walking and talking, and not just limited to voice. So, when the project first started, it was phrased in terms of the '*voice of the child*' in line with the UN Convention on the Rights of the Child. But, increasingly, it became important to look more at drawing on a multi-method approach that could pull on a wider pool of strengths, not just to be limited to the spoken word. Of course, that kind of stretches us to think more in terms of preverbal children as well, and to make sure that that was part of our thinking.

How has this approach been used Internationally?

The Mosaic Approach was a starting point for me; other people have used it in their own way, developed it in ways that are appropriate for their particular context. So, one project has been working with Danish colleagues in a project involving 'Professionals seeking children's perspectives' (see case study in Clark, 2017: 135–141). This project was funded by the Danish Evaluation Institute. They were keen to work with pedagogues in Denmark who were interested in being able to tune in more to young children's perspectives, but we were aware of some of the challenges in terms of the time it takes and the skills needed.

We worked over several months, looking at The Mosaic Approach as a starting point and then with different kindergartens working with the ideas and adapting them. One of the areas that became particularly important was to look at the ethical challenges of listening to young children, and a phrase that came from the pedagogues themselves was to think about what they described as wearing an 'ethical cloak'. So that rather than ethics being around signing forms and legal processes, it was around your day-to-day thinking about how you work with young children.

How did they build on The Mosaic Approach?

I think by articulating in a stronger way the ethical framework around The Mosaic Approach and then looking at how they could embed that into their day-to-day practice within their particular context in Denmark. Another phrase that came out was around the importance of pedagogical

(Continued)

improvisation. So rather than saying, okay, when we are listening to children you know we start here, and then we need to bring these tools in and then we do this, it's more a question of almost a dance with children in the sense that you are learning to take the lead from the children, looking at what tools you need to bring to that listening, and being flexible and adaptable. During the study most of the pedagogues adopted an exploratory understanding of children's perspectives, seeing this as 'a never-ending process' and one that opened up new questions to be curious about and challenges to preconceived ideas (Clark, 2017: 138).

Can you give us an example of any recent projects where children's voices are being taken seriously?

A second project that I've been working on more recently has been a children's photographic project in Norway. The group of kindergartens (Early Childhood Centres) have been working with the National Photographic Museum, which is called the Preus Museum. This was a project working with Early Childhood education lecturers from the University of South-Eastern Norway and kindergarten children who were leaving to start school, so they were five going on six years old. The project was around 'What was important to them in their kindergarten? What do they want to remember?'. It was an interesting change. Usually in the projects that I have led, my initial question has been 'What does it mean to be in this place?' So, I am looking at trying to find out what it means for the children to be there. I wouldn't use that sentence to the children, but I'm interested in what's important to them. So, in the Norwegian context they were particularly interested in these oldest children, what memories they would take with them, using the tools of The Mosaic Approach to tune into these young children's perspectives. They particularly worked with the tools in The Mosaic Approach that use photography. These involved children walking around the space taking photographs of what was important to them, and then talking with the children around the photographs. It was a fascinating project because the particular kindergartens that were involved had children from diverse backgrounds and photography opened up many different conversations, as well as, I think, raising the status of these youngest children (in terms of how society might view them). It raised the expectations, I think, around what young children can achieve aesthetically as well in terms of some very beautifully composed and fascinating images. So, this project led to an exhibition within the museum. I think it's one of the first examples of young children's photographs being part of a National Archive, which is really exciting, because it is moving beyond 'Oh, that's a great photograph kind of thing, isn't that clever?' to seeing this photography as a serious way that young children can document their lives and for that to be respected.

Why use image making as an integral tool for this approach?

Reflection on the photographs with children and families opens many opportunities to explore interests and cultural values. Children will take photographs/draw pictures of surprising things. I guess those moments are intriguing because there's such a difference between what we may expect as an adult and what the children do. I think as a researcher I'm always interested in those moments when there feels like there's the widest gap between what I was expecting and what happened.

I guess that's another thing that happened within the Danish project. They thought about 'What am I curious about?' as a starting point for listening to young children and I think that then became a very helpful thread leading to the question for the pedagogues to think about – What am I puzzled about? What am I intrigued about? The things I see children being interested in or involved in … and how to use that phrase as a starting point.

We have talked quite a lot about photography but in The Mosaic Approach the idea is to draw together a range of different ways of communicating. We should not be just be reliant on one particular research tool but revisit this with the children and see what they say, or maybe this is something that drawing will open up to tell us more. It is important not to see it as a magic tool because we will always be interpreting what we think with children.

So, in thinking about the incredibly young children, preverbal children, babies, how would you say that this kind of approach could be used?

I think with the preverbal children … one of the things that emerged out of the first Mosaic Approach project was the importance of listening to as wide a group of people as possible who knew the children well. In that first project, I actually worked with siblings of some of the youngest children in order to build up a *mosaic of* what they saw as important to those children. In the third edition of *Listening to Young Children* (Clark, 2017), I explored a setting working with the under threes. The preschool realised that it was important to involve the perspectives, not just of the key worker working with those children, but also maybe a practitioner who didn't work day to day with the child, but had maybe seen a different perspective, a different way of thinking about them. So, I guess it was learning how to build up a more detailed picture using people with different perspectives, and including parents. Observation is a tool in The Mosaic Approach and underpins the other tools. It is a fundamental part of listening, particularly with the youngest children. So, in the Danish study, there was some interesting work with two year-olds when one of the pedagogues looked at how she could use young children's photographs. So, children took photographs. It was a project around the outdoor play space and she was interested in how the children were using the space and what was important to them. So, working with these two year-olds, they took photographs outside. These two year-olds placed a circle of their photographs on the floor and that became a talking point, an exploring point, as somewhere to crawl over and touch. Parents would also come in and sit with the children in among these photographs so the photographs themselves became a talking point with parents as well as with the children. So, I think there have been some quite innovative ways of adapting The Mosaic Approach to work with younger children.

How would you know you had successfully implemented The Mosaic Approach?

Well, I think, as a practitioner, if you've been surprised by what you found out, whether you feel you know the children better, and in more depth, and that the children have enjoyed communicating with you in new ways. I would add that a success might also be if you found something out of concern to a child and you were able to change something as a result.

Reflection Point

Reflect on the interview in the case study above. How have you used the elements of
The Mosaic Approach?
What tools support you in advocating for young children?

Tools for Supporting Participation

There are many socio-cultural views on how to support participation, including Harts' (1992) and
Shier's (2001) participation frameworks to support citizenship, which move away from former
imperialistic and paternalistic ways of working. Building on this, Harrison and Harris (2020) took
inspiration from the world of creative arts in devising their topology for meaningful listening, supporting the participation of children and their primary carers within the context of Early Childhood.
Their model, The Helping Hands of Participation (see Figure 2.1), provides a framework to reflect
upon, discuss and action processes to develop and sustain active participation and empowerment
for all.

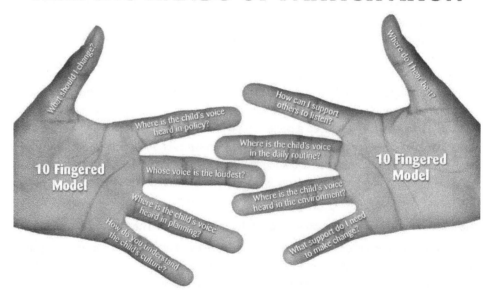

Figure 2.1   The Helping Hands of Participation framework (Harrison and Harris, 2020)

High Scope offer many tools to support you to work and engage effectively with young children. They focus on children's strengths, developing the active learning environment to support children to be creative. Practitioners and parents work together to support children in a sensitive way and encourage thoughtful interactions, including 'holding, playing alongside children and toddlers at their pace, communicating in give-and-take exchanges … respecting children's choices and encouraging their efforts, acknowledging children's strong emotions, and involving children in resolving conflicts' High-Scope (2020)(https://highscope.org/our-practice/infant-toddler-curriculum/). Close observation is essential to understanding the child's interests and to enable practitioners to develop the environment to create opportunities. Observation is also key when entering children's play. In order to be fully respectful of the child, it is encouraged that adults will:

Silently
Observe what the children are doing
Understand what is happening
Listen carefully to what children are saying (in whatever language they are using).

This simple 'SOUL' strategy allows you to enter play appropriately, enabling the adult to be truly part of the exchanges that are taking place. It also allows you to develop learning, to stop play becoming dangerous without disciplining and to develop more meaningful relationships where power is equally balanced.

What Should Listening to Children Look Like in Practice?

Stand aside for a while and leave room for learning, observe carefully what children do, and then, if you have understood well, perhaps teaching will be different from before.
(Malaguzzi, 1920–1994)

Everybody is capable of observing children in their natural environment. However, it takes a skilled practitioner to understand and hold the child in mind. Early Childhood professionals have recourse to different observation methods and tools to capture the learning and development of children. What is captured and how the information is used marks or underscores the professionalism of the Early Childhood educator. Malaguizzi's '100 Languages of the Child' poem highlights children's abilities to communicate in many different ways, in their thinking, articulation and expression. It serves as a clear framework for practice, identifying and reminding the observer that children are competent individuals, that there are many actions to contemplate as the child uses different actions, movements, words and gestures to research, explore and connect with their environment (www.reggiochildren.it/

Plan   Do

Review

Figure 2.2   Plan–Do–Review cycle

en/reggio-emilia-approach/100-linguaggi-en/). Reflection on action through internal dialogue, by the exchange of ideas with others and by the application of child developmental knowledge and learning theories, is an essential skill. The depth of thought, recognising different possibilities of meaning for the child's groups and encounters, with the ability to offer further opportunities for learning, signifies the graduate skill of the professional/pedagogue. In the implementation of this encounter and leading and mentoring colleagues on pedagogical practice, the Early Years professional needs to be aware of and use theories of reflection. In an Early Childhood context, the work of Schön and Brookfield provide informative and relevant frameworks. Schön (1991) identifies processes to enable reflection in and on action, linking to a continuous cycle of review and refinement of the pedagogical offer. Brookfield (2017) builds on Schön and advocates that we also need to include the thoughts and perspectives of others within these reflections to enable us to see the world from the student's perspective. Both support the implementation of curricula, policy and variations of pedagogy, and the specific approach – the Plan–Do–Review cycle – is endemic within the professional's skill set.

Reflection Point

In your professional life, how do you implement the Plan–Do–Review cycle, individually and as a team?

As part of constructing an enabling environment which allows the voice of children to be heard, Harrison and Harris (2020) identify the need to create meaningful spaces for encounters between children and Early Childhood professionals. This is the identification of physical space and time within the day for a collective discussion to complement the individual dialogues that all professionals hold with children. Adaption of Mosley's circle time for young children (2014) can provide this forum. It is an approach that can seamlessly work with different pedagogical ethoses and curricula policies. Practitioners need to be able to understand how this time can support emotional resilience and social development through providing a space to discuss, explore, reflect and listen, to share ideas, to debate and to feel part of this group – a group of citizens who have a place in this community and can therefore have agency within the setting and their own life.

Top Tips for Circle Time

Circle time can be an important and integral part of the day if used effectively. It encourages children to verbalise and join discussions, providing a structured place for participation to be visible. It does not matter what pedagogical approach or curricular framework you use as this global tool can complement it as collective participation is a right. The 'Circle' in circle time (Mosley, 2014) stands for:

Considered/planned

Interesting

Relevant

Concise

Laughter (it has to be fun!)

Equal

Task

Observe a circle time and evaluate this session using The Helping Hands of Participation model described above (Figure 2.1) and the mnemonic for CIRCLE.

The relationship between adults, particularly caregivers, and children must never have the character of a struggle for authority and rights: caregivers have an obligation to skilfully arrange conditions under which children may freely develop in the fullness of their rights. (Janusz Korczak, 1999)

Advocacy for Early Childhood can have an internal or external focus. It can be focused within the setting, relating to the immediate context for the child and their family, and it can be external to the setting, advocating with and about the wider environment at the local, national and international level, involving legislation and policy. The underlying premise for this comes from a range of advocacy perspectives, including:

Ethical perspective	Is underpinned by morals and values
Capitalist/economic perspective	Investment in preventative measures saves money for the state at a later date
Individual perspective	Maximising personal contributions
Collective perspective	The responsibility of citizens for individuals

All of these perspectives come from a social justice point of view, aiming to enhance the quality of children's lives by providing equity for children through learning and living, and promoting intellectual, social and economic wellbeing through reconfiguring resources and policy.

Liebovich and Adler's (2009) research highlighted that Early Childhood professionals are more confident and prefer to advocate for children and their families from within the setting. There is a focus on a developmental perspective of advocacy through securing resources, particularly for children with special rights, who have additional needs. Thinking about the child through a developmental lens enables the practitioner to use their specialised knowledge, so advocacy from this perspective – the developmental perspective – should become an everyday skill. Effective advocates need to be skilled communicators: skilled at listening and skilled at analysing and presenting information. A graduate practitioner should be able to encompass other forums for advocacy for children and their families, looking outside the setting, using different communication strategies to influence relevant factors in their locality, having the self-belief and confidence to contribute to wider policy initiatives, and seeking to have the voice of the Early Childhood community heard in national and international policy and legislation.

Case Study

Examples from the field

The narratives of graduate practitioners Nowshin Sweety and Cynthia Adewole highlight how Early Childhood professionals can and do advocate for children through listening and under-standing the context of their lives. Both of these students reflect advocacy through international perspectives.

Nowshin reflects:

As a graduate practitioner, I strongly believe that all people involved in the Early Childhood sector need to advocate for young children both inside and outside the settings. Early Childhood professionals need to strive to create an enabling environment for young children, so that children develop to the best of their abilities. For this to occur, legislation that supports practitioners and allows them to create an enabling environment need to be implemented. Our society is constantly changing. Therefore, children need to be supported in ways that aid them in developing all skills and knowledge that will help them to deal with what the future holds.

From a young age, I understood the importance of supporting young children's development. I was born in Bangladesh and came to this country when I was five years old. Before coming to this country, I had never been to school, never studied, nor did I speak any English. After two weeks of being in the country, I started attending a primary school. Within the first month of being in school, the support that I was receiving from my year one teacher allowed me to settle in comfortably and learn the basics of the English language. The feeling of being supported stayed with me and I have spent all my life trying to make changes for young children.

During my time in school, I was part of several Model United Nation conferences that took place among school, colleges and universities. Students of all ages from different institutions in the UK and from other countries, such as the USA, would get together to discuss world issues. No matter what the conference topic was, one of the solutions that would be concluded at the end of every conference was to provide good-quality education in a safe environment to all young children. This is a solution that participants agreed upon.

One key skill needed to advocate for young children is to be able to have good communication skills. This is a skill that I developed from participating in the Model United Nation conferences for many years. It was important for all participants to listen to each other. I strongly believe that people who work in the Early Childhood sector across the world need to be able to communicate effectively with children, parents and their colleagues. Additionally, individuals need to be able to work alongside policymakers and to talk on behalf of young children's rights.

Through my experience and studying about children's learning, I have learnt about the best ways children learn. This allowed me to implement new strategies within my setting: for example, the importance of outdoor play and the types of activities to carry out in the outdoor environment that support children in all areas of development. Moreover, I discuss the knowledge I have with my colleagues and I encourage them to implement it in their paradigm. I have been able to use my languages as a bilingual practitioner to talk with children and families in their home language and then share information with my colleagues who do not have access to the children's and families' language. It is essential to value all languages and ensure individuals are not disempowered through language challenges.

I always ensure that I am up to date with current information regarding what my local community is doing to support Early Childhood. I have subscribed to organisations such as OMEP (World Organisation for Early Childhood) to gain knowledge on what is happening on an international level for Early Childhood education. My dream is to be able to attend an OMEP conference, which will allow me to gain further knowledge and make changes in children's life on an international level.

Cynthia reflects:

In 2017, I had the opportunity of spending some time in Northern Nigeria in a home for children affected by the insurgency crisis. The children in this particular house were from early childhood up to the early teenage years. They had been orphaned and/or displaced from their homes as a result of insurgency. A mother figure provided

(Continued)

for these children in this setting. This was my first time working with children who had experienced trauma. I did not know what to expect.

I observed and was amazed at how much I learnt from them. I did not understand the main language spoken in this household and I found that it had no bearing on my understanding each child. It was important to provide developmentally-appropriate activities. The older children were able to re-enact their culture from some of the basic items we had purchased from a local artisan. They enabled them to share details of their culture with one another. So, I learnt more about them from them. We had conversations about their interests.

From this experience, I learnt that to really advocate for children, I had to be:

- An objective observer (present, notice what's happening before me).
- Humble. By this, I mean an acceptance that it is the child's wishes and needs that matter. My role here is to listen to the child and act in their best interest.
- Consistent in my approach and with my presence.
- As an advocate it is important to share what is happening with leaders within the community.

To honour the child, I have to present myself in a humble manner, observe and respond appropriately. I have to constantly ask myself, 'Is my voice the voice of this child? Am I speaking in the interest of this child?' When I can say yes, then it means I have advocated on behalf of the child.

Reflection Point

What skills do you bring to the Early Childhood community that you can use to advocate for children and their families?
How can you help colleagues to advocate for young children?

Summary

Meaningful participation of children within the context of Early Childhood requires a commitment to listening to the voice of the child and a willingness to consider seriously how to value the child as an equal citizen within the community. Respecting the *civicness* of the child needs to be visible in practice as well as evident in policy frameworks and codes of practice. A graduate professional is an individual who understands this concept and has depth of knowledge on child development, pedagogy and social and political issues. Using this knowledge, the Early Childhood professional has the skills and strategies to co-research with children, following the child's interests, understanding how to observe, how to listen and when to provide a link to prompt new thoughts and responses to the environment. The confidence that emanates from professional knowledge should enable the graduate practitioner to engage in complex situations, to have demanding conversations with children, to acknowledge with them the important issues in the children's lives and to admit to the children that the adults do not know everything.

A formulaic approach to implementing policy is disrespectful to the uniqueness of the child and their family. Looking and learning from the established Early Childhood community should provide inspiration and insight as to how to empower children and their families. This focus needs to be located within and outside the setting. There is more to be learnt from pioneers such as Montessori and the McMillan sisters (Giardiello, 2013; Liebovich, 2018) than 'the prepared environment', and the 'value of play' and the interconnection between health and learning. These early pioneers were advocates for children and their right to high-quality learning and education, no matter what their circumstances. They raised this on the national and global stage, by using their voice, their 100 languages and by astute use of connections. (How else was the concept of free school meals initiated within the UK at a sociological time when women's own rights were only just emerging?) Today's graduate practitioners should be able to use their voice to comment on and initiate policy at a local and national level, not just speaking on behalf of children and their families but actively providing tools so that participation is a reality for all; benevolence, however well-meaning the original intent, is extinct.

Key Points

This chapter has explored many aspects of listening to children to promote a democratic Early Childhood experience for all children. It has looked at:

- How past Early Childhood pioneers and theorists inspire practice today
- Contemporary approaches to supporting young children to have a voice and to participate in encounters in their own life
- Children's rights as citizens
- Strategies to support professional practice in listening to children and advocacy in Early Childhood
- The Mosaic Approach as a tool for participation.

Further Reading

The texts and resources below have been chosen to enable you to explore further the tools of participation and to understand further specific curricular approaches and ethoses, which promote participation and listening to children:

Clark, A. (2017) *Listening to young children: A guide to understanding and using the Mosaic Approach* (Expanded 3rd edition). London: National Children's Bureau UK.

Clark, A. and Moss, P. (2011) *Listening to young children: The Mosaic Approach* (2nd edition). London: National Children's Bureau for the Joseph Rowntree Foundation.

Paley, V. G. (1991) The boy who would be a helicopter: The uses of storytelling in the classroom. Cambridge, MA: Harvard University Press.

International curricular approaches include:

- HighScope: https://highscope.org/our-practice/curriculum/
- Reggio Emilia: www.reggiochildren.it/en/loris-malaguzzi-international-centre/ and www.reggiochildren.it/en/reggio-emilia-approach/100-linguaggi-en/
- Te Whariki: https://education.govt.nz/early-childhood/teaching-and-learning/ te-whariki#:~:text=Te%20Wh%C4%81riki%20Te%20Wh%C4%81riki%20

The following two international organisations work on a global context both locally with children and with policymakers, advocating for social justice for all children through changes in policy and distribution of resources:

UNICEF: www.unicef.org

UNESCO: https://en.unesco.org/

Chapter 3

PROMOTING HOLISTIC CHILD DEVELOPMENT

Tanya Richardson

Chapter Aims

This chapter will consider ways in which you can promote and support young children's holistic development. It will build on the knowledge that you will have gained as an integral part of your degree and begin to consider how to apply this knowledge to practice. The chapter will acknowledge the holistic nature of an Early Years degree and consider this by discussing how this area can be promoted not just through Early Years settings, but also within the fields of health and social care. By engaging in this chapter, you will have opportunities to reflect upon and extend understanding of how to:

- explain, justify and apply in practice, knowledge of how infants and young children develop from conception to the age of eight in terms of:
  a) Neurological and brain development
  b) Cognitive development
  c) Communication and language development
  d) Personal, emotional and social development
  e) Physical development (Graduate Competencies 2.1).

- demonstrate and apply knowledge to practice of the factors that promote and impede holistic development and long-term outcomes. These include:
  a) Individual circumstances
  b) Family circumstances
  c) Attachment
  d) Physical health
  e) Mental health
  f) Personal, social and emotional wellbeing
  g) The impact of disadvantage and adverse childhood experiences

h) Relationships with friends and adults

i) The importance of learning through play

j) The role of creativity

k) Policy (Graduate Competencies 2.2).

Introduction

This chapter does *not* set out to provide detailed knowledge on holistic child development, as it is recognised that this will be a thread that runs through your degree programme. What this chapter will do is build on that knowledge and consider the implications for practice: how to promote child development within a working environment, whether it be in the field of education, health or social care. Whichever field of work you are hoping to go into, this chapter will reflect upon how you can promote holistic development throughout your work with young children and families.

A Sum of All Parts

Although Competency 2.1 asks you to explain, justify and apply in practice knowledge of how infants and young children develop within five different areas, the interconnected nature of development also needs to be recognised. Each and every child is a sum of all parts. Lindon and Brodie (2016) assert that a whole-child approach is necessary when looking at child development, ensuring that each child is seen as an individual and all different skills and areas of development are intertwined. This chapter will therefore focus on this interconnected nature of development.

This section will outline some key theory relating to each area of development and will allow you to refresh your knowledge of child development. The table below is a reminder of some key theorists within this area and the stance they take.

	Nature	Nurture	Combination of both nature and nurture
Language development	Noam Chomsky (1928–) Language Acquisition Device (LAD) biologically prepares infants to learn rules of language through universal grammar	B. F. Skinner (1904–1990) Children learn through operant conditioning (reinforcement) and imitation	Michael Tomasello (1950–) Inner capacities and environment work together; social context is important

Cognitive development	Core knowledge theorists believe that all children have the biological ability to understand crucial aspects of learning (Spelke, 2004)	John Locke (1632–1704) Children are born as blank slates – 'tabula rasa' – and it is the role of the adult to educate Lev Vygotsky (1896-1934 – Cognition is based on social interaction and language	Jean Piaget (1896–1980) Child is pre-programmed to learn but needs adults to facilitate learning
Physical development	There is little dispute in this area that physically children develop based on their genetic make-up and the environment in which they find themselves. Look at the work of Gallahue and Ozmun (1998) for some key theory in this area		
Social and emotional development	Work with very young babies has asserted that the development of early emotions is an innate trait. Experiments such as the still face experience are shown to evidence this (Moore et al., 2001)	John Bowlby (1907–1990) Bowlby's theory of attachment asserted that the relationship with the mother figure was crucial to a child's emotional state and the way that they developed future relationships	Lewis (2010) argues that this area of development is constructed with *primary emotions*, those reflexes that are present at birth, and *self-conscious emotions*, those that require self-awareness and come from interactions

Although it is important for you to understand the respective theories, it is equally important for you, as practitioners, to reflect on your own stance on children's development. This will impact on how you practise, and on your pedagogical stance. Your personal views of childhood will influence your approach to development. In the case study below, Adelola Fadina, a student at the University of Northampton, explains how her pedagogy has been shaped by her views and experiences.

Case Study

Student voice: Adelola Fadina reflects on her pedagogical influences

Due to my own childhood experiences, I feel that it is really important that I adopt a child-led practice when working with children. One way I have done this is through providing children with open-ended resources used in a way that provides provocation. I talk to parents to understand

(Continued)

more about the interests of the child and use this information to provide them with provocations that can extend their learning. I understand, though, that adult engagement is also important. Therefore, I would demonstrate ways in which the children could use the provocations, giving them ideas on how to achieve the best outcome, while still allowing them to take full rein on the activity. This approach aligns with that promoted by Froebel, who says that although children flourish under a free regime, adults should be ready to engage to boost their learning where possible, and there should be a balance between adult-led and child-directed learning. Froebel further suggested that self-directed play is an expression of a child's imagination and creativity, and therefore, by me demonstrating the provocation to the children, it could be argued that I take this opportunity away from the children. I also recognise, as Froebel suggested, that taking a didactic stance could undermine a child's autonomy, therefore it is important to me that I carefully judge when it is best to intervene in a child's provocation. I would carefully intervene with open-ended questions, and give them the opportunity to reject my ideas for their own, therefore allowing them full autonomy. I recognise that autonomy is best achieved when an adult carefully intervenes to get them to make use of the tools in the most efficient way possible. Therefore, although my provocations are provided to the children with me adopting the role of a demonstrator, it can be argued that this allows the children to get the most out of their learning.

Take some time to consider the Reflection Point below.

Reflection Point

What stance do you take when thinking about how children develop?
How does this manifest itself in the way you work with children?
How does this align with other people you work with or have worked with?
Do you think it is possible to work with people with different viewpoints or does every-one need to agree?

The knowledge that you have within this area on how children develop can be applied alongside developmental milestones, such as Mary Sheridan's work (Sharma and Cockerill, 2014) or national developmental guidance (Early Education, 2012). This links with Competency 4 (see Chapter 5). You will need thorough knowledge of how children develop in order to be able to effectively observe, listen and plan for their progression.

Practical Applications of Child Development Knowledge

If we adopt an approach where we consider nature and nurture to be equally important, we need to remember that the way that children learn and develop is dependent on their surroundings and the interactions that occur within those environments, as well as their genetic construct. We need to recognise that our view of development can combine elements of nature and nurture and therefore this needs to be taken into consideration when applying theoretical knowledge to the reality of children's lives. It is also important to note that what has gone, as in what children have been exposed to in the earlier days, also impacts on the here and now.

To illustrate this point further, in the case study below, David and Michael, same-sex parents, explain their experiences of working with children and the impact that children's individual and familial circumstances can have on those children's development.

Case Study

Interview with David and Michael about their experience of adoption

Can you give a brief background of your situation and what made you decide to adopt and foster?

After being together 20 years, we approached the local authority and at the time they were not overly supportive. Another nearby authority had been set a target to be more diverse in their adoptive families and they were very keen to have same-sex couples adopt. Before we knew it, we had adopted a little boy, and went on to adopt two more boys over the next few years. All the boys were born with either alcohol or drug dependencies and therefore had to spend time in hospital once born to wean them off their substance addictions.

Last year we decided to venture into fostering, wanting to help babies going through the rehab process as we had experience in this area. We wanted to give something back as our first two boys had had really good foster experiences and those good relationships were noted to be really beneficial in their early development. What happened, though, was that we ended up being asked to take three siblings, a seven-year-old girl and her twin siblings, a boy and girl aged five, one of whom has special needs.

What have you noticed about the children that you care for, with regards to the impact that their individual and family circumstances have on their development?

One of the twins we are fostering has some kind of developmental delay and due to the Covid-19 pandemic the diagnosis has been really slow. We believe that there may be genetic issues, but also the child's dad was heavily involved with alcohol. We are waiting for the formal diagnosis, though. Our adopted children have been lucky in that they had fantastic relationships from day one, with either foster carers or ourselves, and they began to develop attachments very early. Our oldest child was in a hospital room on his own for 12 weeks, but he was very much loved and looked after. The two younger adoptees' mother didn't have alcohol dependency, just drugs. We have not seen any long-term impacts from that – they are very bright. The nursery and preschool that they attended in the early days helped and, as they came to us at an early age, we were able to offer the consistency and love that they needed. The youngest child was placed with us before he was born, and as soon as he arrived we were in the hospital giving

(Continued)

kangaroo care (skin-to skin contact). That was phenomenal. He got out of hospital in 5½ weeks whereas the others took 5–6 months. I think that that was down to a very forward-thinking consultant at the hospital who encouraged us to trial this kangaroo care. There do not appear to be any long-term issues. At the moment, none of them is presenting with any major issues.

Can you tell us about how you see attachments developing or not developing with the children you care for?

Our three adopted boys are very secure and are very good with adults and know the boundaries, whereas the three foster children are different. An example of this – we had a family friend visit the house two days after they arrived to stay with us and the girls were sat on his lap within 30 seconds of him being here. Now our boys would never have done that. The night that the foster children arrived, they were alive with nits and were very bedraggled. They came in and had dinner, they chat, chat, chatted and then one-by-one they went upstairs and washed their hair. They sat on the table waiting to have the lotion put on and carried on chatting. I was amazed – if that was our boys and they had been taken away from us, they would have been so distressed. We couldn't believe that they allowed us to do these things and were so compliant. What their attachment is like we have no idea. They are very attached when they go to see their mum – she buys them things and presents.

At school they are quite friendly, they do make friends. They are very social. They will attach to anybody and they are quite intense with their friendships. For example, a friend at school called one of the girls a name during the first week of school and it was a huge issue, it was massive for her – it was like someone had hurt her. They are hyper-sensitive.

Do you notice a difference in the way some of the children play? Do their adverse experiences impact on the way that they behave?

The attachment issues mentioned above do impact on the way that the foster children play with others. If they get something, it's theirs, but if they see something that belongs to one of our boys, then that's to be shared. When they first arrived everything was coveted, so if I gave one of them a Barbie, that was never to be seen again – it was hidden away in her room. Things are stored away and kept safe – even stickers. Say she finds one on an exercise book, it will be taken off and put away somewhere. Whereas our boys are more 'easy come easy go'. Christmas was magical – the foster children had never had a Christmas stocking, never had a Christmas tree, so that was massive for them. Saying that, they definitely know right from wrong. They are obedient, but not in a frightened obedient way. I think mum tries, but the company she kept, and the lifestyle she led, didn't work. The foster children also tend to exaggerate things – and there is lots of storytelling. Things such as, 'in our garden we had an orchard and we had a new car every month'... it was all about fitting in.

The oldest foster child has mentioned 'what went on at home wasn't right. We didn't have lunch and sometimes we didn't have dinner, we only got crisps for breakfast'. She looked after the younger two when in the home environment and when they first arrived with us, she would want to help read a bedtime story, she would want to be there when they were bathed, she would watch me get out their clothes and help to decide what they were wearing that day. She was seven years old. I did end up saying 'that's not your job anymore, you don't have to do that', and she understood that and she very quickly pulled back and started to do her own thing. You could tell it was a relief – she could be a child at last. This summer was amazing... paddling pools, roller skates, going to the beach, zip wires, that kind of thing. They had never done any of that.

One thing to say is that our boys have been really good. We briefed the boys a few days before they came and our oldest has been a real advocate for them. He sat with them on the first night and said, 'I was taken away from my mum, she couldn't look after me. These guys are OK', and he was instrumental in the foster children settling down. On paper, all of these children shouldn't work particularly well together, but it does work. And that is because of the boys and our strong relationships.

The case study above links to Competency 2.2 (points a to h). David and Michael talk honestly about factors in all of the children's lives that could impede, or indeed be used to promote, holistic development and long-term outcomes. Imagine caring for these children in an Early Years context, be it through working in a setting, a health context or a social care environment. Now consider the Reflection Point below.

Reflection Point

What are the main points that you take from the conversation with David and Michael?
How would this conversation influence your practice with these children?
What could you do to assist the foster children's development?
What do you think the longer-term implications may be for the foster children?

One of the main points of learning from the above case study should be that there should not be a 'one size fits all' approach to children and their development. What David and Michael's situation highlights is that each child is unique in the way that they process, translate and react to what is happening in their social construct. Bronfenbrenner's (1979) theoretical approach to development (see Figure 3.1) highlights an importance placed on the community and society in which the child grows up in and it is noted that this has a large part to play with the children in this example.

David and Michael talk of positive outcomes, thus far, for the children in their care, and yet this story could be so different. It is also worth noting that the effects of Early Childhood, especially from conception and the first two years of life, can last into adulthood (1001 Critical Days, 2019), and the nurturing and caring environment that these children find themselves in should assist them as they continue throughout their lifespan. Using Bronfenbrenner's model, it is possible to consider the various factors that could impact on a child and their development. What should be noted is that these aspects are not always permanent for all children. In the case of the children in the case study, for example, the microsystem has changed considerably over time and this microsystem is impacted

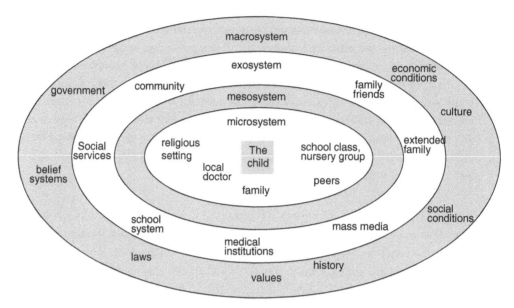

Figure 3.1   Bronfenbrenner's model of ecological development (1979)

by the outer systems, so the influences that are part of these children's lives are not static concepts; instead they can be quite chaotic, and it should be considered how this can impact on young children's development over a longer term.

Reflection Point

Put a child you know into the context of Bronfenbrenner's ecological system. What are the influences on the way that they develop?
Now consider the foster children in the case study above. How does their situation differ?
Thinking more widely than your own individual practice, what do you think can be done to assist children's development when considering the context in which they grow up?

Factors that Promote or Impede Holistic Development: A Health Professional's View

In the first practical example of this chapter, we considered, in the main, how the context in which children are born and nurtured throughout their Early Years can impact on their learning and development. We focused on the *nurture* of young children. In this section, we will focus more on the *nature* aspects and how these can influence a child's outcomes.

Sharon Smith is an Associate Lecturer at the University of Northampton. She is an experienced Health Visitor and former children's nurse with a particular interest in childhood nutrition and family health promotion. She is a member of and author for the All Party Parliamentary Group on a Fit and Healthy Childhood.

Case Study

Interview with Sharon - how health can impact on children's development

Sharon was asked to share her views on how she felt aspects of health can impact on children's development. She said:

> Health is the foundation for holistic development – the Early Years lay the foundations for lifelong health and wellbeing. Health starts in preconception – the health of the parents will determine the health of the pregnancy and therefore the health status of the baby. For example, the impact of a mother smoking, maternal diet, stress and alcohol consumption affect all aspects of development from birth and potential mortality (e.g. due to low birth weight).
>
> Nutrition in the perinatal period is key for strong growth and development in infancy and childhood, and so the promotion of breastfeeding is fundamental to this best start in nutrition. Breastfeeding rates in the UK are currently the lowest in the world and childhood obesity is the highest in Europe, with 10% of 4–5-year-olds being obese in 2019 (Public Health England, 2020). We must invest in preventing childhood obesity; it is associated with an increased risk of adult obesity and chronic diseases such as type 2 diabetes. Childhood obesity is also associated with emotional and behavioural problems from a very young age and often results in lower levels of physical activity and increased school absence. These factors impact on all aspects of development, for example not being able to optimise motor skill development and socio-emotional difficulties can present due to difficulties in socialising with other children. Physical activity does not need to be organised activities or held in a structured class environment – movement is the key, whether its tummy time, nappy changing stretching or trike laps! Promoting the outdoors as a healthy environment physically and mentally, not to mention the benefits for language development, needs to be highlighted more by Health Visitors and suggestions provided in health promotion literature.
>
> Development can be affected by common health conditions, such as vision or hearing difficulties. For example, 'behavioural' problems in nursery may purely be due to poor eyesight or hearing loss or even a chronic itch due to poorly managed topical eczema. Health Visitors work with families as part of the 0–19 Healthy Child Programme, but, in my experience, it is essential to remember the importance of

(Continued)

relationships and that a 'one size fits all approach' does not work when meeting individual child and family needs. Universal services tend to focus on healthy nutrition, including oral health, physical activity and healthy weights. The importance of promoting perinatal mental health and parenting support, for example sleep support, cannot be underestimated in managing some of the 'physical health' needs identified. In the early days and weeks, the mother's mind could be described as the baby's environment, and so maternal mental health and physical health are entwined tightly and impact directly on how their children develop.

Sharon provides suggestions of how Health Visitors can assist in this area. However, it should not just be down to health professionals to make such contributions. Whichever field of Early Years you work in, there is a responsibility to support children and families with health promotion. Sharon's statement above – *'in the early days and weeks, the mother's mind could be described as the baby's environment'* – gives us real food for thought and shows the importance of not only the Early Years but also the period of conception. Maternal mental health is a pivotal aspect of children's development, with perinatal mental health problems affecting between 10% and 20% of women at some point during pregnancy, and for the first year after birth, with around 10–15% of women experiencing common mental health problems such as perinatal depression and anxiety (Bauer et al., 2014). It is also important to note that only around half of all mothers with perinatal depression and anxiety are identified (Hearn et al., 1998).

Thought also needs to be given to fathers. Much emphasis is placed on the mother figure, but the mental health of fathers can impact on children and families too. The NSPCC (2011) report that this is an under-researched topic and stress that it should be an area of focus due to the fact that it can not only have a direct impact on the family due to the father's state of mind, but can also impact indirectly by making a difference to the mental health of the mother. It is also reported by the NSPCC (2011) that a serious shortcoming of assisting mothers with regards to mental health has been the failure to engage with fathers and other members of the family, and therefore not gaining a whole view of the situation and potential solutions.

Reflection Point

Reflect on the thoughts that Sharon shared with us in the case study above. What can you do as practitioners to assist in this area?

How do you think the aspects that she discusses – obesity, breastfeeding, mental health, nutrition and health complications – can impact on a child's development?

What can you plan to assist children's learning and development if they are affected by physical health conditions? What about mental health problems?

Practical Ways of Engaging with Children and Encouraging Development

Whatever field you work in, you are likely to have direct contact with children and their families. Whether working in an Early Years setting, a health environment or a social work context, you will need to engage with children with the aim of promoting development and improving long-term outcomes. It is likely that the best way to engage, in whatever field, is through the medium of play. Moyles (2005: 4) explains that the concept of play can be compared to 'trying to seize bubbles, for every time there appears to be something to hold on to, its ephemeral nature disallows it being grasped'. This indicates that the nature of play is hard to define. That said, it is widely recognised that there is a need for children to be exposed to high-quality play-based experiences (Sylva et al., 2004). Olusoga (2014: 63) states that a practitioner's responsibility with regards to play is to 'reconcile children's learning and developmental needs with wider societal concerns'. This leads us back to Bronfenbrenner's model (1979), which was discussed earlier in this chapter, and forces us to consider how play aligns with the expectations of parents, professional colleagues and with society as a whole.

The definition of creativity, like play, is diverse and varied (Fisher, 2004), but there are multiple benefits of allowing creativity in the context of learning and development. Eisner (2002) compiled a list of ten benefits to learning and development, through engaging in creativity. These are:

1   The arts enable children to make good judgements about qualitative relationships.
2   Problems can have more than one solution and questions can have more than one answer.
3   The arts celebrate multiple perspectives (there are many ways to see and interpret the world).
4   In complex forms of problem-solving, purposes are seldom fixed, but change with circumstance and opportunity.
5   The arts make vivid the fact that neither words in their literal form nor numbers exhaust what we can know.
6   Small differences can have large effects.
7   The arts allow us to think through and within material.
8   The arts allow us to say what cannot be said (a work of art can allow a release of poetic capacities to find the words that will do the job).
9   The arts give us experiences we can have from no other source and, through such experiences, allow us to discover the range and variety of what we are capable of feeling.
10 The arts' position in the school curriculum symbolises to the young what adults believe is important.

If we think back to the conversations in the case studies in this chapter, we can appreciate the need for open definitions and the need not to be constrained by a particular construct around play or creativity. However, both play and creativity are extremely valuable for all children, irrespective of context. It should be noted that when considering factors that impede young children's development (as Competency 2.2 asks you to do), then, based on the points made above, it is likely that when children are not able to play or be creative, it can have a detrimental effect.

What Does All of this Mean for Practice?

The conversations with both David and Michael and with Sharon highlight the need for practitioners, in whatever field they may be working in, to really know the children and families that they work with. This links closely with Competency 7 (Partnership with parents and caregivers) and indicates the interconnectedness of the competency evidence. Please refer to Chapter 8 for information and support on how to work with parents and caregivers in order to maximise plans for learning and development.

When acknowledging the need for play and creativity to promote holistic development, let's think back to the twins in David and Michael's conversation. As a reminder, the twins are five years old, a boy and girl, and are in foster care after a tough start in life. Consider how you could encourage development, through play and creative approaches, within each of the key areas of development. Now complete the table below with your thoughts:

	What activities could you do to encourage this area of development?	What benefits do you think that this may have?	Any special considerations/factors that you would need to take into account?
Physical development			
Cognitive development			
Language development			
Social development			
Emotional development			

Summary

The Graduate Practitioner Competencies aim to allow you to develop and evidence 'the skilful application of knowledge to practice and practice to knowledge' (ECSDN, 2019). This chapter has provided opportunities for you to do just that. The golden thread that has run through this chapter is that each child is unique, and each family is a unique construct in itself. Your main take-away from this book should be that 'one size does not fit all'. It is important to apply what you learn in the lecture room about the key theories of child development, but it is equally important to keep the child, and their family, at the centre of everything that you do.

Key Points

This chapter has, through the use of conversations, explored various aspects that can impact or impede young children's learning and development. It has:

- Revisited key theory around the areas of development
- Reinforced the need to adopt a holistic approach to development
- Applied knowledge of child development to practice
- Considered how factors such as individual and family circumstances promote and impede holistic development and long-term outcomes
- Reinforced the concept of the unique child and the need to deal with each child and their family as individuals – avoiding the 'one size fits all' approach
- Reflected on the impact of community and society on development
- Heard, and reflected on, the viewpoint of a health professional regarding the implications of physical and mental health on development
- Considered the role of play and creativity and how these can aid development.

Further Reading

The texts and resources below have been chosen to enable you to explore further specific aspects of child development. It is important that you keep up to date in this area. New theories of learning and development are constructed as access to medical science becomes more sophisticated, so this is an area that can advance over time.

Gopnik, A. (2016) *The gardener and the carpenter*. London: The Bodley Head.

Free Online Courses | Harvard University https://pll.harvard.edu/catalog/free

OpenLearn - Open University – all courses are free https://www.open.edu/openlearn/free-courses/full-catalogue

Early childhood development | UNICEF https://www.unicef.org/early-childhood-development

Home • ZERO TO THREE https://www.zerotothree.org/

Chapter 4

WORKING TO PROMOTE HEALTH, WELLBEING, SAFETY AND NURTURING CARE

Helen Simmons and Carol Fenton

Chapter Aims

This chapter contextualises health and wellbeing and the competencies which will need to be demonstrated. By the end of the chapter, you will have had opportunities to reflect upon and extend understanding of how to:

- demonstrate the application of knowledge about health, wellbeing and safety to practice and apply data protection legislation to practice (Graduate Competencies 3.1, 3.2 and 3.3)
- know and demonstrate how to complete a risk assessment and apply it in practice (Graduate Competencies 3.4)
- understand factors which influence nutritional health and integrate knowledge about current dietary guidance into practice, including early feeding and weaning (Graduate Competencies 3.5)
- demonstrate the application of knowledge and understanding about the importance of respectful nurturing care routines, support children with ongoing health conditions, and facilitate the promotion of health and education (Graduate Competencies 3.6, 3.7, 3.8)

Introduction

This chapter focuses on the importance of promoting health, wellbeing, safety and nurturing care. It will consider how the Early Childhood Graduate Practitioner should lead practice within the Early

Childhood context and demonstrate the application of knowledge regarding health, wellbeing and safety in practice. This chapter will also consider the importance of respectful nurturing care routines and the role of the Early Childhood Graduate Practitioner in working with other professionals, children and families.

The Importance of Policies and Legislation and the Application to Practice

First, we will explore the legislation that underpins work with children. Legislation is the process of making or enacting laws and is a fundamental aspect of society. It has various purposes, but the general objective is to ensure societal health, safety and welfare. You can explore the general legislative framework in the United Kingdom at legislation.gov.uk/understanding-legislation.

Parker-Rees and Leeson (2015: 234) encapsulate the idea of policy development with the analogy of the 'black box', in which inputs are entered and outcomes emerge. The information is the input. Consultation takes place and the output is the legislation.

Specifically, social policy is an aspect of policy whereby a social issue is identified. This can be as a result of research, media input, serious case reviews, lobbying or a combination of these. *This is the input.* Campbell-Barr (2015) acknowledges the aim is to improve outcomes for society. Significantly, it is noted that governments impact the lives of children through social policy, therefore policy can be viewed as a social construct of childhood. Baldock, Fitzgerald and Kay (2013) would agree with this idea. They note that social policy will undoubtably change over time because it is placed in the contemporary social and cultural context in which it is devised. Take, for example, the many revisions of the Children Act 1989 (Legislative.gov.uk, 1989). *This is the output.*

Reflection Point

Consider the impact of changing governments on social policy. Reflect on the effect this has on the role of the Early Childhood practitioner.

Clearly, it would be unreasonable to expect that every setting has access to every piece of legislation that affects children. Instead, we use setting-specific policies as an interpretation of the law, and this is what provides an outline of practice. You should have access to the policies in your setting and it is good practice to ensure you are up to date with these documents. Each policy should have a review date, at which point it may be updated, so the importance of being up to date with the policy development in your setting cannot be underestimated. Not all setting policies will refer specifically to children; some will underpin the health, safety and welfare of staff. As a result of the information input, an eventual setting policy is developed.

Reflection Point

Why is it important that you as a practitioner adhere to the policies in your daily practice?

Let us now look at some specific legislation that underpins practice with children, its evolvement over the last 30 years and its application to practice.

The Children Act 1989

The Children Act 1989 (Legislation.gov.uk, 1989) arose as a result of some high-profile child abuse cases in Cleveland. Due to the actions of social workers, the primary function of the Act was to ensure that the welfare of the child was paramount and the child's wishes were taken into account when making decisions about them. The Act provided boundaries for outside intervention based on the premise that children are best cared for by their own families. Intervention, however, was possible if families were non-cooperative.

Task

The Children Act 1989 was intended to balance the right to family life (privacy) with the responsibility of the state to protect children from harm. Consider and write down how this might be achieved in practice.

The Children Act 2004

The safeguarding and welfare requirements for children were improved in the Children Act 2004 (Legislation.gov.uk, 2004). In addition, it amended sections 17 and 47 of the 1989 Act to give children a right to express their views in child protection enquiries. The Every Child Matters: Agenda for Change (ECM) (DfES, 2003) was enforced by the Act as a result of the serious case review of Victoria Climbié (Laming, 2003).

Every Child Matters

Every Child Matters: Next Steps (Department for Education and Skills (DFES), 2004) led to the merging of schools and other child services. Five key themes – being healthy, staying safe, enjoying and achieving, making a positive contribution and achieving economic well-being – underpinned the new approach to the wellbeing of children.

It provided the basis for the development of the Social and Emotional Aspects of Learning (SEAL) programme in schools. This is an example of social policy development in action. However, the focus of government policy can change with a change of government which has a different ideology.

The 2010 Coalition government moved away from the ECM agenda, moving the focus from the idea of wellbeing, towards achievement.

Task

The Local Safeguarding Children's Boards (LSCB), which coordinated relevant local organisations to safeguard and promote children's welfare, were introduced in the Children Act 2004. They became a point of reference for settings when abuse was suspected. Consider which policies a setting may have to develop in order to underpin the support that could be given by the boards.

The Childcare Act 2006

The Childcare Act 2006 (Legislation.gov.uk, 2006) was pivotal in that it was the first to be concerned with Early Childhood and childcare. It presented an integrated education and care framework for preschool children and instigated the non-ministerial Office for Standards in Education Children's Services and Skills (Ofsted) childcare register. Significantly, it introduced the Early Years Foundation Stage (EYFS) (Department of Children, Schools and Families, 2008)) and tasked the local authorities with improving outcomes for 0–5 year-olds, and the ECM outcomes, thus reducing inequalities for children.

The Early Years Foundation Stage (revised)

The revised *Early Years Foundation Stage Framework* (Department for Education, 2017) is mandatory in England; it has to be adhered to by providers on the Early Years Register and all providers registered with an Early Years' childminder agency. It sets the standards for Early Childhood providers in learning and welfare in early childhood, and was based on research that stated that children's learning and development would best be supported with good-quality childcare.

Reflection Point

Consider the implications of the Childcare Act 2006 and the subsequent EYFS framework for early childhood practitioners. How do you see this implemented in practice?

The Children and Families Act 2014

In order to ensure that all children, regardless of background, are given the opportunity to succeed the Children and Families Act 2014 (Legislation.gov.uk, 2014) was introduced. The Act is in two parts: the improvement of services for vulnerable children; and supporting the childcare sector to, in turn, support families and children. A single assessment process was introduced to provide support from birth to age 25. The process combined an Education, Health and Care (EHC) plan, which replaced statements of special educational need.

The Health and Safety at Work Act 1974

The Health and Safety at Work Act 1974 (Legislation.gov.uk, 1974) is a crucial Act that details the duties of employees, employers and members of the public, towards themselves and each other, as far as is reasonably practicable. The Health and Safety Executive (2009: 1) states that 'all workers have a right to work in places where risks to their health and safety are properly controlled'. In short, your employer must:

- risk assess any harm you could be subject to
- explain how the risks will be controlled
- work with you, contractors, other employers and the Health and Safety Executive to protect you from harm
- provide health and safety training
- provide, toilets, drinking water, washing facilities and first aid facilities
- report major incidences
- insure you while at work.

You have a responsibility to:

- follow the training you have been given
- take reasonable care of your and others' health and safety
- cooperate with your employer
- report breaches of the legislation.

This may not appear to be legislation that you would consider to be part of the work in Early Childhood, but consider aspects of risk assessment, first aid, fire safety, the administration of medicines, manual handling, the safe disposal of waste and food hygiene in Early Childhood settings. These are all part of health and safety at work.

Reflection Point

Reflect on which aspects of these you have been involved with in your setting.

The General Data Protection Regulation 2018

The General Data Protection Regulation (GDPR) 2018 (legislation. Gov. uk, 2018) replaced the Data Protection Act 1998 and primarily states that 'you must have a lawful basis in order to process personal data' (Information Commissioner's Office (ICO), 2018). It gives individuals more control over their personal data, privacy and consent. Personal data can be considered as name, address, health data and photos, to name a few. Unlike the previous Act, the GDPR emphasises the need for transparency and accountability which is clearly demonstrated and documented. At least one of the following principles must apply:

- Consent
- Contract – necessary if entering into a contract
- Legal obligation – in order to comply with the law
- Vital interest – protection of life
- Public task – necessary to perform a public interest task with a clear basis in law
- Legitimate interest

Source: (ICO, 2018)

This is a very good example of the development of contextual policy. The notion of personal data has seen a significant shift with the advent of information technology in the last 20 years. Thus, the GDPR reflects contemporary society.

For aspects of legislation in Scotland, Wales and Ireland, please see the Further Reading section at the end of this chapter.

The Identification of Risk, Completion of Risk Assessments and their Application to Practice

Identification of risk

There are a number of elements to risk. The Project Management Institute (PMI), cited in Pritchard (2015: 4), identifies a six-step approach to the management of risk. This is a business model (the setting in which you work is a business and should be following this broad plan as part of the Health and Safety at Work Act). If followed, it will encapsulate the elements of risk that you may come across in your practice in Early Childhood settings, which you, as an employee, are responsible for. It is most likely that the leadership team will plan risk management and undertake action to reduce risk. However, you may be asked to:

- identify risks
- qualify risks

Figure 4.1   A risk analogy (Ropeik and Gray, 2002: 23)

Hazard: ketchup
Exposure: to increased pickle consumption
Consequence: how much harm does the hazard do?
Probability: the risk is only there if you are allergic to pickle

- quantify risks
- plan risk response
- monitor and control risk.

Ropeik and Gray (2002: 4) advocate keeping in mind two vital elements of risk: exposure to a hazard and negative consequences. They present a very good analogy that perhaps makes the concept of risk assessment less intimidating (Figure 4.1).

Hopkin (2013) notes that a clear understanding of the risk is required. He advocates that in all businesses the main objective is the delivery of a service. Therefore, the purpose of risk management is to achieve the best possible outcomes by preventing the negatives, thus by minimising the damage.

Risk assessments

Perry (2016) defines a risk assessment perfectly, stating that it is a review of the dangers in an activity and an evaluation of the consequences. If the dangers are too high, control measures should be put in place to reduce the risk to an acceptable level. If we consider the aspects of the Health and Safety at Work Act 1974, it follows that employers need to ensure that employees are safe in their place of work. In practice, they can do this by undertaking risk assessments. This, of course, requires that the member of staff carrying out the risk assessment has sufficient competence and knowledge of the consequences and can control the hazards identified. Extend your knowledge by reading the *Health and Safety Guide to Risk Assessments and Safety Statements* (Health and Safety Authority, 2016), which can be accessed at https://www.hsa.ie/eng/publications_and_forms/publications/safety_and_health_management/guide_to_risk_assessments_and_safety_statements.pdf

Application to practice

Task

You are planning a trip to the local farm for a group of Key Stage 1 children. You have to hire a bus to make the journey. Write a risk assessment, covering all the aspects you need to consider. You can use the risk assessment grid we have provided to help you make your decisions.

- The journey
- The ratio of children to adults
- The safeguarding requirements
- Any allergies a child may have
- Personal hygiene
- Parental consent
- Cost

Complete the risk assessment to help you make your decisions.

Risk	High, medium, low	Action	Member of staff responsible	Level of reduced risk
Journey				
Staff/child ratio				
Safeguarding				
Allergies				
Personal hygiene				
Consent				
Cost				

Take these points into consideration:

1   The risk assessment has to be shared with all adults that are on the trip.
2   They have to sign to say they understand their responsibilities.
3   Has everyone had access to the setting policy on school trips?
4   Remember GDPR regulations. What potentially confidential information may you be sharing?
5   Do you have a registered first aider accompanying the trip?
6   Has anyone carried out a pre-visit to the location?
7   Has the travel company been cleared to transport children?
8   Do you have children with special educational needs?

Safe Disposal of Waste and Medicines

As we have discussed, an employer has a duty to ensure as far as is reasonably practicable the absence of risks to health for employees. There is also further legislation that details specific aspects of health and safety. Here we will look at the safe disposal of waste. Much of the control of hazardous waste regulations refers to waste that, as an Early Childhood practitioner, you will most probably not be subject to. However, The Controlled Waste Regulations 1992, as part of the Environmental Protection Act 1990 1(2) (a), details waste as:

Any waste which consists of wholly or partly of human or animal tissue, blood or bodily fluids, excretions, drugs or other pharmaceutical products, swabs or dressings, syringes or needles or other sharp instruments, being waste unless rendered safe may prove hazardous to any person coming into contact with it. (Legislation.gov.uk, 1992)

You can appreciate here that, while working in a range of settings, including Early Childhood, schools, health or social care environments, you may be exposed to a number of aspects of this definition of controlled waste. As part of your duties as an employee under the Health and Safety at Work Act 1974, you are responsible, along with colleagues, for the safe disposal of these types of waste.

In addition, The Control of Substances Hazardous to Health Regulations 2002 (COSHH), again part of the Health and Safety at Work Act 1974, includes using, handling, storing and transporting hazardous substances. It follows, then, that the management of waste is essential as there is a potential risk of infection. The Health and Safety Executive (HSE) (2021) state that the following aspects need to be taken into consideration:

- Infection control and health and safety legislation
- Environmental and waste regulations
- Transport legislation.

This will clearly impact your practice. Your setting should have a number of policies that detail the control of substances hazardous to health, and you need to be familiar with them.

Reflection Point

Reflect on the differences between Early Childhood settings and the responsibility for the safe disposal of waste and medicines. How will practice differ in a nursery or a school?

Good Hygiene, Including Food Preparation

The Food Standards Agency (2020) provides a checklist for settings that offer food on their premises. Depending on the answers, there are two different procedures to be followed. Broadly speaking, if there is provision of meals, snacks or drinks or food provided by a parent needs to be reheated, the *Safer Food Better Business for Childminders* (Food Standards Agency, 2020) should be followed. This covers aspects of cross-contamination, cleaning, chilling and cooking. Additionally, specific advice is provided for babies and children. If the childcare is provided on non-domestic premises, the *Safer Food Better Businesses for Caterers* (Food Standards Agency, 2015) should be followed. Regulations are also detailed in the EYFS (Department for Education, 2017). Schools and colleges follow different regulations.

Food and drink are also covered in the EYFS (Department for Education, 2017: 28). There is a stipulation that food and drink must be healthy, balanced and nutritious, and some settings may have a Food and Drink Policy and Procedure.

Maintaining equipment and accessing training

It is essential that all equipment is well maintained and that staff are trained for its use.

There should be a health and safety policy in place, in all settings, which includes procedures for identifying, reporting and dealing with accidents, hazards and faulty equipment, to ensure the safety of the children and staff. Statutory guidance is provided by the Health and Safety Executive (2012)

Case Study

Voice of the Early Childhood Graduate Practitioner: Chloe, University of Derby

During all my placements I have always been given a brief training session around safeguarding and child protection. This would usually consist of reading through the setting's policies and procedures with my supervisor at the setting and also them giving me the basic information around safeguarding and child protection, for example, who the safeguarding lead is, who to report any concerns to and my role within safeguarding and how I should always report issues to a member of staff, no matter how small the issue may be. In regard to health and safety, I have found that it has always been general information about ensuring all children are registered, all outdoor doors are locked so no children can escape, and risk assessments are done on a regular basis on the classroom to ensure it is safe. My first placement also gave me training on completing a risk assessment when doing a food activity, as we were using a cooker and a microwave. This also links on to food hygiene, as children were handing the foods. So the class teacher went through the basic food hygiene we needed to ensure that we were meeting its requirements, such as washing hands, wiping the surfaces and tying long hair back. In terms of first aid, I was told information on my induction around first aid and who was first-aid trained, so I was aware who to report any accident to. In my second-year placement, there were sheets around the school and in every classroom about who was the first aid monitor. I found this really helpful as not being there all week, I sometimes forgot who to report accidents to.

I learn better when I see practice. So I had a conversation with the teaching assistant in my classroom, who was a trained paediatric first aider, to see if I could join her when it was her day to be the first aid monitor. I actually found this really helpful and ended up doing it with her quite a few times.

Unique Child, Unique Parents

We know that long before a child is born, new parents face important decisions, with contemporary parenting often bringing with it much pressure and scrutiny. Whether via health professionals, Early Childhood practitioners, parenting books, online platforms or friends and family, new parents may look for help, advice and support from many different sources. Because of this, parents can often find themselves navigating conflicting and overwhelming advice about the meeting of basic care needs of their child, including attachment, feeding, sleep and early social interaction.

For all new parents, it is important that those who support them have a good level of understanding about the pressures of modern parenting and have an awareness of where parents may look for support. It is important to be informed about contemporary debates within modern parenting and to ensure that anyone supporting new parents is well equipped to recognise each family as unique, diverse and requiring individualised support.

Contemporary Issues

Early feeding and weaning

One of the first decisions a new parent will have to make once their child is born relates to early feeding. Recognising that breastfeeding is the best scenario in terms of nutrition and attachment for a new child, it is important that new mothers are supported to breastfeed. It is also important that mothers who are unable to breastfeed, or who choose not to, are supported and respected as autonomous and agentic members of society.

Recent research by Simmons (2020: 86) highlighted some worrying examples of women not always feeling comfortable when breastfeeding in public, while others recalled challenges in finding support and information if they decided, for multiple reasons, not to breastfeed. For example, below are extracts from two participants reflecting on their antenatal classes:

> We had a very pushy woman talk to us about breastfeeding. She refused to speak to us about bottle feeding at all.

> There was no information provided on other ways to feed your baby if and when it was needed. The classes should have supporting families at the heart of them, not pushing a particular agenda.

It is important to note that, while these quotes from participants highlight some frustrations, practitioners who support new parents in such forums do so under guidance of the World Health Organisation (WHO) and (in England) the Department of Health (DfE).

Guidance, policy and early feeding support advocate the message that breastfeeding is 'the best start for babies' (Musgrave, 2017: 91) and encourages the promotion of this guidance through support and intervention for new parents. This is an important message because the benefits of breastfeeding include a reduction in (Musgrave, 2017: 91):

- lower respiratory tract infections and urine infections
- wheezing
- non-infective gastroenteritis
- otitis media (ear infection)
- lactose intolerance
- asthma
- infant feeding difficulties
- gastroenteritis
- eczema
- infant feed intolerance
- obesity in later life
- diabetes mellitus in later life

Issues may arise, though, if practitioners are in some way constrained from supporting new mothers who may wish to make different choices or may simply like more information about all the options available to them. To ensure that new parents can make an informed choice, the role of empathetic and supportive practitioners is crucial, and this is not always easy in an Early Childhood workforce that is 'dominated by a strongly positivistic and regulatory discourse' (Moss, 2017: 11).

As stated by Burman (2008: 80):

> the decks are heavily loaded in favour of breastfeeding: what mother can resist the injunction to foster the development of her child, or worse, impede it by failing to provide 'baby's birthright'? What of the mothers who do not have 'the choice' not to work, or who cannot for other reasons breastfeed their babies?

It is essential that new parents, especially new mothers are supported in the decisions that they make. These decisions are not made lightly, and it is an important part of the Early Childhood Graduate Practitioner role that respectful and individualised support is ensured. Helpful guidance from the Royal College of Midwives (2020: 3) states that:

> With the right support and guidance, most women are able to breastfeed. However, the parents of infants that are formula fed, whether exclusively or partially, need accessible evidence-based information to enable them to do so safely.

As children move towards weaning age, new parents continue to require support which reflects and responds to their individual and diverse circumstances. The World Health Organisation recommends that complementary feeding begins at six months old. It offers the following information as part of their guide *Complementary Feeding: Family Foods for Breastfed Children* (WHO, 1948):

> Ensuring that infants' nutritional needs are met requires that complementary foods be:

- *timely* – meaning that they are introduced when the need for energy and nutrients exceeds what can be provided through exclusive breastfeeding;
- *adequate* – meaning that they provide sufficient energy, protein and micronutrients to meet a growing child's nutritional needs;
- *safe* – meaning that they are hygienically stored and prepared, and fed with clean hands using clean utensils and not bottles and teats;
- *properly fed* – meaning that they are given consistent with a child's signals of appetite and satiety, and that meal frequency and feeding are suitable for age.

Parents should be supported to understand the most recent guidance regarding weaning, including support for when to wean, what dietary factors need to be taken into consideration and how to choose an appropriate method for weaning their child. As stated by Musgrave (2017: 92), 'weaning is another aspect of baby care that has become a source of anxiety and mystique for parents'. It is therefore important for parents to be informed and supported in making decisions within the context of their own unique family.

Reflection Point

Consider the feelings of new parents that have been discussed in this section. How can you as an Early Childhood practitioner ensure that you support these parents at this time?

Where new parents go for support

Throughout history, new parents have sought and accessed the popular 'expert' in terms of child rearing and parenting. In his presentation of the history of childhood in Britain over the last 100 years, Cunningham (2006: 202) notes that:

> The first half of the twentieth century can be seen as a terrain on which a battle was fought between behaviourists and psychologically informed views of childhood. The victory went to the latter. Its impact was to place the spotlight on the family, not so much its adherence or otherwise to the gospel of hygiene but for its ability to mould the character and personality of the children who were placed by now so firmly in its care.

From the 1940s onwards, popular child-rearing figures included Fredrick Truby-King, John Bowlby, Donald Winnicott, Penelope Leach and, more recently, Jo Frost and Gina Ford. As explored by Cunningham, the popular figure or 'experts' of the day often relate to the social and cultural constructs and dominant discourses of that particular time.

With the rise of modern technology, new parents now use the internet as a source of support and advice. This includes accessing parenting forums such as the UK-based Mumsnet (Mumsnet, 2000) or Netmums (Netmums, 2000) to pose questions to a community. While parents have always shared experiences with each other, modern forms of instant connection have provided increased opportunity, according to Pederson (2016: 32), for 'internet discussions forums and social media to create and disseminate their own (parents) personal view'. This also includes accessing blogs and social media sites such as Facebook (Facebook, 2004) and Instagram (Instagram, 2010). This plethora of platforms to turn to for advice and support means that, more than ever before, new parents can access instant advice and ask questions about any aspect of their child's development.

As with all such advances, although being extremely helpful, these platforms can also bring with them the potential for some degree of harm, especially in relation to mental health. Scrutiny and judgement through social media is an inevitable facet of modern living, and the impact on new parents is something that needs to be thoughtfully considered. It is important that those who support new parents have this understanding.

While providing opportunities for new parents to 'turn to the internet as a source of community, which helps them connect, communicate and share' (Valchanov et al., 2015: 51), it is also important to remember that such platforms can exacerbate feelings of inadequacy for new parents and increase potential feelings of being judged by others.

Just as it is important for children, it is important for new parents to be well supported by empathic and well-qualified practitioners who can recognise the importance of supporting the individual. This support includes the facilitation of activities and advice for new parents to explore their new role in a safe and non-judgmental environment. As stated by Hardyment (2007: 305):

> It is the isolated nature of modern parenting that creates anxiety. Getting in touch with likeminded people eager to help and share does far more good than the most enlightened of advice manuals.

Reflection Point

How can the notion of 'expert advice' potentially undermine confidence in new parents? What is the role of the Early Childhood Graduate Practitioner here?

Along with the context of unique families, it is important for the support for new parents to progress into this support offered within the early childhood setting. This includes strong partnership working and respectful care routines.

Respectful Routines

As explored within the previous section, it is important to recognise children as individuals and this recognition and value must extend to parents. As children enter education and care settings, the partnership between parents and practitioners is a fundamental aspect of facilitating the development of children.

This partnership includes sharing of information about the individual needs of children and the diverse contexts of each child's home life. When supporting a child within a setting, this partnership can help to support attachment, security and a positive environment in which young children can flourish.

Respectful nurturing care routines

When families are exploring Early Childhood settings for their child to attend, it is important that they can feel confident that their voices and wishes are heard and that practitioners within the setting will work with parents to ensure a smooth transition. Parents will want to know about the rest, sleep and 'quiet' time facilities, and how these can support and align to the home environment as closely as possible.

As stated by Nutbrown and Page (2008: 90) 'the environment should be created such that children, where possible, have choices about where they are when they sleep and can go to their sleeping space themselves'. Children and their parents can be supported through strong communication and through practitioners taking the time to understand the child's home life, encouraging families to bring in objects from home, particularly those that will support sleep, rest and security.

Through a well-thought out space and an understanding that children, like all human beings, will take some time to settle into an unfamiliar environment, it is possible to support a sense of belonging that will facilitate resilience and development. Providing thoughtful and respectful sleep routines, personal care opportunities, mealtime routines and play opportunities will support this development and early social interaction and attachment within the Early Childhood setting.

Through daily routines, practitioners, including, for example, the key person, can take the time to get to know each child, learn about their preferences and support the child to feel valued and heard. As pointed out by Glazzard, Potter and Stones (2019: 35), 'the key person plays a crucial role in developing children's confidence and self-worth and these factors will impact positively on their ability to be resilient in a range of settings'. Providing the time and space through daily routines will support attachment and development and is also a fundamental aspect of promoting self-regulation.

In recent years, links have been made between the importance of self-regulation and its association with school readiness (Department for Education, 2017), with the early fostering of independence and the promotion of resilience serving to help to equip children with ability to adjust to a new environment and cope with the demands of school. From an Early Childhood perspective, although the long-term benefits of well-fostered self-regulation are recognised to be important, the promotion of these skills are valuable for the very young child as a standalone period of their life. This links to the ongoing frustration from those within the discipline and practice of Early Childhood that this stage is often viewed as a stepping stone to the next phase of development, rather than being valued as a fundamental time in human development.

Glazzard et al. (2019: 56) state that, within the Early Childhood setting, 'infants are exposed to a series of new and different experiences involving people, movement and sounds; they are dependent on a safe, caring adult who is in tune with their needs to regulate their responses'.

In their book *Meeting Mental Health Needs of Young Children 0–5 Years*, Glazzard et al., (2019: 57) offer some useful strategies for practitioners to support self-regulation. Some examples for toddlers aged 1–2 years are:

- Children can sometimes find it hard to complete tasks when required, so it can help to offer choices. For example, if a toddler is reluctant to put on a coat to play outside, they may respond better to 'left arm or right arm first?'
- This age-group may enjoy imitating actions and songs with gestures that encourage memory, waiting and recall.
- Games with simple rules can be introduced – such as taking turns to throw beanbags into a box or roll a ball down a tube.
- Adults who are attentive and in tune with a young child's needs are on hand to guide and help manage emotions.

It is through the promotion of positive relationships and 'anchored attention' (Roberts, 2010: 73) that resilience and self-regulation can be supported. Everyday routines and opportunities to facilitate independence and choice, along with clear links to and communication with the home environment will all help not only to build the foundations for later development, but also to ensure the best possible childhood experience within these important early years.

Working together

Along with strong partnerships with parents, the relationships between practitioners themselves is also a fundamental aspect of providing a positive environment in which young children can flourish. The promotion of positive relationships can help to support wellbeing, self-esteem and resilience in young children (Fenton, 2021). Children will respond to the atmosphere they are in, and it is essential that communication and teamwork are fostered within all Early Childhood settings, schools, health and social care environments.

This partnership working extends to the relationships between all professionals within the setting. Effective teamwork includes communication, sharing of information and working together to ensure the promotion of health and education of children and families. Teamwork and communication go hand in hand, and it is important for the professionals who work together to consider the best methods of communication for sharing of information. As explored by Yates et al. (2021: 25), the best way to share information will differ and must be done within an appropriate forum:

> Some information can be shared in group contexts such as staff meetings, while sensitive, confidential information may need to be discussed with specific individuals or professionals with specific responsibilities, such as the SEN coordinator or the child's parents/carers.

Critical reflection

An essential aspect of the Early Childhood Graduate Practitioner role includes recognising the importance of critical reflection. Engaging with continuous critical reflection is fundamental to effective teamwork. This is not an easy process and can lead to some uncomfortable reflections, but it is essential for personal development, as stated by Bolton (2014: 52): 'Critical reflective practice is risky, leading to unsettling development of one's own practices and to demand for change.' It involves engaging with critical approaches and debates in relation to Early Childhood and applying this to practice. Early Childhood Graduate Practitioners can practise and support colleagues in the practice of the following levels of critical reflection:

A Descriptive Level – Describing the event in question

A Reflective Level – Thinking about the event

A Critical Level – Questioning the circumstances of the event and viewing this from different perspectives in relation to power relationships. (Yates, 2020: 118)

As leaders and agents for change, the Early Childhood Graduate Practitioner will continue to support those they work with to engage in reflection and professional development. As stated by Nahmad-Williams and Oates (2018: 487):

> by working with others, we can be offered an alternative perspective that allows us to develop new ways of thinking, opening up different possibilities that would not have been explored without their contribution.

Such opportunities can support the development of the individual and, ultimately, raise the profile and status of the Early Childhood workforce.

Case Study

....

Voice of the Early Childhood Graduate Practitioner: Chloe, University of Derby

Through the graduate competencies I have learnt more than I expected in terms of working in partnership with parents, professionals and other agencies. I have 100% built on my confidence in terms of partnership working and I now feel more confident in working as a team than I did when I first started this course. The different tasks of the competencies have helped me build on this by taking me out of my comfort zone, which really showed me what I am capable of doing even though I never thought I could. There were two competencies which really pushed me out of my comfort zone: Competency 3.8 about promoting health to children and families, which I was nervous about completing as I have never had direct contact with parents before, but once I had done it, I felt confidence in myself that I can essentially do it; and Competency

(Continued)

4.9, which was planning activities. At the time I was in a mixed year 1 and 2 class, doing the National Curriculum, which I had never done before. I found it daunting at the time but I expressed my concern around planning activities for that age group with the class teacher and he really supported me by directing me to helpful resources. We worked together to plan a few activities first, then I planned my own, but he was fully supportive throughout.

Critical reflection allows us as practitioner to reflect on what we have done and how we can improve it. It allows us to consider questions, share ideas with each other and also consider different perspectives. Critical reflection enables me to have a deeper understanding of the subject or idea and also ensures the quality of education and care is top quality for all children.

Reflection Point

What skills do you have that will support your practice in Early Childhood and ensure you are meeting the legal requirements of the setting?
Consider how you can support new parents in an empathetic and individualised way.

Summary

It is important that the Early Childhood Graduate Practitioner is able to use their experience and knowledge to support the children and families that they work with. This includes taking a critical approach to practice, ensuring that diversity within families is celebrated and supported, and recognising the importance of strong teamwork between all professionals.

Well-fostered working relationships and good communication between teams and with parents lies at the heart of effective practice. Children will benefit from this on a practical level with effective sharing of information, and the promotion of health, safety and education. Children will also benefit at an emotional level through support from multiple attachments, providing opportunities for diverse early social interaction and the development of an environment where they and all their earliest caregivers are valued, recognised and listened to.

Key Points

This chapter has explored how we work together to promote, health, wellbeing, safety and nurturing care. It has examined:

- The process of legislation within Early Childhood settings
- Social policy development
- Some specific legislation relevant to children's care and wellbeing and its application to practice
- The identification of risk, completion of assessment and application to practice

- Safe disposal of waste and medicines
- Good hygiene practices
- Contemporary issues within modern parenting, including early feeding, weaning and sources of support
- Respectful and nurturing care routines
- Working together.

Further Reading

The following resources will support you as you explore education, policy and provision in the four countries of the UK.

Northern Ireland

Department for Education: www.education-ni.gov.uk/topics/support-and-development/early-years-education-and-learning (accessed 20 April 2021)

Scotland

Early Education and Care: www.gov.scot/policies/early-education-and-care/ (accessed 20 April 2021)

Education Scotland, Scottish National Improvement hub: https://education.gov.scot/improvement/practice-exemplars/a-summary-of-elc-resources/#:~:text=The%20Early%20Years%20Framework%20(2008,the%20best%20start%20in%20life'.&text=Within%20CfE%2C%20children%20are%20entitled,until%20the%20end%20of%20S3 (accessed 20 April 2021)

This education hub incorporates information and resources for professionals and parents and includes a national e-learning tool.

Wales

Early Years Wales: www.earlyyears.wales/en (accessed 20 April 2021)

The following texts explore the importance of critically reflecting on important aspects of practice, including teamwork, multi-agency working and working together:

Hayes, C., Daly, J., Duncan, M., Gill, R. and Whitehouse, A. (2017) *Developing as a reflective Early Years professional: A thematic approach* (2nd edition). St Albans, UK: Critical Publishing.

This text includes the exploration of a range of themes, including global childhood poverty, observation and assessment, leadership, and multi-professional working, highlighting the importance and application of reflection throughout these areas of research and practice.

Mac Naughton, G. (2005) *Doing Foucault in Early Childhood Studies: Applying poststructuralist ideas*. London: Routledge.

Case studies and examples taken from real situations are used and will be of interest to anyone studying or researching Early Childhood practice and policy.

Chapter 5

OBSERVING AND SUPPORTING CHILDREN'S WELLBEING, EARLY LEARNING, PROGRESSION AND TRANSITIONS

Gayle Blackburn and Jan Grinstead

Chapter Aims

This chapter will support your knowledge and understanding of how to observe, listen and plan for the implementation of high-quality experiences and activities to support and progress young children's wellbeing and early learning, taking account of individual children's needs and the range of transitions children may experience during early childhood. By the end of the chapter, you will have had opportunities to reflect upon and extend understanding of how to:

- know and understand the relevant Early Childhood curriculum frameworks and apply them in practice (Graduate Competency 4.1)
- apply a range of observation and research skills to co-construct young children's development, play and learning, encouraging independence and next steps, in partnership with parents and/or caregivers and colleagues (Graduate Competencies 4.2 and 4.5)
- evidence the application of different theoretical perspectives when planning to support during practice, including young children's social and emotional development and any transitions they may experience (Graduate Competencies 4.3 and 4.4)

- demonstrate knowledge and skill in listening to and communicating verbally and non-verbally with children and how to encourage their communication skills, including situations where a child has special educational needs and/or disabilities and English as an additional language (Graduate Competency 4.6)
- identify and apply pedagogical knowledge of how to develop enabling environments indoors and outdoors that support children's language and literacy, mathematical development, use of technology and their understanding of the wider world (Graduate Competencies 4.7, 4.8, 4.9, 4.10 and 4.11)

Introduction

Competency 4 (as in all competencies) is interconnected and integral to the professional skills of the Early Childhood Graduate Practitioner as the learning and knowledge related to these skills will continue to develop and change throughout a career working with children and their families. The *Early Years Foundation Stage Framework* (EYFS) (Department for Education, 2017) is statutory and used as the foundation for the development of professional skills in England. When practising in an educational setting in different parts of the United Kingdom (UK) it will be necessary to have the knowledge to implement the curricula of the devolved governments of Scotland, Wales and Northern Ireland.

Different job roles across the Early Childhood sector will require knowledge of and the skilful application of a variety of methods and different types of documentation that are used to gather information about children's learning and developmental needs. You should expect your own learning and application of skills to develop consistently from level 4 to level 6 and beyond, because all children are unique. Listening to the child's voice, as clearly advocated in Chapter 1, is not limited only to verbal communication, but also to their many different languages, such as body language and drawings. As Nutbrown and Carter (2012: 120) wrote, 'Watching children as they learn and understanding their learning moments is complex and difficult work and places the highest of demands upon their educators'. Your knowledge and skills to assess aspects of child development will develop with experience, and a good foundation from which to enhance these skills is to be familiar with developmental milestones, as advised in Chapter 2. Easy-to-read and accessible resources are *Development Matters in the Early Years Foundation Stage (EYFS)* (Early Education, 2012) and the more recently published *Birth to 5 Matters: Guidance by the Sector, for the Sector* (Early Years Coalition Partners, 2020).

Observation and Research Skills

It is important for Early Childhood Graduate Practitioners to think about and note their own values and principles about observing and assessing children. Be mindful to respect the values and principles of others, such as parents and family members, colleagues in the team and those you may work with in multi-agency teams centred around the family. It is vital to be familiar with the range of methods used across the sector and to practise skills ethically at every opportunity.

Carr (2001: 148) advises practitioners to think about their own perspectives of observing and assessing children's learning and development and advocates having discussions with adults centred around the child to consider whether:

- parents should be involved in the assessment of their children
- all adult staff should be involved in the process of assessment
- children should be involved in the assessment of their own progress and development
- all aspects of a child's development should be recorded and valued for assessments, such as social and emotional relationships and self-regulation
- assessments of individual children should be used in planning activities for those children
- assessments over a period time should be used to review and evaluate provision during their time.

Collecting Information: Documentation

The ability to observe and record efficiently and effectively is a skill that is learned and developed over time and with much practice. During practice, it is vital to reflect about the different documentation in use across the sector to achieve the competencies. The current *Statutory Framework for the Early Years Foundation Stage* (Department for Education, 2021) advises practitioners to collect and maintain necessary information about children but not allow the maintenance of such documentation to take precedence over interaction with the children. Documentation takes many forms across Early Childhood settings, for example, narrative observations, learning stories/journeys, time and event sampling, checklists and sociograms, to name but a few. These different methods have their advantages and disadvantages and are useful for gathering information for assessment (see Further Reading section at the end of this chapter).

- Essential information is needed for most observation documentation when gathering evidence for evaluation and competencies, for example: Note the aim – what children's skills and knowledge do you intend to find out about?
- Name/code of child/ren
- Age/s of child/ren
- Context
- Setting

- Time duration – start and end time
- Additional adults if present

Experience during practice should assist practitioners to develop the skills of observing and responding to children's learning and development in the moment (Chilvers, 2020): for example, initiating conversation about their interests, offering guidance and, during interactions, saying 'I wonder if...' or 'Tell me about...' when interacting with children. A pocket notebook and pencil for making notes can be useful as prompts to use when analysing and discussing information with colleagues. Some terms are used more often when notetaking and can be shortened for speed or convenience, such as child – c, adult – a, or a type of text language of abbreviated words or expressions can be used and then translated for completing the actual documentation.

Learning Stories and Journals and Portfolios

Carr et al. (2000) conducted an assessment project, supported by the New Zealand Government, to look at the key outcomes from the Te Whariki curriculum (New Zealand Ministry of Education, 1996). They developed a tool of observation and documentation which they called Learning Stories (Carr, 2001; Carr et al., 2010) that practitioners could use to aid the development of assessment ideas and procedures to enhance children's development.

It avoids the use of over-formal methods, as the practitioner watches and listens as children explore through play. It is a good way of meaningful communication, helpful for practitioners, interesting for families and supportive of learners (Carr, 2001; Carr et al., 2000). Learning Stories (or learning journeys) are always positive about the children's strengths and ideas and can be added to learning journals to document the children's next steps. Using a variety of methods to track children's progress within an Early Years setting, they can contain photographs, 'wow' moments, written narratives, drawings by the children and also contributions from parents. They are useful because they can be shared with other agencies that may be working with the children. Thus, regardless of the job role you are in, if you are working with young children, the likelihood is you will see a learning journal. They are also a great way of developing communication with parents and carers as the latter can contribute too. Many learning journals are now digital, so parents and carers can have access to them at all times.

Many settings collate, maintain and share with the child and their parents or carers a learning portfolio of the child's time at the setting. Seitz and Bartholomew (2008) found that the portfolios can be created with intentional goals and purposeful artefacts that help the child, practitioners and parents share monitoring and feedback.

Task

Using the case study below, reflect on how you could use the information in the case study to design and write a learning story to add to a learning journal. Also, consider which schemas Krista may be displaying (schemas are discussed below).

Case study

Krista: 40 months in a voluntary preschool

Krista has been attending her local preschool for two months and has settled fairly well. Krista likes tying things up and has been seen wrapping paper in elastic bands or sticky tape from the mark-making area, using pipe cleaners to tie up clothes in the home corner and when she found a long piece of rope, she began wrapping it round and round one of the posts in the outdoor area. Another two children in the block area were busy making a den using tables and chairs. Krista went to the dressing-up area and dragged a large meringue-like wedding dress to the block area and began draping it over the tables and chairs. Krista and the other two children began creeping under the satin to play.

Observing and recording schemas

Learning stories and journals can be a good format to record observations and respond to children's schematic behaviour. Athey (2007: 5) defines schema as 'patterns of behaviour and thinking in children that exist underneath the surface feature of various contents, contexts and specific experience'. According to Brodie (2015):

> You can use this intrinsically motivated, deep level learning in planning for the children by including suitable activities. This also personalizes the process of planning, because you are planning for the needs of the unique child.

From experience, a thorough knowledge of schemas and enabling environments, practitioners can feed children's schemas in a similar way to providing a healthy diet. Examples of schemas that are easily observed, and what they tell us about a child's development, are described in Table 5.1.

Observing social and emotional aspects of development

As previously stated in Chapter 3, child developmental areas, such as social and emotional development and cognitive development are interrelated and interconnected. Observing children's free

Table 5.1   Schemas and what they reveal about a child's development

Schema	What a child can be observed doing, drawing or making, or being interested in	Concept development
Enveloping	Wrapping things up Making and/or going into tents, dens, tunnels, boxes Painting over a picture or drawing Burying objects in sand or mud Hiding	Capacity and volume
Enclosure	Putting fences around animals or walls around cars Drawing borders around drawings Putting smaller objects into separate compartments, e.g., bun trays, chocolate boxes	Area Sizes Pattern
Transporting	Moving objects or themselves from one place to another Putting objects in bags, boxes, prams and moving them to another place Getting into a trolley or on a pedal toy and moving it to another place Taking toys outside Taking water from a tray and putting it in the sand	Distance Spatial awareness
Trajectory Movement of up and down and side to side	Throwing objects Games involving throwing and movement, dice games, kicking and throwing balls, skittles, bursting bubbles, throwing bean bags or stones Joining in with action games and songs	Weight Height Speed Direction

and spontaneous (child-initiated) play can be a firm starting point from which to build a child's learning story. Ferre Laevers' (1997, 2000) and colleagues in Belgium developed the Leuven 'scale of wellbeing and involvement' (Table 5.2) which links particularly to assessing children's personal, social and emotional development during play. This scale is commonly used and popular, and using it can help practitioners to understand what makes a setting a quality one. Laevers (1997) proposed that the activities offered and the children's involvement in the activities are key factors of quality.

Task

Using Leuven's scale of wellbeing and involvement in Table 5.2 (Laevers, 1997), observe a number of children in various contexts. Reflect on the scale. Is it helpful? Why? How could it be used to enhance the environment and child/adult interactions?

Using observations to inform planning activities and experiences

Gathering observational evidence, by finding out and getting to know the child, and documenting this evidence begins the cycle of planning – often referred to as the Plan–Do–Review cycle

Table 5.2   Leuven's scale of wellbeing and involvement (Laevers, 1997)

The Leuven Scale for Wellbeing		The Leuven Scale for Involvement	
Extremely Low 1.	Child lacks interest in their environment, is withdrawn and avoids contact. Shows signs of distress, crying, screaming, dejected, sad, frightened or angry. Child may show aggression towards self and or others.	Extremely Low 1.	Child seems to be disengaged and passive, displays no energy and may stare into space, looking around the environment absently. Activities are simple and repetitive.
Low 2.	Child shows signs of level 1 but not the whole time. Child does not show signs of being at ease in their actions, stance or facial expressions.	Low 2.	Child is engaged some of the time. Activities are disrupted for moments of inactivity, when the child is staring into space or distracted by what is going on in the environment.
Moderate 3.	Facial expressions, stance and actions show little emotion. There are no indications of sadness, pleasure, comfort or discomfort.	Moderate 3.	Child is busy at a routine level with few signs of engagement. Child makes some progress but lacks energetic engagement and is easily distracted by what is going on in the environment.
High 4.	Child shows many signs of satisfaction, although not constantly or as intensely as at level 5.	High 4.	Child is engaged with some intense moments of high involvement. Child is not easily distracted.
Extremely High 5.	Child shows high levels of energy, looks happy, cheerful, smiles with pleasure. Actions and stance can be expressive and spontaneous. Child can be heard talking playfully, humming and singing. Child is responsive and engages openly with the environment. Child is relaxed, showing no signs of distress or tension, and expresses self-confidence and self-assurance.	Extremely High 5.	Child is wholly engaged and their involvement is intense, thoughtful and creative throughout almost all of the observed activities.

(see Figure 2.2). It is a simple framework to meet the learning and developmental needs of children. It helps practitioners to identify and reflect on the following:

- What is there to see?
- How best can we understand what we see?
- How can we put our understanding to good use?

This approach can take time to do but it helps to identify the complexity of individual differences. Drummond (2003: 175) concluded: 'Children's learning is so complex and various that the task of trying to understand it is necessarily complex too.'

Vygotsky's theory of scaffolding (1978) suggests the observation of what the child can do without help informs thinking about what could be offered to the child to enhance these abilities. Bruner's cognitive development theory (1986) and Moyles' Play Spiral Theory (1989), (moving between free, structured and free play), also illustrate to the practitioner that children's development and learning begins with finding out about the child and getting to know each other, and then building on this to fulfil the child's potential. Practitioners then can use their observations to plan the next steps in building on the child's stage of development. When planning next steps, Sylva et al. (2004) suggest that to extend children learning and development, good practice involves providing a balanced mixture of child-initiated, adult-extended and adult-led activities and experiences within the environment.

Case Study

The voice of the practitioner: Alex Lock, ECGPC graduate, University of Sunderland

I would observe a child from a distance and record any points on an assessment sheet. One child was showing a particular interest in animals and Africa. I used this detail from the observation to take the child to a computer and set up a drawing app for him, where he proceeded to make a picture of a lion. I put this picture into his learning journal and detailed his next steps immediately. This spontaneous planning ensures that the child's interests are maintained.

Another example of how observations have informed my 'in the moment planning' was when a group of children showed an interest in fishing. Based on this, we gathered sticks from outside and I attached string and magnets and we made some letter sounds on fish pictures which were differentiated to meet all the needs in the class. These were colour-coded so we could guide the children on which colour they should reach for. All children were involved and all needs were met. The children with EAL [English as an additional language] were encouraged to match the colours so they could still feel involved and were a part of the game.

As with observation documentation, planning documentation can take many forms within Early Childhood practice across different sectors. It is important for practitioners to familiarise themselves with the procedures and documentation used for planning in the context of the work setting. For example, an after-school club will have different procedures and planning from a nursery school maintained by the Local Authority or a Family Support team working within Social Services.

Table 5.3 Pro-forma to be used in planning activities and experiences for children

Planning adult-led activities/experiences (increase size of boxes using computer to add detail)	
Focus of activity/experience:	
Date:	Duration of activity/experience:
Number of children	Competencies addressed:
Girls: Boys:	
Chronological age of youngest and oldest	
Links to the curriculum and or intentions for use:	
Prior learning:	
Learning and development intentions (refer to the curriculum you use):	
1.	
2.	
3.	
(Add/reduce as appropriate)	
Differentiation:	
Resources:	
Key questions:	Key vocabulary:
Organisation (include account of activity/experience, practitioner strategies, timings as appropriate): *What the practitioner will do? (pedagogical approaches):* *What the children will do? (behaviours and actions, language and evidence of thinking):*	
Differentiated success criteria (outcomes):	
Assessment strategies (show knowledge and understanding of appropriate approaches used to record the outcomes for each child in the activity group based on your identified learning intentions):	

The example in Table 5.3 may be useful for you to plan activities and experiences for children to engage with, in sufficient detail to meet the requirements of the competencies. You should always work closely with the setting to ensure you capture everything they need while observing the children. Designing your own plan based on your learning during practice is a graduate skill. You should try to use a range of observation methods to ensure your skills are continually developing and reflect on these methods as you use them.

Moyles' Play Spiral (1989), which builds upon the child's play activities, can be used to document information about a child and inform planning as an ongoing process. The example in Table 5.4 shows how knowledge of the children and activities/experiences based on their interests can be offered to assist the children in developing connected and sustained thinking.

Communicating with Children, Parents and Colleagues

Communicating involves transmitting and receiving information using dialogue (verbal, pictures and written), body language and gestures. Breakdowns in communication can take many forms,

Table 5.4   Documenting a child's progress using Moyles' Play Spiral technique (Moyles, 1989)

Date	Free Play: M aged … is sitting at the modelling table and has been watching other children playing with dough and clay for a couple of days but has never sat down to try it herself. Today she explores the dough by pushing and squeezing it and making holes with her finger.
Date	Free play. M plays freely several times over the next few days and becomes more and more skilful in the way she handles the dough.
Date	Adult offers structured play: baking dough shapes. When the Early Years practitioner sets up a dough baking activity to make fruit shapes for the shop, M is interested and joins in.
Dates	Free play. Over the next few weeks, she develops real skills in modelling dough.
Date	Free play. M begins to investigate clay, exploring it using fingers to poke and squeeze.
Dates	Free play. Adult observes (perhaps because she is experienced in modelling dough) M's skills with clay grow more quickly.
Date	Adult offers a structured play activity: making biscuits. M is interested and joins in. To make biscuits, M rolls out the paste and cuts out the biscuits with control.
Dates	Free play. M is observed playing with the cooking utensils in the role-play area.
Dates	Free play. M develops her play and adults observe a rich sequence of imaginative domestic role-play based on cooking.
Date	Adult offers structured play activity: cooking bread. M is really interested and enthusiastically joins the cooking activity.

with either the transmitter and the receiver. Sharing children's interests and developmental outcomes with parents and colleagues is regarded as vital to the relationships that develop between them and the children. It is important to reflect about how communications can be disrupted, and how to respond and understand the impact such disruption can have on these relationships. As a practitioner, and as a team, it is your collective responsibility to respond to disruptions empathetically and not allow relationships to deteriorate to such an extent that they become irretrievable. Chapters 7 and 8 will provide more detail on working in partnership with families and caregivers and in collaborating with others from multi-agency teams when working with children across the sector.

Children Who Speak English as their Additional Language (EAL)

Children who are learning a different language from that or those those spoken at home should be acknowledged as developing appropriate communication skills if they understand others and are understood by them. Children learning English as an additional language (EAL) may be assessed as having a development delay when measured against the English language developmental milestones. This is to be expected. Speaking more than one language should be celebrated and bilingual learning should be valued. Crosse (2007: 12) stated: 'Children from minority religious, ethnic and cultural groups can contribute a wealth of experiences and knowledge to benefit all the children attending the setting'. It is important that practitioners learn and use the key words and phrases of the home language of the children they support so that the children can feel a sense of belonging and social wellbeing. Parents and family members can be the most helpful source to assist with your learning. You can research the cultural background of their home language to assist with their inclusion in the setting. Building relationships with families is crucial to ensure that your skills develop effectively in this area as EAL may not be supported within the home environment.

For all children, play is central to language learning. Children can learn their new language in a context which is meaningful to them. It is therefore crucial for practitioners to observe children's play, follow their interests and their readiness to engage and communicate in English. Young children do not need to learn English through meaningless vocabulary lists but by using language in contexts that are relevant to them, for example, in role-play. Hearing the use of English by their peers and adults in context enables them to make sense of what they are hearing and to try it out when they are ready (Crosse, 2007).

Transitions Children May Experience during their Early Childhood

All children experience change in various forms and aspects of life as they grow and develop. Bronfenbrenner (1979) defined this as when their position in the social context changes as the result of a change in role, setting or both. Changes in routine, family members, where they live, and in accessing and moving though care and education can be positive or adverse to their development, depending on a child's developmental stage, interactions with adults and environmental interaction. Children who have developed self-regulation skills tend to respond and adapt to change more readily and seamlessly (Florez, 2011). Newman and Blackburn (2002) found that children who are resilient can recover faster and more completely from traumatic experiences, are better able to cope with change and can resist stress. Observations of changes in a child's behaviour can often indicate a child's response to experiencing immediate changes and forthcoming changes, for example, the fire alarm sounding a drill, toilet training, the birth of a sibling, moving to another school and family break up. You should consider all of the transitions you experienced as a child and think about the support mechanisms that were in place and how successful these were. Why were they successful and how can you replicate them for the children you are supporting in your work environment? As a practitioner working with children, in whichever setting, it is vital that you are aware of any transitions a child may be experiencing. You should really develop your knowledge of all children in your care so that any changes, however slight, can be noticed. Good communication with parents and carers also contributes to this as they can inform you of anything they may be experiencing.

Enabling Environment

As you develop as a practitioner, your observations should be used to inform the planning of your environment. They should be used to assess how successful your resources are and how effective the layout of your room and outside areas are. Which areas are being used by who and why? Which areas are engaging the children? You should always ensure the children in your setting have access to an enabling environment, regardless of which role you have when using your Early Childhood Graduate Practitioner Competencies (ECGPC).

An enabling environment is a rich and inviting space where children can develop and express themselves freely and safely. The space should feel welcoming to all children to encourage a sense of belonging. Resources and activities which are provided by the practitioner should be based on the interests of the children and should encourage the children to be challenged, engaged and motivated. There should be a balance of child-initiated and adult-led activities and you should show evidence of these. The ages of the children should always be considered and planning adapted to suit – this may be babies or children up to Key Stage 2.

You should not think of an enabling environment as simply being the resources in a room or the layout of a room. You should consider the environment as a 'third teacher' Strong-Wilson, 2007). The environment relates to indoors and outdoors, and also the 'feel' which is inherent throughout it. The children should feel comfortable and confident, and feel safe with their peers and the adults within this nurturing environment. The environment should support the holistic development of the child – that is, their behaviour and their cognitive, physical, language, emotional and social development. Child-initiated activities should be encouraged, as discussed by an ECGPC graduate in the case study below.

Case Study

The voice of the practitioner: Helen Haygarth, ECGPC graduate, University of Sunderland

Children of any age learn effectively when they feel they have ownership and their views are valued. As a practitioner, I have followed many different curricula and pedagogies yet always appreciate and enjoy the spontaneous moments which are instigated by a child's interest, and often these are best found outdoors.

It is a privilege to be able to harness this and follow the child's lead. It is not always easy, but I tend to find children will create their own learning if you facilitate it. My knowledge of child development ensured that I could enhance their chosen task by introducing concepts such as creative thinking, mathematical language, encouraging them to expand their language and utilising the resources around them. My role as a practitioner is to expand on their imagination and give them tools to broaden their learning.

This highlights the importance of using resources which offer open-ended opportunities: e.g., a cable drum can become anything for a small child's world; den making will support any area or theme; junk materials and loose parts can nurture heuristic play. Children are experts at transforming an item to a purpose.

Nurturing planning around child-initiated moments creates a more meaningful process which can be tailored to meet the individual needs of any child. As such, it was always reflected within my practice; observations reflected individual planning which was then reflected in assessment and next step planning.

All the while, children focused on fun!

The Outdoor Environment

Ensuring children have adequate outdoor opportunities is vital. As an ECGPC practitioner, you must ensure children have access to the outdoors at some point in their day, regardless of the settings they are accessing. Child-initiated play is often something those working with children can be unsure of due to feeling that they are not able to 'control' the activities. Early Years curricula play a key role in supporting the learning journey of a child and ensuring that this journey is based on their interests. You must ensure that you do not make assumptions on these interests and listen to the child by reviewing and evaluating your practice and taking note of the child's interactions effectively. Mathivet and Francis (2007: 9) acknowledge that practitioners need to develop skills to recognise these needs of children and how they communicate them: 'the development of language and communication skills is … more than a … checkpoint on a … chart. It is an essential aspect of being human, … of sharing thoughts and ideas…'.

An enabling outdoor environment encourages a child to use their senses, develop their curiosity, and allows them to adopt a sense of exploration and enquiry. Children also take more risks outside, which contributes to the development of their resilience. Risk taking is and should always be viewed as a natural and inherent part of play, as children seek to experience new sensations and experiment to test their limits (Little and Wyver, 2008).

The resources provided for the children should be of high quality and should contribute to all areas of development. Try to divide your outdoor area into smaller areas – little places where children can hide and develop their imagination. Nooks and crannies are great for encouraging a little bit of calm

Table 5.5 Developmental opportunities for indoor and outdoor play

Area	Development opportunities	Example evidence
Sand	Use of different containers Measuring Balancing Shapes Mathematical language Problem solving, e.g., how many jugs of sand are needed to fill the bowl?	Activity plan Photographs Observations
Mud	Drawing shapes in the mud with a stick	Photographs Observations
Nature	Using leaves – sorting leaves, measuring leaves, using leaves for measuring, talking about shapes of leaves	Photographs Observations Evaluation of activity Reflective account
Building a den	Size and shape of the den discussion How many people will it hold? Problem solving – design Group work Estimation	Activity plan Examples of den plan from children Reflective account Witness statement from other staff members
Exploration of the wider local environment	This could be a historically-based walk, a geographically-based walk or a focus on the child's senses and the nature which is all around them	Risk assessment before you go on the 'trip'

into their day. Large open spaces tend to encourage more running-based play, which is obviously great for developing gross motor skills and allowing them to express excess energy, but be mindful to have a balance of spaces also.

An exploration of the local environment can encourage the child to become more aware of the world around them and the learning opportunities are endless. Supporting them to engage in learning opportunities on an everyday basis is a skill that will develop and should also be embedded in your reflective practice. Example activities for both indoors and outdoors are listed in Table 5.5, and a reflective task linked to developing an enabling environment follows.

Task

....

Look at these photographs (supplied by Sarah Dixon Jones of Mill Hill Nursery, Houghton le Spring) and think about how you can extract learning opportunities from them.

Mathematics

Linking your environment to support mathematic development is crucial. This encourages children to be embedded with mathematical opportunities which naturally occur for them. Engagement with play is the main tool which can be used here. Do not feel pressured into counting in pairs just because that is on the planning for that week. You should be allowing the children to explore and 'creating an atmosphere of mathematicalness that is unbounded' (Bottrill, 2018: 89). By allowing children to be free with their mathematical development, it enables the experiences to be fun and joyful and not linked with set activities. Mathematics should be real and purposeful to children, enabling them to participate in activities which encourage problem solving, sustained shared thinking, counting, grouping, matching or identifying shapes, for example. Peacock and Pratt (2011) suggest that to foster the mathematical disposition in children, they should be supported to develop their mathematics outdoors, as this enables children to become aware that mathematics is all around them and is naturally-occurring. You should also ensure that children are not afraid of making mistakes. They should feel safe in their mathematical environment, and this alone will encourage them to explore, investigate, develop their understanding and use their initiative. If they do make a mistake, then encourage them to explore their errors (Gifford, 2015).

Technology

Technology has advanced at a phenomenal rate throughout the last two decades. It is common practice for children to have access to the internet, games, social media, tablets and mobile telephones. McManis and Gunnewig (2012: 16) suggest that the use of technology should be very carefully considered, and practitioners should ensure that it is 'developmentally appropriate', based around the children's interests and 'social and cultural contexts'. This means you should carefully consider how you will use technology in your environments and remember that it can only be successful if you use it well, regardless of what the app, game or piece of technology is capable of.

One way you can use technology is by incorporating it into your use of observations. Technology can be incorporated into a child's learning journey. You can take photographs of a child engaged in an activity and add your links to the curriculum. You can also ask the child to take photographs as they progress through their activity – at different stages of their construction, for example. You can then use these photographs to help other children to develop their own constructions – for example, they can be used to help the children see how the construction progressed and to support them in developing their own. Discussions with the child also can enhance this learning opportunity.

Developing partnerships with home is crucial when using technology with children. It is important to support the development of a child's confidence in using technology, but it is also your role to ensure that children do not overuse it and become reliant on it. Apps which include parents and carers can ensure that they are kept up to date with their child's progress through sharing links to observations on their children, photographs of their children in the setting and access to their learning journals. Feedback from parents and carers about a child's interests should also be used to inform planning and your resources and environments.

One of the greatest benefits of using technology is that it can be personalised to suit the children, their ages and their abilities. This is ideal for supporting children with special educational needs. You can use adaptive technology with children to help personalise their learning. Also, regardless of which supportive career you enter into, you can use technology to support your planning and record keeping, and in communicating with parents and sharing best practice with your colleagues.

Language and Literacy Development

Children presenting with speech, language and communication difficulties when they start school is a continuing concern (Langston, 2014). Research suggests that 'a communication-supportive environment at preschool and the primary school will enhance a child's language at this crucial developmental stage' (Hartshone, Tenenbaum and Pinker, 2018: 12).

Building an environment rich in language is crucial for children. Creating a language-rich environment that promotes language and literacy development is making use of every opportunity to develop these skills. Encouraging language and literacy development in your environment will also encourage social and emotional development as it involves sharing conversations around a focus or a topic, which will encourage language skills and talking. Do not feel pressured to encourage children to write letter symbols. Your environment should help children to explore and develop their social skills and prerequisite motor skills, and the children should be allowed to develop at their own personal level. Children should feel comfortable and confident to try new things with their literacy and language development and it is the role of the practitioner to provide and support these experiences. Mark-making will naturally develop with exploration and discovery. Audits of literacy opportunities, which you can complete based on your setting or placement, are useful to complete as a practitioner.

Task 1

Think about examples of mark-making with water, sand and soil, and about your own setting. Does it offer opportunities like these? Are children given paint brushes etc. to use on walls or fences to practise their mark-making or grasp? Is there a range of resources available which children can access freely?

Task 2

Looking again at the photographs of Mill Hill Nursery, think about what links you can make to learning opportunities in mathematics, technology and the digital world, and literacy development?

Early Years Curricula

Using one Early Years' curriculum, such as the Early Years Foundation Stage (EYFS) (Department for Education, 2017), is a very narrow lens on which to base graduate practitioner competencies. You need to research and compare different Early Childhood curricula approaches in England, Scotland, Wales and Northern Ireland, and internationally, to inform and challenge your knowledge of the EYFS. Revisit Chapter 2 to read about curricula in New Zealand, Denmark and Italy.

It is important to be responsive and reflective about new ideas in pedagogical approaches and perspectives, because more is being learnt about responding to the unique child and assisting children to develop their full potential. The Learning Stories approach (Carr, 2001) was new to the sector in 2000 and its use as a tool to gather knowledge and document observations to assess children's development was widely debated. Now it is a regular approach in Early Childhood settings.

Different curriculums have different approaches, and it is important to be critical of these. You can consider the different approaches at a surface level, focusing on the subjects or topics which are going to be considered in the curriculum. You can then critique them with regards to how they are going to be delivered in the setting., For example, are they play based? Which pedagogical approaches are being used? Are the children being assessed? The final critique can be viewed through the government policy lenses: which governmental policy practices have been adopted by the curriculum's framework, for example, accountability, observation and assessment of the children and staff, standards, funding, etc. (Wood and Hedges, 2016)?

Summary

Practitioner observational and listening skills will develop with experience of working with children, their parents or carers and colleagues across the Early Childhood sector. Documentation and methodology to gather knowledge about children's development will vary in different job roles within the sector. Primary schoolchildren will be observed to gather different types of information for assessment from that needed by a social worker or playworker. The main purposes for observing children are for the practitioner to gather knowledge – to get to know the children in their care – to use that knowledge proactively to assist children to develop to their full potential and to share this knowledge proactively with the child's family.

Key Points

- Be prepared to familiarise yourself and engage with the variety of different documentation used in practice across the sector to record informally and formally about children's learning and developmental abilities and needs.

- Keep in mind that many curricula are used when working with children. Be mindful of these different approaches.
- As a practitioner, do not be afraid to allow children to engage in free play. Use free play regularly to gather the relevant information you may need about the child, their environment, the resources they are engaging with, and the adults round them.

Further Reading

Further reading is necessary for academic learning and the development of skills to gather evidence for the competencies at level 4, 5 and 6, regardless, whether or not a level 3 qualification has already been gained.

Brodie, K. (2015) *The power of schematic play*. Available at: www.kathybrodie.com/articles/schematic-play/ (accessed 19 January 2021).

Kathy Brodie illustrates the types of observations in table form, which can be a useful aid to familiarise yourself with them and to develop knowledge for practice. The table is free to access using the website: www.kathybrodie.com/observations-guidelines

Drummond, M. J. (2012) *Assessing children's learning* (Classic edition). London: David Fulton.

This classic edition provides practitioners with case studies of children to reflect upon and to develop their practice and to value children's learning and development.

Palaiologou, I. (2008) *Child observation*. London: Learning Matters/Sage.

This book provides students with practical examples to use to develop their observational skills.

Smidt, S. (2015) *Observing young children* (2nd edition). Abingdon, UK: Routledge.

This book discusses all aspects of the practical application of the observation and planning cycle.

Early Education (2012) *Development matters in the Early Years Foundation Stage (EYFS)*. London: Early Education.

Early Years Coalition Partners (2020) *Birth to 5 matters: Guidance by the sector, for the sector*. Available at: www.birthto5matters.org.uk/ (accessed 4 February 2021).

These are easy-to-read and accessible documents to assist with a general overview of child development stages.

Chapter 6

SAFEGUARDING AND CHILD PROTECTION

Eunice Lumsden and Emma Twigg

Chapter Aims

This chapter introduces you to the global and national context of safeguarding and child protection and provides opportunities to reflect on the knowledge and skills required for Competency 5:

- know the wider legislative and statutory guidance for safeguarding and child protection
- recognise when a child may be in danger or at risk of serious harm and the procedures that must be followed, including when to signpost to other services or designated persons
- appreciate the importance of working with others to safeguard and promote the wellbeing of infants and young children
- evidence advanced knowledge about child abuse, the wider theoretical perspectives about the causes of abuse and the potential implications for young children's outcomes
- apply knowledge of adverse childhood experience, including child abuse to individual planning for children

Introduction

Infants and young children have the right to protection from violence, abuse and exploitation wherever they live in the world. There is a plethora of research evidence about the impact of these areas on infants and young children's holistic development that you need to engage with during your studies. This evidence informs legislation, child protection policy and procedures that reflect, for example, the culture and political ideology of individual countries.

As a student you need to understand:

- the global breadth of violence experienced by infants and young children, including war, conflict, maltreatment, sexual exploitation and exposure to the digital world

- how to differentiate between safeguarding and protecting children from harm, what constitutes abuse, the social-ecological causes of abuse, including Adverse Childhood Experiences (ACEs) and intervention methods
- how living in and experiencing violence, abuse and the breadth of ACEs impact on early childhood development, health, wellbeing and early learning, as well as the lifelong consequences
- the legislative, statutory frameworks and policy aimed at prevention, identification and intervention, and how these are reflected in practice
- the importance of and challenges in multi-professional and inter-agency working.

It is this foundational knowledge that you will draw on in different ways depending on what career pathway you follow. For example, if you become a social worker with children and families, you will have specific statutory duties to follow. You will also have the knowledge and skills to identify, assess and intervene when child abuse has happened, and the ability to work across agencies and with different professionals. As a teacher, you need to be able to identify concerns, follow procedures, appreciate how the child's experiences are impacting on their learning and may be reflected in their behaviour, and support appropriately. If you are working in an ECEC setting, you also need to identify cases of abuse and follow procedures, but you will also use your knowledge of the impact of abuse and adversity on a child's holistic development and provide rich opportunities to mediate this, for example, by focusing on language development, decision making, fine and gross motor skill development and self-efficacy.

There will be challenges in your gaining extensive practice experience in child protection. However, there is a range of case study and interactive resources that you will be able to use to develop your competence in this area and evidence your skill in applying knowledge to practice and Level 6.

By the final assessment for the competencies, you should be able to:

- clearly articulate the relationship between theory and practice in safeguarding and child protection
- evidence how you would apply this knowledge in different practice contexts
- critically evidence the tensions between theory and practice.

To support you with this, this chapter is presented in two sections. The first part introduces you to the global context of violence against children and their right to protection. There will be a focus on child protection, the factors that place infants and young children at risk, what constitutes abuse, its causes, the challenges in identification, the legal context, the importance of working with others, the impact of abuse on child development, as well as developing your skills in applying this knowledge in practice. The second part presents four conversations to illustrate different perspectives in this area through the voices of practitioners and the experience of a student. You will also be directed to further reading and resources to support your development in this area.

Taking care of yourself

Child abuse is an emotive area. For some, it can trigger issues from their childhoods. However, if you are going to work with children and families, you must take care of yourself and seek support if issues are raised for you. This could be at any point in your career.

Child Protection in Context

The challenges of protecting children globally are increasing. Digital technology presents new challenges in a world where children already face exploitation and violence, both in their families and in their communities, through acts of commission, such as physical and sexual abuse, or by omission through neglect (Murray 2020). Consequently, child protection is a children's rights issue and those working in Early Childhood settings have important roles in advocacy, prevention, identification and intervention.

Infants and young children are particularly vulnerable to adverse experiences and abuse, especially as they are dependent on the adults in their lives. However, the protection needs of infants and young children can go undetected as they are mainly cared for within the home and have limited contact with professionals. In some cases, when children are seen, their need for protection is not always recognised or acted upon (Coventry Local Safeguarding Board, 2013; Lumsden, 2020).

The protection rights of children for safety, emotional support and provision if abused are defined in Articles 19 and 39 of the United Nations Convention on the Rights of the Child (UNCRC) (UN General Assembly, 1989). The UNCRC also provides the global definition that underpins work in this area, with General Comment 8 (United Nations, 2008: 19) emphasising that violence against children is not acceptable and is preventable:

> The Committee defines 'corporal' or 'physical' punishment as any punishment in which physical force is used and intended to cause some degree of pain or discomfort, however light. Most involves hitting ('smacking', 'slapping', 'spanking') children, with the hand or with an implement – a whip, stick, belt, shoe, wooden spoon, etc. But it can also involve, for example, kicking, shaking or throwing children, scratching, pinching, biting, pulling hair or boxing ears, forcing children to stay in uncomfortable positions, burning, scalding or forced ingestion (for example, washing children's mouths out with soap or forcing them to swallow hot spices). In the view of the Committee, corporal punishment is invariably degrading. In addition, there are other non-physical forms of punishment that are also cruel and degrading and thus incompatible with the Convention. These include, for example, a punishment which belittles, humiliates, denigrates, scapegoats, threatens, scares or ridicules the child.

It is important to note that categorisation of 'harm' can change between time, place and by different individuals, and it can depend very much on an individual's cultural and societal values and beliefs

(Corby, Shemmings and Wilkins, 2012). Abuse is a socially constructed concept, so what society finds unacceptable or not at a given time will influence definitions, which can be dependent on research findings and cases that have been before (Lumsden, 2018).

Even though abuse is an ever-changing concept, all would acknowledge that harm should not be happening to children. For students of Early Childhood, you will need to engage with global, national and local issues in relation to child protection and abuse. You will also need to develop your professional efficacy and reflection skills and those you have developed in research and synthesising knowledge.

Child Protection Practice

In the United Kingdom, Scotland and Northern Ireland have different legislative and statutory frameworks that inform practice in protecting children. England and Wales have the same legislation, although the way it is enacted in each country is different. Furthermore, different professions, occupations and organisations that work with children and families have their own procedures to be followed. These reflect the statutory requirements of the country they are in and the specific remit and culture of the organisation. This section presents England as a case study, so if you are studying in another country, it is important that you access the relevant information. Links for the other nations in the UK can be found at the end of this chapter.

The definitions and categories of abuse that underpin practice and protection procedures in England are contained in *Working Together to Safeguard Children* (Department for Education, 2018). This provides all the information about the child protection system, including legislation and the role of different organisations. Whatever context you work in, you must be conversant with the document and use it to inform your practice. It is updated regularly, as is the guidance in *Keeping Children Safe in Education* (Department for Education, 2020b).

At a local level, every local authority has a Local Safeguarding Children's Board (LSCB) and local safeguarding arrangements that you should also be familiar with. It is an important source of information about local procedures and guidance that follow national guidelines. The boards also publish Child Safeguarding Practice Reviews (formerly known as Serious Case Reviews).

As well as providing an overarching definition of abuse, the *Working Together* document provides greater insights into the different categories of abuse. These are not static and reflect changes in societal views of what children and young people need protection from. They include (HM Government, 2018: 107–108):

- Emotional abuse
- Sexual abuse
- Child sexual exploitation
- Neglect
- Domestic abuse
- County lines and child criminal exploitation.

Activity 6.1 Understanding what constitutes abuse

Access *Working Together to Safeguard Children* (Department for Education, 2018) or the equivalent document in your country of study and answer the following questions:

1. Explore the definition of abuse. How does it compare to the definition provided by the United Nations?
2. Read and reflect on the definitions of the different categories of abuse. Are you surprised by the different categories included?
3. Do you think the range of categories help or hinder the detection and reporting of abuse?

Even though child abuse is categorised into these distinct areas, cases of abuse may not align to one or another. You will find that there is an element of emotional abuse apparent within every one of the other categories of abuse (Moody and Fernley, 2014) and a child may suffer from more than one form.

Case Study

Billy (aged 3 years) lives with his parents, in a flat on the fourth floor. His mother has experienced perinatal mental health issues and has been unable to find employment. His father has just been made redundant and they are claiming benefits.

Every day Billy hears, and at times sees, his mum and dad physically fight and argue. When this happens, he does not always get his tea. He goes to his room and hides under the bed to drown out the noise.

Reflection Point

What categories of abuse can you see in this case study?

Signs of abuse

All practitioners working with children must have a clear understanding of what abuse may look like, so that action can be taken immediately to protect children. However, it is not always clear or easy to detect. In this case study, Billy is not being directly abused but the intimate partner violence occurring in the family, as well as the perinatal mental health challenges experienced by his mother and the wider social ecological factors of unemployment, poverty and housing, could impact on Billy's holistic development, and he could be experiencing emotional abuse and neglect.

When considering child abuse, you need to understand definitions and possible signs and indicators of abuse. It can be said that there are several generic signs that may indicate abuse. Therefore, observation skills are crucial to identify any concerns. In Early Childhood Education and Care (ECEC), for example, Lumsden (2018) identifies these categories:

- Verbal
- Behavioural
- Physical appearance
- Attendance

Activity 6.2 Identifying signs of abuse

Using the working definitions of abuse (HM Government, 2018) or similar definitions, identify which possible signs and indicators may fall into each of Lumsden's (2018) categories?
  How does your list compare to those highlighted by Lindon and Webb (2016: 22)?

- A child's verbal and non-verbal communication may alert you to a child being in pain, or that something has happened to them.
- A sudden change in a child's behaviour, a child may regress in their development.
- A child may become aggressive and act out what is happening to them or what they have observed.
- A child may become very quiet and withdraw from their friends or staff.
- A child may come to the setting unprepared for the weather.
- A child may wear ill-fitting clothes.
- Practitioners may notice marks or bruises on a child.
- A child may need to visit the toilet a lot more regularly or be in the toilet for a longer period.
- Practitioners may notice that a child is starting to have long periods of time away from the setting.

Difficulties in detection

Several studies (Elarousy and Abed, 2019; Regnaut et al., 2015) report on the difficulties in the detection of child abuse by practitioners. Findings highlight the lack of understanding some may have around what they perceive as being child abuse. These findings are important for those working in Early Childhood and reinforce the importance of those studying the Graduate Competencies to develop their knowledge and confidence levels in child protection. In England, for example, all those working with children have training in this area, yet we continue to miss opportunities to protect children. This reinforces the importance of regular communication with colleagues and the importance of regular child protection training (Twigg, 2021).

The NSPCC (2021) cite Reder, Duncan and Gray (1993) when considering the term 'disguised compliance', which refers to the act of parents and carers appearing to be cooperative with professionals in cases of concern, when in fact the opposite is happening. This is difficult, as practitioners need to look beyond what is being portrayed to them. It can only happen if those working in Early Childhood have the appropriate knowledge in the first place.

Children may not talk about the abuse that is happening or has happened to them. At times this is hard to understand, but there may be reasons for their silence. First, some children may not have the language or understanding to be able to verbalise what is happening to them, especially if they are very young. They may not understand that what is happening to them is abuse if it is something they have experienced all their lives. Second, abuse of an individual is about the abuse of power by the perpetrator on the victim. The extent of the power may be so great that children are forced into being silent and do not feel that they have the capability to tell anyone else.

Violence against Children: Theoretical Perspectives

This section considers the ecological reasons that support our understanding of violence against children. It is an emotive and difficult area, and you will need to reflect on how it makes you feel. Social workers, who have a primary role in this area, receive regular supervision. While supervision is vital for all, it is not always available.

There are psychological and sociological theoretical perspectives that enable us to make sense of violence against children (see Bernard and Harris, 2016; Corby et al., 2012). The World Health Organisation (WHO) (2016: 16) stresses the importance of understanding this area through a social-ecological model so that preventative measures can be implemented. The model recognises the following factors:

- **Individual**-level risk factors include biological and personal history, aspects such as sex, age, education, income, disability, impaired brain and cognitive development, psychological disorders, harmful use of alcohol, drug abuse, and a history of aggression or maltreatment.
- **Close relationship**-level risk factors include a lack of emotional bonding, poor parenting practices, family dysfunction and separation, associating with delinquent peers, children witnessing violence against their mother or stepmother, and early or forced marriage.
- **Community**-level risk factors include how the characteristics of settings, such as schools, workplaces and neighbourhoods, increase the risk of violence. These include poverty, high population density, transient populations, low social cohesion, unsafe physical environments, high crime rates and the existence of a local drug trade.
- **Society**-level risk factors include legal and social norms that create a climate in which violence is encouraged or normalised. These also include health, economic, educational and social policies that maintain economic, gender or social inequalities, absent or inadequate social protection, social fragility owing to conflict, post-conflict or natural disaster, weak governance and poor law enforcement.

Violence against children can be a result of several interrelated factors. Further insights are provided by Feletti et al. (1998), whose work has investigated what they have termed Adverse Childhood Experiences (ACEs). These embrace individual experiences of abuse as well as environmental factors and provide a framework for understanding the impact that these experiences can have across the life course. In Scotland and Wales, ACEs are explicitly influencing legislation, policy and practice (see the Further Reading section at the end of the chapter).

Working together

Walker (2018) seeks to define the terminology used within professional contexts when practitioners work together. The terminology covers inter-agency working, multi-agency working and multi-disciplinary working. You will find that these terms are often used interchangeably. Definitions of key terms can be found in the Glossary of this book.

Early Childhood settings involve different types of practitioners working together to gain a holistic picture of the child and family in order to provide support to help in a range of situations. This way of working is reflected in legislation such as the Children Act 1989, the Children Act 2004 and the Children and Families Act 2014, to name a few. Parents and carers and children should be a very active part of the multi-agency team as well.

Task

Think back to when you have been on placement. How many different professionals have you worked with or seen other members of staff work with? Write a list.

There are many benefits in working together, some of which include:

1 Communication – effective, transparent and open.
2 Cooperation – trust between members of the team, with all professionals working to a common goal.
3 Coordination – all members of the multi-agency team work effectively to reach common goals.
4 Coalition – the commitment to joined-up working between professionals.
5 Integration – there is a range of different professionals who come together (Horwath and Morrison, 2007: 56)

However, working together can also present some difficulties. Solomon (2019: 397) highlights some of these difficulties as including 'a lack of shared goals' and 'resistance to shared evaluation', while Walker (2018: 30, 31) cites both structural and individual barriers, which include 'different values, cultures and practice between agencies' and 'lack of clarity in lines of authority and decision-making'.

Lindon and Webb (2016: 64) consider some of the benefits to multi-agency working and encourage us to think about the multi-agency team as 'a jigsaw for which different professionals or services each have only a few of the total number of pieces'. They highlight that it is too easy for professionals to think that someone else is aware of the problem, with the result that they do not take responsibility for it. Consider the case of Victoria Climbié (Laming, 2003), where professionals were aware of her situation and had concerns about Victoria's care and safety, but they all assumed that other members of the multi-agency team were doing something about it.

Case Study

Kaylee

The Context

You are a manager in a preschool setting and have been asked to host and attend a multi-agency meeting following ongoing concerns for Kaylee.

Kaylee has attended the preschool for the last six months; she is 30 months old now. She has had a Family Support Worker working with her and her family since she was born. Her mother was 16 when she had Kaylee and is white British; her father was 24 and is from Somalia. Kaylee speaks Somali and English. They live locally and are housing association tenants. Mum is doing voluntary work at a charity shop and Dad works part-time as a cleaner; although he has a degree, he has struggled to find work. There have been some concerns regarding their parenting styles and home life. Kaylee is eligible for a funded place at preschool and usually attends, although recently she has been absent for a couple of months when they flew back to Somalia to visit family.

The scene

A number of practitioners have gathered in the preschool's story room to review Kaylee's situation and the ongoing concerns about her. Kaylee's father is present, but her mother has not arrived yet and the meeting was due to start 20 minutes ago. The social worker has just turned up, giving his apologies. He had a serious incident he had to attend and he is a little flustered and stressed. The preschool will need the story room at 3 pm, and it is now 1.20 pm.

The health visitor decides to begin the meeting even though some key participants are missing. She begins by noting that she has no concerns. She has been unable to meet with the family regularly because she has struggled to contact Kaylee's parents, but has undertaken Kaylee's health review at age two. The GP, while not at the meeting in person, has provided a written statement, which says he cannot share any information at present, but he has no current safeguarding concerns. Kaylee's key worker at the preschool has been working with Kaylee this morning. Kaylee has limited language skills and uses one- or two-word sentences, but she has drawn a picture with him of her family. Kaylee was keen to draw Daddy standing next to her, but she put Mummy in the corner. They all had straight lines for their mouths. The Family Support Worker has been working with the family since Kaylee was born. Due to numerous trips out of the country and concerns around Kaylee's safety, because of her mother's volatile behaviour, a social care worker has been invited to join the team.

Reflection Point

Identify and list the professionals involved with this case?

Would this case study raise any concerns for you?

What do you think each professional could do after the meeting?

Do you think there are any other professionals who may need to be involved?

Are there any barriers that may be present in this case?

From the case study, the following professionals are involved in this case: the Family Support Worker, Health Visitor, Social Worker, GP and Preschool Manager. Although the parents are not classed as professionals in this case, they are of equal importance in this case. The concerns that you may have identified could include concerns around parenting and Kaylee's home life. The Health Visitor has been unable to meet with Kaylee and her parents for her review at two years. You may also have identified the possibility of domestic abuse.

As we have stressed throughout this chapter, it is important that all the professionals work together as a multi-agency team and devise a plan, together with the parents, that will help to support the family moving forward.

In cases such as this, when working with families from different cultures, it is important, as a practitioner, that you are aware of the social, cultural, 'economic, political, temporal and spatial context' (Laird and Tedam, 2019: 114) of the family. An awareness of these issues, and the effects these may have on the family, will help to form enabling partnerships.

Perspectives on Safeguarding and Child Protection

As a student of Early Childhood, it is important that you understand the different perspectives, roles and responsibilities in the safeguarding arena. This section enables you to explore and develop your knowledge and understanding further by engaging with the 'voices' of three people working in the Early Childhood sector – the two authors of this chapter and a former nursery owner and lecturer in Early Childhood studies. They all share their experiences and interest in safeguarding and child protection, as well as the role of the Graduate Competencies in enabling students to widen their understanding of this complex area and develop their confidence. We also hear from a student, who shares her perspectives on how studying child protection has impacted upon her.

Case Study

A conversation with Emma Twigg, former Nursery Nurse, Adviser in Early Years and now a Senior Lecturer in Early Childhood at the University of Derby

Could you tell me a little bit about your professional experience in working in child abuse?

I qualified as an NNEB Nursery Nurse in 1990 and started working in a nursery. One of my main responsibilities was to ensure that the children were safe in my care, and if I had any concerns, to report them and to make sure that I'd recorded my concerns.

After spending a couple of years in that role, I moved into the role of Nursery Manager, and this gave me a lot more responsibility around safeguarding and child protection. I managed a couple of nurseries with approximately 20 staff.

As Nursery Manager, I became the person who was the Safeguarding Lead and my responsibilities included ensuring that staff were confident in understanding safeguarding and child protection procedures and that they were attending all their required training.

My responsibility was to ensure that if any staff had any concerns about children, and we felt that those concerns needed to be passed on, it was then my responsibility to pass them on to the local Duty Team. I also met with other professionals, working with families. This role really extended my knowledge and gave me lots of experiences.

During those two periods or work, I continued to attend safeguarding training. I attended training through the Local Council, and the Local Safeguarding Children Boards, which are now known as Local Safeguarding Arrangements. Before that, it was the Area Child Protection Committees. There have been lots of changes.

In my role as an Improvement Officer in the Local Authority, in a range of Early Years settings, a large part of my role was supporting childminders. So, any concerns they had, I would support them with those concerns. Childminders need this support because they work very much in isolation. I supported them through the procedures that they needed to follow if they had any concerns about a child. I think this is particularly difficult for a childminder, especially when they are working very closely with families and children.

How do you think you've used this work with students and through the Competencies?

One of my responsibilities at the University is teaching on our Child Protection Module, and so I do talk about my experiences. I personally like to hear other people's experiences because I think it brings things a bit more to life – it illuminates different situations.

I do also encourage students to talk about their experiences as well, so I get any students who are in practice, and any students who have been in placement, to talk about their experiences. Obviously, we must always make sure that confidentiality is maintained through those conversations, but I think it is also good because when it comes to having concerns about children, I think it's very much about our own confidence and what we actually do with that concern.

(Continued)

First, one of the things we can support students with is confidence. Practitioners can be very worried about getting a concern wrong, but we advise that it does not matter – at least they have done something with that concern.

Second, it is about encouraging students to share any concerns. They should never, ever have to carry anything that they feel concerned or worried about, while obviously, again, ensuring confidentiality and sharing that information on a need-to-know basis.

Both aspects are very much about developing confidence in students, enabling them to talk through experiences. During our teaching session we talk about case studies. We use serious case reviews or child safeguarding practice reviews in our sessions and it really brings the subject to life a little bit more.

Why do you think it's so important for our Graduate Practitioners?

I think it is about developing their confidence. It is one of the most important things, if not *the* most important responsibility for an Early Years practitioner, that they need to be very competent and confident within safeguarding and child protection.

Students who are following the Competencies achieve a greater and more in-depth understanding of safeguarding and child protection, particularly in relation to theoretical perspectives and how they can be applied to practice. Students also gain an understanding of legislation and statutory guidance. I do think that that is important so that staff understand their responsibilities, they understand their duties, and I think that is where the Early Childhood Graduates really will have that in-depth knowledge around these areas.

Case Study

A conversation with Eunice Lumsden, an academic at the University of Northampton and a registered social worker

What is your professional experience of working in child abuse?

I spent 20+ years as a social worker, predominantly focused on child protection, safeguarding children, child abuse – the language has changed over time. My work involved assessment, decision making, following legal procedures, court work, working with families and placing and supporting children in alternative care. I also worked with other agencies, professionals, and practitioners. In short, I was involved in every aspect of the child protection system as well as working directly with children, families and their communities. All of those influence all the work I do now.

How do you use this in your work with students and through the Competencies?

For me it's important the students understand the difference between safeguarding as an umbrella term, child abuse, child protection early intervention and different intervention methods. They really need to appreciate the social-ecological factors that can lead parents and carers to harm their children.

The Competencies provide a framework that facilitates thinking about how we can apply our knowledge to mediate the impact of abuse and wider inequalities, including racism, on child development. It's this understanding of the multifaceted nature of development that enables a greater focus on interventions that can enhance outcomes for children.

They also support the students to see the world through the eyes of the child and their experiences, and to advocate for them. For example, they may be angry. Understanding why this is the case will enable appropriately attuned responses, rather than punishment.

Why do you think this area is so important for the Graduate practitioner?

Because what we're doing in this country is not good enough. We invest millions of pounds in protection, intervention and alternative care, but we still fail to protect all children and mediate effectively against the impact of abuse and wider adversity. I'm not saying that investing in Early Childhood is the answer to everything, but if our graduates and those working in the breadth of Early Childhood don't understand these issues, we will continue to fail children who live in the margins of society. They are often invisible, although we know that that is such a crucial time in ensuring we're putting in the building blocks for the future as well as learning so many important skills.

So, for me, the Competencies are about enabling our students, whatever their future career, to have this grounding in understanding that child abuse isn't just something 'out there', and that their knowledge, understanding and skills in relationship-building and in applying their knowledge to practice can make a real difference in the present and across the life course.

Case Study
....

A conversation with Michelle, former Nursery Owner and Early Years Professional

What is your professional experience of working in child abuse?

I am an advocate for children, and it is my statutory duty to take all necessary steps to keep children safe. As a professional working in Early Years settings, I often came across complex family issues that affected the children I cared for. I recognise that there are multiple factors that influence children's enjoyment and experiences of life. Some are 'within' each child, such as their personality or level of resilience. External factors also affect a child's wellbeing and holistic development, such as living conditions or family circumstance and relationships. Following a child-centred approach, I believe in a culture in which children's needs and rights are respected, and they are listened to. Therefore, for services to be effective they should be based on a clear understanding of the needs and views of child. As an Early Years practitioner, I was well placed to be able to listen and observe changes in children's behaviours, indicating that something could be wrong. Through establishing an open and professional partnership with families, I was able to recognise when parents were experiencing difficulties that stretched their capacity to care for their children. I therefore worked with other agencies' support to maintain and improve their parenting and to protect children from harm.

(Continued)

How do you use this in your work with students and through the Competencies?

The students need to understand the roles that relationships and the child's environment play in shaping the child's holistic development. We provide a thorough overview of the different ways in which children might be vulnerable. The ability to communicate with the children about their needs and wellbeing lies at the core of safeguarding. Early interactions with primary and secondary caregivers through touch, face-to-face contact and stimulation through conversation and play, provide the positive experiences necessary to the construction of a rich network of neural connections in the brain that form the basis for cognitive and social development.

Why do you think this area is so important for the graduate practitioner?

Students need to understand and know what their roles and responsibilities are as Early Years professionals in relation to safeguarding children. Students need to be reactive, being able to recognise when there's cause for concern about a child and knowing what procedures to follow if abuse is suspected. The importance of knowing how and when to work with other agencies, professionals or organisations during investigative processes is also another important aspect for students to understand before they go into the workplace.

How do you think the Competency in this area will help improve practice?

The students will gain a deeper understanding about the impact abuse can have on children, in particular when children do not receive the type of sensitive, loving care that stimulates the growth of the brain and promotes the establishment of secure attachments.

It's vital for students to know how to build safe and trusting relationships with children so they can speak out about any problems they are experiencing. This involves teaching children what abuse is and how they can get help. Therefore, our students need to be knowledgeable in this area. A student may just save a child from harm or, even worse, death if they have the skills to recognise abuse and act.

Case Study

A conversation with Tracey, an ECGPG undergraduate at the University of Derby

What have you learnt from Competency 5 that will help you in practice?

This Competency has been explored through a child protection module which students take in their second year. It has helped to widen my knowledge about legislation and statutory guidance as I had a basic knowledge of the present policies and procedures. These skills are now applied to my everyday practice. I am now able to recognise when a child may be at risk or in danger; I understand the signs and symptoms of each component. I now appreciate the importance of working with others, for example, multi-agency working, and how this can go wrong, but through reflection, it supports the next steps to support a child and their family needs.

This module advanced knowledge about child abuse and the wider theoretical perspectives about the many effects and the potential implications for young children's outcomes. I now apply this knowledge in my everyday practice, and I can identify when a child is in need, such as when a child is hungry, unkempt and there are physical signs. I understand the importance of building a child's resilience and emotional wellbeing, because if children do not have these needs met, they are unlikely to achieve their academic potential. I love this module, although it was a challenge at the time due to personal experiences. I am thinking of pursuing a career such as social work or supporting children with ACEs in Child and Adolescent Mental Health Services.

Summary

This chapter has introduced you to the breadth and complexities of safeguarding and protecting children from abuse that underpins Competency 5. Child abuse is socially constructed and what is categorised as abuse changes over time. While there are global definitions of what constitutes abuse, legislation, policies and procedures are country-specific. Therefore, you need to remain well informed and ensure that you are in line with any changes. It is important to note that when navigating the areas covered in this chapter, and when in practice, you will need to develop your personal efficacy skills (see the introduction of this chapter), which will ensure you can advocate effectively for the children you will be working with.

Key Points

This chapter has introduced you to:

- The importance of developing your knowledge of what constitutes violence towards children in local, national and global contexts.
- The importance of your use of reflection and to build on this knowledge in practice.
- The challenges of this area, including the challenges of detection and working with others.
- The different perspectives of practitioners, including a student, when working in Early Years settings.

Further Reading

Davies, L. and Duckett, N. (2016) *Proactive child protection and social work*. London: Sage.
This book considers four main categories of child abuse (emotional abuse, sexual abuse, neglect and physical abuse) by drawing on a range of real-life experiences.
Holt, K. (2019) *Child protection* (2nd edition). London: Red Globe Press.

This book looks at the legislative perspective of child protection, it considers some of the responsibilities of practitioners.

Laird, S. and Tedam, P. (2019) *Cultural diversity in child protection: Cultural competence in practice*. London: Red Globe Press.

This book highlights the difficulties that social workers face when working with diverse families. Although written from the perspective of the social worker, students and anyone working with children will find this useful.

Lumsden, E. (2018) *Child protection in the Early Years: A practical guide*. London: Jessica Kingsley Publications.

This book introduces you to child abuse, the causes, impact, theoretical perspectives, working with others and how to mediate against the effects of abuse in practice.

Perry, B. and Winfrey, O. (2021) *What happened to you? Conversations on trauma, resilience and healing*. London: Bluebird.

This book explores the impact that trauma has over the lifetime, reinforcing early intervention and the importance of understanding how your own experiences may have led to your chosen career.

WebsitesNSPCC: www.nspcc.org.uk

This website contains a wealth of information in relation to all aspects of child protection. The site hosts the repository of child safeguarding practice reviews and there is a range of accessible links to research.

World Health Organisation (WHO): www.who.int

This website includes information on a range of child safeguarding issues from a global perspective.

Children's Commissioner's websites

www.childrenscommissioner.gov.uk (England)

www.childcomwales.org.uk (Wales)

https://cypcs.org.uk (Scotland)

www.niccy.org (Northern Ireland)

These websites inform the reader of the initiatives of the Children Commissioner's Office in the areas stated.

Child Protection system in Northern Ireland: https://learning.nspcc.org.uk/child-protection-system/northern-ireland

Child Protection system in Scotland: https://learning.nspcc.org.uk/child-protection-system/scotland

Child Protection system in England: https://learning.nspcc.org.uk/child-protection-system/england

Child Protection system in Wales: https://learning.nspcc.org.uk/child-protection-system/wales

The above websites provide information on the children protection system, including legislation and policies, for the areas stated.

Chapter 7
PROMOTING INCLUSIVE PRACTICE

Bruce Marjoribanks, Lindey Cookson and Helen Haygarth

Every snowflake is different; no two leaves are the same: similar, sure but not identical. Diversity is the biggest blessing of our existence. (Huffman, 2015: 91)

Chapter Aims

This chapter will support your knowledge and understanding of how to engage with and promote inclusive practice which ensures that Early Childhood Graduate Practitioners, young children and their parents and carers co-participate with thoughtfulness and mutual respect. By the end of the chapter, you will have had opportunities to reflect upon and extend understanding of how to:

- evidence knowledge, understanding and application in practice of pedagogy that supports inclusion (Graduate Competency 6.1)
- know how to identify infants and young children who may require additional support and how to refer to appropriate services (Graduate Competency 6.2)
- demonstrate an understanding of statutory guidance for children with Special Educational Needs and Disabilities and Protected Characteristics (Graduate Competency 6.3)
- evidence skills in appropriate planning to address the care and early learning needs of individual young children with Special Educational Needs and/or Disabilities and Protected Characteristics (Graduate Competency 6.4)

Introduction

This chapter focuses on the importance of inclusive practice in which Early Childhood Graduate Practitioners, young children and their parents and carers work together to create a supportive environment where everyone feels a sense of belonging and connectedness, and where all children have equal access to positive and inclusive learning experiences. It encourages you to consider how the Early Childhood Graduate Practitioner can lead practice within the Early Childhood context with the knowledge, skills and strategies required to include all children and families. The chapter begins by exploring definitions of inclusion and inclusive pedagogy before providing an outline of the legislative framework and policy context for inclusion and inclusive practice. The chapter then goes on to highlight the importance of reflective practice for the Early Childhood Graduate Practitioner and includes a series of examples which encourage you to 'pause for reflection' about how you might consider your own practice as you continue to develop your Early Childhood Graduate Practitioner portfolio. Helen, one of the authors of this chapter, has recently graduated with the Early Childhood Graduate Practitioner Competencies and has kindly shared some examples from her own portfolio in this chapter.

Inclusion and the Child's Environment

The chapter takes as its starting point the understanding that children's childhoods and experiences are influenced and shaped by the wider societies in which they live. That is, 'inequality' does not exist as separate to the communities, institutions, policies and legal frameworks (locally, nationally and globally) that children are born into. Bronfenbrenner's Ecological Systems model (Bronfenbrenner, 1979), which emphasises the cultural and contextual aspects of a child's development, is helpful in thinking about and understanding the issues raised in this chapter. Here, the focus is the relationship and interconnectedness between the developing child (bio) and the 'systems' of the culture and society they belong to (ecological). His 'bio-ecological' model, also referred to as a 'systems' model, is most typically presented visually as a series of concentric circles representing different 'layers of influence' around the child (see Figure 3.1). Bronfenbrenner likened the world of the child to a 'set of Russian dolls' (Bronfenbrenner 1979: 22) with the child at the very centre (the microsystem), surrounded by a set of wider systems radiating out from the child that both directly and indirectly influence their experiences and development. You can read more about Bronfenbrenner in Chapter 3 of this book.

The 'microsystem' represents the child's most immediate everyday context and experiences, which for most children consists of their most intimate family members, their family home and may also extend to close friends, family relatives and Early Childhood settings within their local community. This means that as an Early Childhood Graduate Practitioner working in a professional context supporting young children and their parents/carers, you are a part of the child's microsystem. That is, you are part of the environment in which children first learn about others and become aware of the values, practices and beliefs of the communities they have been born into (Doherty and Hughes, 2009). This immediate environment of familiar routines and first relationships with parents/carers and other close caregivers and professionals is the child's 'core entity for learning about the world', offering them a 'reference point' from which to make sense of the wider world which they gradually become a part of (Swick and Williams, 2006: 372). You are therefore well placed in your role to help young children to develop a 'reference point' which provides a firm foundation of healthy curiosity and acceptance around difference, and one which encourages them to respect other young children and families whom they come into contact within the Early Childhood setting and beyond.

However, again following Bronfenbrenner's model, children's immediate contexts for development and learning are nested within and influenced by a range of wider systems. The macro system represents the wider structures around the child which influence all aspects of the microsystem, for example, the legislative and policy frameworks, political agendas, education, childcare and welfare policies, values and dominant ideologies of a society (Bronfenbrenner, 1979). Where these dominant ideologies contain deeply embedded negative stereotypical beliefs about certain groups of people, this can lead to political agendas, legislative frameworks and practices which discriminate and exclude those people. This is why we have included a section about global and UK legislative and policy frameworks in this chapter to encourage you to reflect upon how children's experiences, and your own practice as an Early Childhood Graduate Practitioner, can be shaped by this context beyond the Early Childhood setting.

Inclusion and Inclusive Practice

People have many different understandings of what inclusion means. Inclusion is associated with equality and diversity and is established as a universal right. The aim of inclusion is to value and embrace all individuals, groups and cultures, irrespective of their differences, background or needs. All people, regardless of their race, age, gender, disability, religious and cultural beliefs and sexual orientation, must be embraced. Inclusion involves making people, whether they are an individual or a group, feel valued and respected for who they are. It is also about recognising and challenging 'exclusion' and working to give equal access and opportunities to everyone in all aspects of life. Children should also be given equitable opportunities, which take into account their differences, to realise their full potential. Inclusion within Early Childhood settings should be an organisational effort and engage practices in which different groups or individuals having different backgrounds are culturally and socially accepted and welcomed, and where their needs are equally treated. This can be achieved through inclusive pedagogy.

Pedagogy is often referred to as 'the practice (or the art, the science or the craft) of teaching', but in the context of Early Childhood this broad definition must also take into account the provision made for play and exploration in the learning environment (Siraj-Blatchford et al., 2002: 26). There are different dimensions to pedagogy, but 'pedagogical strategies' (specific behaviours on the part of adults) and 'pedagogical framing' (the behind-the-scenes aspects of pedagogy which include planning, resources and the establishment of routines) are two aspects of your own practice to reflect upon in relation to inclusion. Inclusive pedagogy therefore involves Early Childhood Graduate Practitioners and other staff working to create supportive environments for development and learning in which all children are provided with equitable opportunities to fulfil their potential. Inclusive pedagogy aims to raise the achievement of children while safeguarding the inclusion of those who are vulnerable to exclusion and other forms of marginalisation. In their early years, children should have access to all the support needed to ensure that they become well-rounded, caring and empathic individuals. They are beginning to learn about themselves, other people and their wider environment. Children's identities are beginning to emerge, and they are developing an understanding of their place in the world.

The need for holistic and flexible curricula and pedagogy underpins inclusive practice and children's wellbeing. All aspects, including cognitive, social, emotional, linguistic and physical development, benefit from this approach.

An inclusive pedagogy takes into account the range of perspectives in a variety of Early Childhood settings and is delivered in a way that strives to overcome barriers to access which young children and their parents/carers might have. It is important to recognise that all learners differ, but it does not mean that these individual differences are unimportant. For example, two children might have difficulties learning to read, but for different reasons. One child might have English as additional language (EAL), whereas the other child might have dyslexia. In these instances, a practitioner has to differentiate the learning and develop pedagogical strategies that enhance both children's learning experience.

A diverse and inclusive setting allows children to be recognised as unique while acknowledging their individual differences. The process of inclusion engages each child, encouraging a sense of self-value, which is essential to the success of their development. Early Childhood practitioners are reminded of this in the *Early Years Foundation Stage Framework* (Department for Education, 2017: 2) which states that, 'You must promote positive attitudes to diversity and difference within all children. In doing so you will help them learn to value different aspects of their own and other people's lives.' It is important to reflect upon and realise that we are all a complex mix of cultural influences woven together and it can be enriching to be responsive to equality and diversity.

Task

Take a few moments to think carefully about what inclusion means to you in your role as an Early Childhood Graduate Practitioner. Jot down key words then try to write a short paragraph that captures your own thoughts about this. No one else will see your notes so aim to be as honest as possible. At the end of this chapter, we would like you to revisit your paragraph and reflect upon whether you would like to amend it.

Legislation and Statutory Guidance

The United Nation Convention on the Rights of the Child (UNCRC) (UN General Assembly, 1989), which all but two countries of the world have signed up to, states that all children have a right to a childhood where they can participate in society. The Convention comprises 54 Articles grouped under what are known as the three Ps: Protection, Provision and Participation. The two most relevant Articles in relation to participation are Articles 3 and 12. Article 3 maintains the best interest of the child shall be a primary consideration and ensures the child such protection and care as is necessary for his or her wellbeing. The UNCRC underlines the importance of obtaining, listening to and responding to the views of the child. This is enshrined in Article 12. The Department for Education's

(DfE) statutory guidance, *Listening to and involving children and young people* (DfE, 2014c: 1), stresses that schools are strongly encouraged to pay 'due regard to the Convention' and outlines that the involvement of children and young people in decision-making encourages children to become active participants in a democratic society, and contributes to the achievement and attainment of children.

Various global reports, such as those by UNICEF (2010, 2015), highlight the social inequalities children experience around the world and the harmful impact these can have on children's developmental and learning trajectories. Strategies and targets are embedded into government policies to address social inequalities worldwide. Some of these policies are to address income inequality and poverty; priority needs and rights of poor, vulnerable and marginalised people; and the empowerment and advancement of women and girls. Globally, it is recognised that children live in acutely unequal societies where prejudice around disability, ethnicity, gender, poverty, and other protected characteristics, are excluding them from reaching their full potential. As noted by Penn (2005: 1), 'what is unarguable is that young children suffer disproportionately from these inequalities'.

In the UK context, the Equality Act 2010 (Legislation.gov.uk, 2010) aims to protect children, young people and adults against discrimination, harassment and victimisation in relation to housing, education, clubs, the provision of services and work. For example, it is unlawful for a school or *other childcare settings* to discriminate against a *child (and their parents/carers)* by treating them less favourably because of their age, disability, gender reassignment, marriage and civil partnership (with some restrictions), pregnancy and maternity, race, religion or belief, sex and sexual orientation. These are called 'protected characteristics'. The public sector equality duty in Section 149 of the Equality Act 2010 requires public bodies, including local authorities, schools and hospitals, to take active steps to eliminate discrimination and take actions to promote equality.

It is *also* unlawful to discriminate because of the sex, race, disability, religion or belief, sexual orientation or gender reassignment of another person with whom the child is associated. In 2014, the Department for Education outlined advice in a document entitled, *The Equality Act 2010 and schools: Departmental advice for school leaders, school staff, governing bodies and local authorities* (DfE, 2014a). The government published statutory guidance in 2015 which relates to children with Special Education Needs and Disability (SEND). This statutory guidance, *Special educational needs and disability code of practice: 0 to 25 years: Statutory guidance for organisations which work with and support children and young people who have special educational needs or disabilities* (DfE, 2015), contains details of legal requirements that practitioners must follow without exception and statutory guidance that must be followed by law unless there is a good reason not to. It explains the duties of local authorities, health bodies, schools and colleges to provide for those with special educational needs under part 3 of the Children and Families Act 2014 (Legislation.gov.uk, 2014). The code, which applies to England, is for headteachers and principals, governing bodies, school and college staff, special educational needs (SEN) coordinators, Early Childhood providers, other education settings, local authorities, and health and social services staff. This is explained on page 13 of the code and section 77 of the Children and Families Act 2014.

All schools should take steps to make sure parents and children are actively supported in contributing to needs assessments, developing and reviewing Education, Health and Care (EHC) plans. The local authority (LA) must make sure parents and children are involved in discussions and decisions about their individual support and local provision. This is set out on page 20 of the code, mentioned above, and section 19 of the Children and Families Act 2014. The EHC assessment should focus on the child as an individual. It should be easy for children and their parents to understand and use clear language and images. The EHC assessment brings together relevant professionals to discuss and agree together the overall approach and deliver an outcomes-focused and coordinated plan for the child and their parents. Other important considerations include children and young people who are looked-after or care leavers; have social care needs, including 'children in need'; are educated out of area, in alternative provision, in hospital or at home; are the children of service personnel; and are in youth custody.

Case Study

Inclusion policies

A governor at a maintained nursery school was contacted by a parent via email to discuss a discrepancy in the setting's Inclusion Policy. The parent felt unhappy that their child was not currently covered by any of the categories identified within the policy but required time away from the nursery to attend hospital appointments in relation to an ongoing diagnosis. The nursery was still charging the parent fees for the missed sessions. The parent felt that the inclusion policy needed to be adapted to consider a wider scope of inclusive issues that could affect the children and families using the nursery school.

The response was a simple one. The governors met to debate and update the policy to reflect a more diverse inclusive arrangement for the setting. This included adding a section related to 'children who required time out of the setting'. Within this, the governors and the head of the school were able to reflect on the different instances where children may miss sessions. With the aim of providing an inclusive approach, they agreed that families should not be charged for missed sessions, provided there was an inclusive requirement. This included long-term illness, organised hospital appointments and also cultural festivals. Within the policy was the notification system – parents were asked to notify the school at the earliest point to ensure the new policy did not impact on staffing and the already restricted Early Childhood budget.

Reflection Point

How would you approach a similar request from parents in your setting? Do you agree with the response from the governing body?

Look at your setting's policy on inclusion. Do you see how the policy complies with the Equality Act 2010?

Do you see any areas for improvement in the policy? Who could you discuss this with?

Reflective Practice for Inclusion

You have now been introduced to some key ideas about inclusive pedagogy, and the key legislation and policy context for inclusion. However, it is still important to remember that inclusive practice can take different forms across different Early Childhood settings (Nutbrown and Clough, 2009). In this section, you are introduced to different types of reflective practice before moving on to some reflective examples. We will introduce you to areas where you can reflect on your own practice to identify potential areas of discrimination, and to promote an inclusive environment where all children are welcomed, respected and encouraged to achieve their potential. Reflective practice is commonplace in Early Childhood settings as it can promote better ways of working with young children, their families and within staff teams. However, like the concepts of 'inclusion' and 'inclusive pedagogy', it can mean different things to different practitioners. Levels of reflection might differ from person to person and may depend on the roles that people hold within the Early Childhood setting.

Early Childhood practitioners are constantly reminded of the value of continuous professional development and reflective practice is at the heart of this (Willan 2017). There are many well-known models of reflection that can be used to support your skills in the reflective practice role (Kolb, 1984; Moon, 2001; Rolfe, 2001; Schön, 1983), and all encourage similar questions on behalf of yourself as a reflective professional. They involve asking you to consider an event, or 'critical incident', in stages: a description of the event, the feelings that were involved, an evaluation of what worked and what did not, what the outcomes were and whether you could have approached the event differently for a more positive outcome. The final reflective question is typically 'what next?', where you are encouraged to consider changes to your practice. These models are really useful for your everyday practice.

Case Study

Reflective practice on inclusion

Ben, an Early Childhood student, shared one of his reflections around inclusion:

A group of girls told me that the boys were not allowed to join them in their play in the home corner because 'boys don't play with babies'. The boys had become forceful in trying to assert themselves in the home corner and I was called in to 'stop them'. My immediate response was to say to the girls, 'that's silly, of course boys play with babies, let them play!', and I intervened by encouraging the boys into the home corner area. However, they were no longer interested by this time and left. Afterwards, I reflected that my response was limited, but I really wasn't sure how I could have responded differently. I discussed this with my mentor, who suggested different ways I could have approached this situation. With continued support from her, I then

(Continued)

developed some further work around gender roles in the home corner. I introduced a more diverse range of dolls (including more male dolls), some 'bathing the baby' activities with myself taking the lead, and displaying images of both men and women caring for babies. I also took the opportunity to include other aspects of diversity in the images, such as same-sex parents, parents and children with disabilities and from different ethnic backgrounds. I informed parents about my 'home corner' project and invited them into the setting to take part.

Reflection Point

How would you have responded in Ben's situation?

How would you feel about sharing this with your mentor?

What else could Ben do to extend this activity?

How else could Ben have informed himself about how to respond to situations like this?

Have you observed children conforming to gender stereotypes in their play?

Have you observed children resisting and challenging gender stereotypes in their play?

Where can you find resources to support your knowledge and understanding of gender diversity and inclusion?

Reflecting Critically for Inclusive Practice

At graduate level, and for you as an Early Childhood Graduate Practitioner, there is an expectation that reflection should be more 'critical', taking into account your developing theoretical knowledge, which, when applied to critical incidents like Ben's, leads to 'theorising practice'. Your reflections on practice, and the changes that you make in response to a more critical reflection, then become evidence-based, or 'informed practice' (Hanson and Appleby, 2015). Critical reflective practice is complex and must also take account of wider socio-political and ideological contexts to expose some of the areas that may not be so obvious at first. Wood (2008: 108) notes that such deeper reflective practice in Early Childhood settings must go beyond reflecting on whether we are delivering the curriculum and following policy to achieve learning set targets and learning outcomes. Reflective practitioners, with an ethical and political commitment to children and their families, and who develop inquiry-based approaches to their own practice in Early Childhood, can become active agents of change who can 'transform, rather than merely implement policy frameworks' (Wood, 2008: 108). Returning to Bronfenbrenner's (1979) model, discussed earlier in the chapter, there is a comprehensive set of equality legislation and policy framing the context of your own practice, although it is up to you to commit whole-heartedly to applying this legislation and policy to your own practice with young children and their parents/carers, in ways which are inclusive and meaningful to them.

Case Study

....

Inclusion and inclusive pedagogy

Helen (contributory author) used her Level 6 assignments from her BA Hons Childhood and Society Studies degree module entitled 'Equality and Diversity' as part of her portfolio to demonstrate her developing knowledge base underpinning her work towards these Competencies. In her ECGPC viva presentation, and discussion of her portfolio, she was able to articulate her critical reflections using newly developed knowledge and theory from the module, in relation to her own practice and understanding of inclusion. She was able to provide thoughtful and 'informed' examples of how she had developed inclusive pedagogy in this area.

Reflection Point

Take a look at some of the examples from Helen's portfolio on pages 121–127.

How can *you* develop your own knowledge of theory in relation to inclusion and inclusive pedagogy?

Task

....

Find out who the key writers and researchers are in the field of inclusion and Early Childhood Studies. What are their key ideas?

Reflecting on Your Own Values, Biases and Attitudes

In relation to reflecting upon inclusion in your own setting, a very useful starting point is yourself. 'Reflexivity', whereby you interrogate and identify your own biases, attitudes and values in the process of reflection, can be a very challenging process, but one which is completely worthwhile for your own development as an Early Childhood Graduate Practitioner committed to inclusive practice. This level of reflection requires listening skills, self-awareness, honesty and self-regulation (Hanson and Appleby, 2015), but can allow for deeper changes as you reflect more honestly on your own unconscious biases. Such close examination of your own beliefs – and even to go so far as recognising that you may have unintentionally contributed to another person's experiences of marginalisation and 'exclusion' – is not intended as a process to make you feel guilty. Rather, it is about acknowledging that as an Early Childhood practitioner, your own unconscious biases might affect the way you work with children and families, which might lead to their exclusion. Acknowledging and reflecting honestly on your own biases then helps you to consider ways forward in developing a more inclusive approach.

Being reflexive in this way does not need to be a 'lone venture'. For example, 'watch, listen and learn' from other practitioners whom you respect and who inspire you; don't be afraid to admit areas where you feel confused; ask your mentor to discuss these with you; ask others to share useful readings, resources and websites with you; be upfront about your lack of understanding and your desire to learn more to address these gaps in your own knowledge, understanding and practice. Adding this emotional dimension to your critical reflection supports your own personal growth and is key to transformational learning (Schunk and Mullen, 2013).

Case Study

Critical reflection on practice

Louise, an Early Childhood teacher, kindly shared with us her very honest example of how the recent Black Lives Matter movement stimulated her own critical reflection about an aspect of her own practice.

> I was planning a lesson about describing Handa from *Handa's Surprise* and I wasn't sure how to approach it. I wondered if I should use the term 'Black' to describe Handa because I wouldn't usually use the term 'white' to describe a character. I discussed it with my colleagues, and we decided it was important to mention that Handa is Black and to use the politically correct term to avoid misconceptions. We recognised this as being particular important in our school, where most of the children are white British; they need to know the correct words to use. I had read *Handa's Surprise* to children many times, and I have used it as a teaching resource for a similar lesson, but this was the first time I actually took a step back and thought about how I would approach this. It seems so obvious now, and I feel surprised with myself to say this, but I had just not thought of inclusion in this way before. So, the Black Lives Matters movement, and the associated discussions around it, certainly encouraged me to question my own attitude and my approach to teaching. Not only me, though! Following this discussion about *Handa's Surprise*, we met as a team to discuss how we should approach Black Lives Matters in our school. We all realised that we had not been taught about Black history at school and that we really needed to learn more about this before we could incorporate it into our curriculum and teach our younger generation. We also started to look closely at our environment and identified areas where we could make positive changes to make our curriculum even more inclusive for all. We engaged with and discussed the possibility that our use of *Handa's Surprise* could potentially reinforce stereotypes rather than challenging them. Our leadership team also took part in these conversations and responded positively to our request for more training in this area.

Reflection Point

What was your own response to Louise's reflection?

Have you had similar reflections and conversations with colleagues over aspects of your own practice?

Are you aware of resources that can help you to understand the experiences of children and families from diverse backgrounds?

How can you use these resources to support your own and colleagues' inclusive practice in this area?

Reflecting on the Ethos in Your Setting

The success of a setting bases itself on the ethos and leadership that drive and ensure the celebration of richness and diversity, and places positive value on its benefit to the setting and community. Practitioners should encourage children to look at differences and diversity through the eyes of others who may be different to themselves, as children often may not have encouragement to do this at home. Staff in settings need to take a 'make it happen' approach to inclusive practice, with constant flexibility in practice to ensure that all children's needs can be met. Discriminatory expressions and actions should be questioned and addressed when they occur. How adults interact and model views, opinions and behaviour helps to create the ethos required. Practitioners can again take guidance from the *Early Years Foundation Stage Framework* (Department for Education, 2017: 22), which reminds us of the role of adults, including parents/carers and practitioners, and that 'Children need adults to set a good example and to give them opportunities for interaction with others so that they can develop positive ideas about themselves and others'. Real commitment to inclusion and anti-discriminatory practice is to accept that it is not just for minority parties, but is crucial for all young children and adults within a setting.

Children spend more time with their families and the wider community than in a setting, and therefore the home learning environment plays a significant role in a child's learning. The Early Years Foundation Stage statutory guidance states that a partnership includes parents, families and practitioners working together to benefit children (Department for Education, 2017). The guidance also emphasises that identified key workers need to communicate with parents, update the parents on their child's progress, report any observations they might have, involve the parents in any potential assessment, and offer them guidance and support to enhance the home learning environment. There must be a foundation of trust between the key worker and the parents, from which they can work together to develop shared expectations and support the child's learning. Of course, like any relationship, the build-up of trust takes time and genuine commitment to want to make the relationship work.

Ensuring practitioners are respectful, transparent and honest with parents/carers and colleagues is vital in inclusive practice. When children are allocated a nursery place, good practice would involve a home visit being arranged in order that the child and parents/carers can meet the staff. At this visit, information is shared and exchanged. Practitioners are able to carefully ask questions to gather as much information as possible. This building of the relationship continues as parents are regularly invited to attend workshops and consultations and are invited to contribute to their child's learning journal whenever they want.

Having the confidence to ask a parent about a situation can solve many misunderstandings. Often the parent/carer can be involved in sharing knowledge with the children to educate them about differences, for example, sharing stories in a different language, celebrating festivals within settings and inviting parents/carers to share cultural differences. Positive relationships with parents/carers will provide trusting foundations whereby staff can encourage conversations that remind parents/carers about the inclusive ethos of the Early Childhood setting. Practitioners must also be mindful of the wishes of parents/carers and not rely on assumptions. For example, one of the examples Helen spoke about in her viva involved a Chinese child who attended the setting and whose parents requested that only English be spoken to her. They wanted her to be exposed to English and to learn as much as she could while she attended. This situation proved challenging for the child. Practitioners used strategies to support communication and language in more simplified ways, utilising body language, images and gestures. While these were strategies devised for one child, they are the same strategies that can be used for general language delays, which is an ongoing consideration in many Early Childhood settings. According to Pollard (2008), accepting a child's first language helps to develop their self-image and supports inclusion. However, he also highlights that children are entitled to learn English, and therefore failing to teach them could limit their life chances.

Task

How does your setting support the development of English language for children with EAL in an inclusive way that takes into account the considerations of the parents and the needs of the child?

Reflecting on the Physical Environment and Resources

When young children and their parents/carers enter the setting, they should feel like they belong. It is worth reflecting on the entrance to your setting and what young children and their parents/carers see, hear and feel when they enter. The physical space should be set up in ways that allow equality of access to all areas, and images displayed throughout the setting should reflect positively the diversity of young children, their families and their lifestyles.

Physical space must be accessible and able to alter and evolve to meet the ever-changing needs of young children and their parents/carers attending your setting. Ideally, buildings should have wheelchair accessible doors and be on one level. If they are not, then adaptions must be made. Corridors should give adequate space and allow access to disabled toilets, along with a hygiene room. Lots of space ensures children with disabilities can move around freely and do so in accordance with the disability characteristic of the Equality Act 2010 (Legislation.gov.uk, 2010). However, these allowances for children with disabilities must consider the health and safety of other children: for example, a child's wheelchair must be stored away from doorways and not block access. Tables should have adjustable legs in order to alter height if required.

Resources should be wide and varied, offering sensory experiences for all children. Where possible, such resources are available as continuous provision, accessible and clearly viewable or with photo labels. Resources reflecting diversity need not be costly. The creative use of resources can reflect the varying needs of children. For example, in Helen's setting, a child was new to wearing glasses and needed an eye patch. Aware of the need to support the child's positive identity, Helen made glasses from pipe cleaners for one of the dolls in the role-play area and placed a patch on a teddy bear, thus giving the child an opportunity to incorporate his additional need into his play. This simple but effective change to the resources in the setting also helped other children in the setting to be familiar with the child's new look (see Table 7.2 below to view this activity in Helen's ECGPC portfolio).

Task

To support her own development and understanding of the competencies in this area, Helen created a table to capture and reflect on the use of inclusive resources in her own setting (see Table 7.1).

Look at Helen's list of resources to promote inclusion that she noted in her own setting and use the list to evaluate the resources used in your own setting. Think about how they are used, how often they are used and why they are used?

Can you add to Helen's list or amend it to reflect your own setting? Is there anything on Helen's list that you disagree with?

Final Task

At the beginning of this chapter, we asked you to make notes and write a short paragraph about what inclusion means to you. Having come to the end of this chapter, we now suggest that you revisit your notes or paragraph and think about anything you might now like to change. As a final reflective task, Helen has kindly shared the examples that she used in her own portfolio to demonstrate the competencies 6.1, 6.2, 6.3 and 6.4 (Table 7.2). Take a look at Helen's portfolio and think about the kind of examples you might provide in your own portfolio.

Table 7.1 Helen's table of inclusive resources in her setting

What?	How Many? And how often used?	Comments
Images and photographs	In every area Used daily	Images are altered according to the needs of children and cohort. Wide range of gender challenges, such as female firefighters and mechanics and male nurses.
'Welcome sign' and books/ stories	In entrance to setting and in book/reading area Used daily	Welcome in different languages on entry to the setting. Wide range of books on lifestyles, homes, celebrations, etc. Maps of the world and globe. Usborne *My First Words* in Polish, Arabic, Russian. Most modern stories have elements of diversity within them, but we also have specific books by Oxfam which have a wide range of diverse topics and images.
Small World Toys	Used daily and alternated, as and when required	A vast range reflecting the diversity of families and lifestyles, ages and abilities. Small World people are used flexibly, staff will make wheelchairs and SEN-related items if required. Staff have made Small World mud huts, etc. to demonstrate different homes.
Food and role-play resources	Used daily and alternated, as and when required	Resources reflect a variety of homes and lifestyles: Chinese/Indian/Italian food Chinese and Indian (endless) Crockery/pans/woks/chopsticks Toolkits Hairdressing kit Real-life home items A range of dolls.
Puzzles jigsaws	Resources reflect diversity and are used as and when required	Puzzles showing ethnic diversity, family diversity, disability. Puzzles showing 'People who help us' with non-gender-specific job roles. Puzzles at different levels to include all children.
Musical activities	These are always provided and are accessible in the book corner	Wide range of cultural instruments and music genres.
Dolls and puppets	Used daily and changed regularly, as required	White, Black, Chinese, male and female. One Black speech and language puppet. Several persona puppets. Puppets are used effectively … staff will often add glasses, bandages, eye patches, etc. to demonstrate children's changing needs and differences. Puppets are interactive so children are able to put their arms inside and make the puppets talk.
Fabrics	Used daily	A wide variety of mixed fabrics, voiles and scarves of differing colours, designs and textures. Children use these fabrics to dress up in rather than having set costumes – this adds to flexibility.

Table 7.1 (Continued)

What?	How Many? And how often used?	Comments
Paints, crayons and scissors	Used daily	A variety of colours to reflect different skin tones. Staff also mix paint accordingly, as and when required. Two sets of training scissors are available for use when required.
Sensory resources	Used daily	A wide range of sensory materials and resources are available. These are used according to the needs and interests of the children.
Makaton Signs and symbols	Used in the environment daily	A few basic signs are displayed in priority areas of the room. Staff use signs when singing songs with the children.
Visual timetable and choice wall	Used in the environment daily	Images are used to create timetables. The images are actual photographs which help give children a reference object to relate to.
Staff and school values	Daily	Staff ratios comply with the EYFS statutory guidance. Staff are the best resource acting as positive role models. Being creative and flexible gives children the best opportunities for inclusion and all staff model behaviours and values of treating everyone equally and with respect for differences.

Table 7.2 Helen's portfolio demonstrating Competencies promoting inclusive practice

6.1 Evidence knowledge, understanding and application in practice of pedagogy that supports inclusion

Environment audit to ensure inclusive practice can be embedded.

Low-level photo choice boards for all children to access and use regardless of ability and language capability.

Photos are regularly updated to include current cohort, adding a sense of belonging and relatability.

(Continued)

Table 7.2 (Continued)

6.1 Evidence knowledge, understanding and application in practice of pedagogy that supports inclusion

Witness testimony from mentor about.

- Supporting a child with EAL.
- Use of Russian picture word book to support during sessions along with Russian songs and music.

Observation of same child whereby her first language is integrated in her play.

Focussed Observation

Pupil:	Date and Time: 16th January 2016
Social context: Solitary Play CI	Learning context: M

Observation:

XXXXX was exploring the pompoms at the playdough table. She removed each pompom one at a time. She appeared to be counting to herself. As I listened it

became apparent she was counting in Russian (having looked in the Russian phrase book).

1-	Adeen	один
2-	Dva	два
3-	Tree	три
4-	Chtiri	четыре
5-	Pyat	пять

I began to count the pompoms with her in Russian. I then began to count in English and XXXXX joined in, able to count clearly 1-5 in English.

Assessment of significant learning:
Maths: Numbers
Recites some number names in sequence (22-36).

Next step:
We will continue to model counting in English with XXXXXX 1-10.

Completed by
Helen Haygarth

Table 7.2 (Continued)

6.1 Evidence knowledge, understanding and application in practice of pedagogy that supports inclusion

Frequently sought help from male support staff within school to try to encourage and expose children to positive male role models, e.g., accessed time in sensory room with male teacher, enjoyed watching caretakers, etc.

Large-scale display depicting children from around the world, flags and greetings in differing languages along with photographs of diverse use of music in practice.

Interactive display for children to explore the globe and discuss their world. Books depict homes and play from around the world. Linked to UNICEF articles.

Observation/Planning/Assessment Cycle which is reflected within learning journeys.
All planning is based upon individual needs of each child and reflects child initiated learning.

6.2 Know how to identify infants and young children who may require additional support and how to refer to appropriate services

Display to share targeted strategy to identify gaps in language and literacy skills.

(Continued)

Table 7.2 (Continued)

6.3 Demonstrate an understanding of statutory guidance for children with SEND and protected characteristics

Talk Matters language and literacy screening tool.

Low scores indicate need for intervention and/or referral to SALT [Speech and Language Therapy]. SALT referral and shared with parents/carers.

Referral to Small Steps for a child with additional needs awaiting assessment from an educational psychologist. Small Steps staff attend and intervene in both home and setting to ensure the needs of the child are universally addressed.

Individualised planning, observation and assessment cycle ensure children's development is monitored and reviewed.

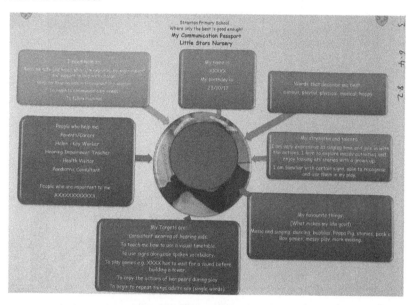

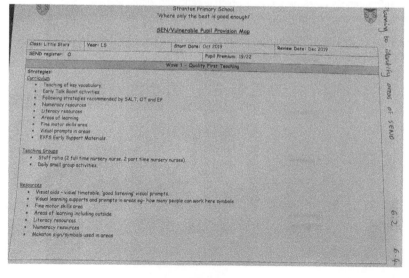

Table 7.2 (Continued)

6.4 Evidence skills in appropriate planning to address the care and learning needs of individual young children with SEND and/or protected characteristics

Communication passport created to record the individual needs and plan for a two-year-old with SEND, which includes agreed review date and is to be shared and signed by parents/carers.

Pupil Provision Map, identifying targeted children and interventions.

Academic essays at Level 5 and 6 (both graded firsts). Assignment titles:

'Analyse approaches to diversity and inclusion and make justified proposals to improve practice in your setting.' This included environment audit, SWOT analysis and action plan.

'The effectiveness of "inclusion" for children with special educational needs and disabilities within the UK educational context.'

Clear display/accessibility of setting Inclusion policy on parent noticeboard.

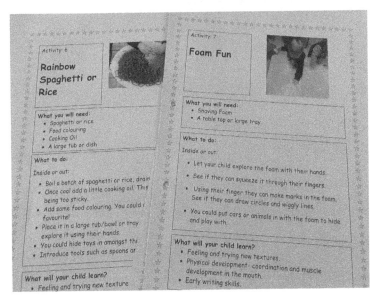

(Continued)

Table 7.2 (Continued)

6.4 Evidence skills in appropriate planning to address the care and learning needs of individual young children with SEND and/or protected characteristics

Words and pictures document created for a child with ASD to support understanding of role of family worker.

During lockdown, I prepared a pack of resources for a family with a child with ASD. These activities were intended to support a structure to their day while helping him learn through play.

Training and reflective assignments: *Understanding and applying good practice for people with autism*

Exploration of music as a tool to support social communication skill approach for a particular child.

Two-year-old boy was required to wear an eye patch during the day. To support this in nursery, we gave our circle time puppet a patch too.

Child assessed with ASD and EAL. Staff shadowed/mimicked her actions one-to-one to attempt to join her world rather than expect her to join ours.

Information pack designed to give simple information and strategies for parents/carers and staff on how to understand and meet the needs of children with autism.

Summary

Values should be at the heart of a setting's inclusion policy and practice, which should reflect an ethos embedded in promoting equality and positive social outcomes for all children and their families. Above all, an 'inclusion policy' should not be a tick-box exercise or be a document in a file that is never looked at. Although some values are considered more important than others in certain professions, there are some universal values that should be, and usually are, held and practised in all of them. The values of respect, dignity and equality are enshrined within key policy and legislative contexts and should form the basis of current Early Childhood Graduate Practitioner Competencies. These values should be demonstrated through all our professional relationships and practices. The connections between values and practices need to be regularly considered over the course of an individual' career. This is an important part of being a critically reflective and enquiring practitioner. You should aim to improve your own practice, by evaluating it, learning from the effective practice of others and from evidence. You need to be motivated and able to take increasing responsibility for your own continuing professional development.

Key Points

- Inclusion is to value and embrace all individuals, groups and cultures irrespective of their differences, backgrounds or needs.
- Critical reflection and continuous professional development are key to inclusive practice.
- Inclusion involves engaging every member of the setting and external stakeholders.
- Existing legislation and policy around inclusion is constantly developing and evolving.

Further Reading

Borkett, P. (2018) *Cultural diversity and inclusion in Early Years education*. David Fulton: London.
This book highlights the impact of culture on children's development and identity. The book discusses the importance of reflection for practitioners to appreciate cultural difference, value diversity and ensure inclusive practices.

Brodie, K. and Savage, K. (2015) *Inclusion and Early Years practice*. London Routledge.
This book comprises an overview of concepts, issues and perspectives of all aspects of inclusion and provides examples of practitioners' 'real' experiences and reflections.

Devarakonda, C. (2020) *Promoting inclusion and diversity in Early Years settings*. London: Jessica Kingsley.

This book raises awareness of diversity and inclusion and provides strategies for practitioners to proactively support marginalised children.

Edwards, M. (2015) *Global childhoods: Critical approaches to the Early Years.* St Albans, UK: Critical Publishing.

This book examines the experiences of children and their 'childhoods' in a global context. Chapter 7 examines global inequalities and the impact on children.

Hamilton, P. (2021) *Diversity and marginalization in childhood: A guide to inclusive thinking 0–11.* London: Sage.

This book introduces students to key perspectives around inclusion, exclusion and integration. Key chapters include contemporary issues, such as transgender children, children with mental health conditions and looked-after children.

Leonard, M. (2015) *The sociology of childhood and generation.* London: Sage.

Chapter 5 of this book, 'From Rights to Citizenship: Transformation and Constraints', recognises children's rights and outlines how children become citizens.

Chapter 8

PARTNERSHIPS WITH PARENTS AND CAREGIVERS

Julie Sealy

Chapter Aims

This chapter will introduce you to building partnerships with parents and caregivers. Key themes embedded throughout the chapter will support your understanding of how you, as a graduate practitioner, can build a practice that places parents and caregivers at the core of your work. Upon completion of this chapter, you will be better able to:

- understand the importance of partnership with parents and/or caregivers in their role as infants and young children's first educators
- demonstrate in practice the co-construction of learning in respectful partnership with parents and/or caregivers
- apply knowledge to practice about the diversity of family life and society
- demonstrate skills in communicating and working in partnership with families.

Introduction

When we talk about partnership with parents and caregivers, what exactly do we mean? In this chapter we will look at the nature of this partnership and what is expected of the Early Childhood practitioner when creating and nurturing a successful relationship with parents and caregivers. The chapter will explore the current evidence supporting parent partnership and the policy that guides this practice. Building partnerships with parents and caregivers can be tricky for some practitioners, especially early career practitioners (Ward, 2018), and in this chapter we will outline some of the challenges that Early Childhood practitioners may experience, along with examples of what successful collaboration looks like.

What Do We Mean by Partnership with Parents and Caregivers?

Throughout this chapter the terms 'partnership' and 'collaboration' will be used interchangeably to describe the involvement of parents and caregivers in Early Childhood settings. While there is UK policy support for building parent and caregiver partnerships, there is no blueprint for how this looks in practice (Ward, 2018). This involvement can take many different forms and childhood settings vary in how they collaborate with parents (Share and Kerrins, 2013).

When I ask Early Childhood students to share their experiences of working with parents and caregivers, their examples most often include sessions where parents are invited in for specific projects, such as a 'stay and play' session or a 'culture day'. However, some Early Childhood students are involved in more in-depth work with parents and caregivers. While research has demonstrated the effectiveness of parent involvement programmes, there remains a lack of consensus on what constitutes good collaboration (Hornby and Lafaele, 2011). For example, is parent involvement the same as parent engagement? Some researchers suggest that parent engagement goes beyond simply involving parents in structured activities (Ferlazzo, 2013), whereas others feel that these are two ends of a continuum (Goodall and Montgomery, 2014).

Reflection Point

What do you think? Are parent engagement and parent partnership the same thing?
Is inviting parents in for specific setting activities a good example of parent collaboration?

Respecting Diversity

When we think about working with parents and caregivers as part of a family system, we need to be mindful of not framing parents as one homogeneous group but respecting the diversity of families that we work with (Cottle and Alexander, 2014). Families are shaped on a micro level by personal, religious and psychological factors and on a macro level by historical, social, economic, cultural and political demographic forces, resulting in diverse socialisation and caregiving patterns within families (Bornstein and Putnick., 2012). Parents and caregivers also come in many diverse forms and a reflective practitioner is aware of celebrating this diversity in everyday interactions with children and families. It should be evident in your practice, in the books you read with children and in the activities you plan, and should shape the ethos of your organisation.

Embracing the diversity of the families you work with should be central to your work with parents and caregivers. Critical Race Theory brings awareness to the pervasive nature of implicit forms of discrimination that intersect along the lines of race, ethnicity, disability, religion, gender and sexual orientation (Bradbury, 2020). Prejudices can be open or hidden, and discriminatory practices can be subtle due to unconscious and implicit bias, whereby we can make quick and sometimes unconscious judgements about others based on our own personal beliefs, backgrounds and cultural identities (Atkinson et al., 2018). Your ability to embrace an anti-discriminatory approach in your work with children and families rests on the time and effort that you invest in ongoing reflexive practice to continuously evaluate your own 'blind spots' to examine the conscious and unconscious biases that you may hold (Henry-Allain and Lloyd-Rose, 2021: 8).

These blind spots can be in areas that you may not have thought about in your practice but can be devasting for families. Parents with English as a second language not only face language barriers but also cultural hurdles. For example, in the case study below, a parent shares an experience that reveals how school meals became a source of stress for the whole family during their transition from their homeland to the UK. Her moving reflection on the family's transition to life in the UK demonstrates how practitioners need to be sensitively attuned to what the parent and family may be experiencing. Observing, listening and trying to understand their subjective, lived experience is the foundation for mutual trust and a supportive relationship.

Case Study

A parent's reflection on relations with school

As parents moving to England 11 years ago, we could not speak any English. It was challenging to start a new life in a socially and culturally different country without support. Everything was new and we needed to learn everything. It was very hard, tiring and upsetting sometimes. We often felt frustrated and isolated. Like every other mum and dad, we wanted the best for our children: we wanted to see them be happy and successful.

Education was always important for my family. However, in England, I could not participate in their education as much as I did in our home country as we faced so many challenges, because of the language barrier and the unfamiliar education system. For example, every year my daughter had different teachers and often had new classmates and was separated from her friends. This was new to us, as in my home country children usually stay in the same classroom for years.

Even though the schools offered some help to my daughters, home–school communication was extremely limited. I translated every letter, school newsletter and report, but we still missed important occasions either because of misinterpreting, or not understanding the real meaning of words. For example, I missed the first assembly because I did not understand that parents could attend.

Parent evenings were particularly hard and frustrating for us. We sat in big, noisy halls with around a hundred other parents and teachers and could not make a conversation. I could not talk because I had no confidence in my English knowledge, therefore I could not ask questions and I absolutely could not understand what the teachers told me about my daughters. The teachers were very nice and kind, they smiled a lot at my daughters and me. From their gestures, I took the message that my daughters are doing well in school.

For me, it was unquestionable that whichever country we will end up living in, we will keep our Hungarian traditions and language. It was hard for us, but I wanted to make sure that my children could maintain their connections with friends, family and culture back in Hungary. Simple things, such as school dinners, were very difficult for us, and my daughter barely ate anything in school. She did not know how to ask for the food she wanted, she felt embarrassed when she could not understand the dinner ladies and found it easier to take only familiar foods, such as yoghurt and fruit. After a few days of arriving home starving, I went to school and talked about the issue and an office worker offered to print out a weekly menu so we can pick the meals in advance. Unfortunately, this did not solve the problem, as she still came home without eating much in school because the food was so different from what she was used to eating.

In an attempt to resolve this, I met with the school and through drawing pictures and writing down words we came up with a plan for me to take warm, freshly cooked Hungarian food for my daughter each day. My daughter was happy, I was happy, but before long her classmates started to bully her because of the dishes she was eating, and she asked me to stop. I visited the school once more and they gave me some ideas for packed lunches. After months of going through a very stressful situation, my insistence on liaising with the school paid off and a solution was found.

My worst memory related to a behavioural incident when my daughter was wrongly accused. Because of the language difficulty, she could not explain what happened and the school did very little to try to fully understand the situation. Instead, the school blamed my daughter and threatened her with future disciplinary action. This only added to the stress that the family was already experiencing due to the difficult transition to life in a new and different culture.

Not long after my daughter started school, she became ill, and it showed us that the transition was stressful and tiring for her. As she became more familiar with the school, learned the language and gained friendships, the illnesses reduced. Fortunately, one staff member was supportive – this was not a professional member of staff but an office worker. She was an angel to me, and I am so grateful for everything she did for us. Without her, we might be not here today.

On a positive note, when my seven-year-old daughter participated in the Young Voices event in Manchester, we were there to watch and sing along with her. No one could tell that she had only started to learn the English language. Our house was loud from her singing for months. Even when she was not well, she did not want to miss this fantastic opportunity. We were all very proud of her.

Reflection Point

What are the gaps in your own knowledge and understanding of diversity and anti-discriminatory practice?

How does your organisation foster an ethos that celebrates diversity and makes everyone feel fully included?

How do you ensure that you are truly working to understand the experience of the parents and families you work with?

As an Early Childhood practitioner, how do you engage in reflexive practice?

Why Do We Need Partnerships with Parents and Caregivers?

You may, like many Early Childhood educators, be wondering why you have to build partnerships with parents. Many Early Childhood practitioners feel that this role sits outside their responsibility (Hughes and Read, 2012). In addition, Early Childhood practitioners often do not feel equipped to engage with parents, citing a lack of training for this role (Sutterby, 2016) and many younger practitioners find the experience intimidating and stressful (Ward, 2018).

You may be surprised to learn that your Early Childhood Studies (ECS) education and training has provided you with the knowledge and skills to be able to develop successful partnerships with parents and caregivers. Early Childhood Studies is an interdisciplinary field that is underpinned with research across several academic disciplines. Within your ECS programme you will have covered critical theories that span disciplines such as sociology, health and social care, education, social policy and psychology (Taylor, Woods and Bond, 2013). Your ECS programme prepares you for multi-disciplinary practice and to work from a multi-professional perspective. As an Early Childhood professional, you will be expected to work as part of a multi-professional team that may include educators, social workers, SENCOs, psychologists, various therapists and, importantly, parents and caregivers (Jones, Powell and Holmes, 2005). The importance of working as part of a multi-professional team has been prioritised by government in response to the failure of safeguarding practices that resulted in tragic events, such as the death of Victoria Climbié (Laming, 2003).

Government initiatives, such as *Every Child Matters* (Department for Education and Skills (DFES), 2004), clearly articulate the expectation that the work of Early Childhood professionals will span professional boundaries, particularly integrating the fields of education and social care. At the core of this work are the partnerships we develop with parents and caregivers. Within education, research has shown that parents want to be involved in their children's education (Williams, Williams and Ullman, 2002). In the UK, the Effective Provision of Preschool Education (EPPE) project (Sylva et al., 2003) provided evidence to support parent involvement, demonstrating that the stronger the relationship between preschool and the home the greater the learning and development outcomes for children.

Greater involvement of parents and caregivers results in children experiencing fewer disciplinary issues and greater progression to higher education (Mapp, Lander and Carver, 2017). When parents are actively involved in their children's school life, their children have been found to develop more positive attitudes towards school (Sanatana, Rothstein and Bain, 2016), have a higher level of social engagement, and achieve greater academic success (Sheridan et al, 2019,). Lawson and Alameda-Lawson (2012) remind us that good parent–school partnerships, which promote parent and caregiver engagement, build social capital, that is, social resources that are developed through building networks, contacts and reciprocal social relationships. Increased social capital is associated with positive outcomes for children's learning and development, and can reduce inequalities, particularly for parents and caregivers from ethnically diverse or disadvantaged populations (Crul et al., 2017).

Reflection Point

How do you feel about approaching parents? Do you feel confident or does this make you anxious?

What do you think would make you feel more confident in building partnerships with parents and caregivers?

How Has Your ECS Programme Prepared You to Work with Parents and Caregivers?

Although we have the evidence to support developing strong parent and caregiver partnerships, many Early Childhood students do not feel confident to implement this in practice. A goal of the Graduate Practitioner Competencies is to ensure that as you complete your ECS programme equipped with the knowledge, skills and belief in your ability to embed working with parents and caregivers into your professional practice. You are encouraged to develop your critical thinking skills to be able to challenge policies and practices that do not promote best practices. As an advocate for young children, you are expected to enable and empower parents and caregivers as equal partners, although research suggests that power imbalances exist within parent–practitioner relationships (Hornby, 2000).

Within your ECS programme you will have developed an understanding of why building respectful partnerships with parents and caregivers should be at the core of your practice. You will have covered critical theories, such as attachment theory, as much of what we know and understand about building healthy relationships with children and parents is based on the extensive attachment literature, spanning over 50 years. The work of John Bowlby and Mary Ainsworth laid the foundation for the development of a body of multi-disciplinary knowledge that now informs our understanding of the critical importance of developing secure attachment relationships (Ainsworth, Bell and Stayton, 1971; Ainsworth et al., 1978; Bowlby, 1973, 1980, 1982). The work of Bowlby (1969) demonstrated how infant–parent/caregiver bonding in early life increases the infant's capacity for survival and is dependent upon warm, nurturing attachment relationships. The quality of this relationship co-constructs the infants' inner working models, shaping their representations of the world as either an emotionally safe, secure base or an unpredictable, anxiety-provoking place that can impede learning and development.

As an Early Childhood practitioner, you play a critical role in the nurturing of infants' and children's psycho-social wellbeing as their secondary attachment figure (Cottle and Alexander, 2014). Throughout your ECS programme you learn how the development of secure attachment relationships underpins children's healthy social and emotional development across the lifespan.

The question many Early Childhood students ask is how to apply this theory in practice. How can an understanding of attachment theory help to build healthy and successful relationships with parents and caregivers? One simple way is through observing parents and caregivers interacting with their children. You may be in a setting where your parent involvement and engagement are minimal, but simply observing parent–child interactions during pick-up and drop-off can give an abundance of information to help you to develop your relationships with parents.

Some Early Childhood professionals will choose to work in practice settings where the involvement of parents and caregivers is at the core of their practice, such as in family support work or work in specialist centres. In these settings, you will have more structured opportunities to work with parents. However, all Early Childhood students will be exposed to interdisciplinary theories and research that support practice with parents and caregivers. You will have been encouraged to observe and ask questions about the parent–child relationship. For example, why is it that some parents seem naturally attuned to their child, while others appear to struggle with this relationship? This may be more noticeable when there are disruptions in the parent–child relationship due to personal or family difficulties, or when the child has a special educational need or disability (SEND) or other emotional challenges. It is important that we take a critical pause here and acknowledge that observing parents should always be done in a respectful manner. Keep in mind that at the core of your work with parents and caregivers is the development of trust, which requires you to adopt a non-judgemental approach within a pedagogy of caring.

Building on the work of Bowlby and Ainsworth, evidence across disciplines narrows the lens to examine the more discrete components that support attachment security, such as parent–child interactional synchrony (Feldman, 2012) and parental reflective functioning (Fonagy et al., 2002; Slade, 2005). The neuroscience literature covered on your ECS programme provides theoretical understanding of the way the caregiving environment can affect the emotional and adaptive coping capacities of the infant (Schore, 2017).

Neurobiology presents evidence of the way regulatory processes and the stress responses of infants are affected by their perception of safety (Porges, 2005). Examining this question from a strength's perspective rather than from a deficit model (Saleeby, 2002), the overarching questions that these theories attempt to answer is what mechanisms are in play when practitioners observe a strong, resilient, attuned, healthy parent–child interaction? Later in the chapter we will look at some examples of interventions that support parent and caregiver collaboration and we will explore some of the barriers that can disrupt this practice.

Reflection Point

How do you think your understanding of attachment theory can help you to build stronger relationships with parents and caregivers?

How can understanding your own attachment relationships support your work with parents and caregivers?

What Does Good Parent and Caregiver Partnership Look Like in Practice?

As stated earlier, there is no template for developing parent partnerships and there is great variation in how they look in practice. For example, partnerships in Early Years settings are going to look very different from those in social care facilities and programmes that offer universal provision will look very different from parent programmes that are developed for a specific population. However, while the manner and the degree to which you will be involved with parents may vary, successful partnerships with parents and caregivers rely on the building of trusting relationships where parents and caregivers *feel* that they are at the apex of a 'triangle of care' with professionals and the community (Ball, 1994).

One example of an initiative that offered universal provision to parents and caregivers is the Sure Start programme that was introduced by the UK government in 1998. This offered support to socially disadvantaged children and families and has since become part of the Sure Start Unit, introduced in 2002. In 2009, there were 3,632 Sure Start Centres across disadvantaged regions (Cheater, 2019). They aimed at reducing the impact of poverty through early intervention with a joined-up approach, providing greater access to early education, family support and health care within communities (Eisenstadt, 2011). Sure Start services are tailored to meet the needs of the local communities and go beyond early education to include parenting support and advice on health and employment issues along with drop-in facilities for parents and caregivers. Evidence from national evaluations of the Sure Start programme suggests that involvement in Sure Start Centres promotes improved home learning environments and a reduction in child behaviour disorders (Belsky, Melhuish and Barnes, 2007; Sylva et al., 2015). Later research has demonstrated an association between the home learning environment and externalising behaviour problems, specifically demonstrating that richer home learning environments result in decreased externalising behaviour disorders in young children (Hall et al., 2019).

Globally, parent programmes have found similar results. Programmes in developing countries which involve parenting interventions that included parent training or coaching incorporating feedback from observations of the parent–child interaction have shown success in increased parent competence and reduced parental stress and depression, particularly with socially disadvantaged families (Mejia, Calam and Sanders, 2012). In the USA, community programmes such as 'Parent Corp', which offer parent support and education for families, with sessions facilitated by teachers and mental health professionals, have shown significant improvement in children's school behaviour and effective parenting practices (Brotman et al., 2011). In Latin America and the Caribbean, home visitation programmes that provide training and education for parents have demonstrated positive developmental outcomes for children (Leer and Lopez-Boo, 2019).

As an Early Childhood professional, you may work in health and social care or other family support settings where you are involved in intensive work with parents and caregivers, such as 'Minding the Baby', an intensive, interdisciplinary home visiting programme that supports young mothers and their families who have experienced trauma. This programme is aimed at addressing disruptions in the parent–child relationship (Sadler et al., 2013). You may be involved in other intensive parent programmes, such as the Incredible Years programme, which has been found to support parents and children with Attention Deficit/Hyperactivity Disorder (ADHD) and conduct challenges (Leijten et al., 2018), or the 'Parent Child+' programme, which supports the home learning environment (Cullen, Cullen and Bailey, 2020).

Whether you work with parents and caregivers as part of an intensive parenting programme or as a practitioner within Early Childhood settings, your work should be grounded in professional standards and ethics. Establishing a culture of mutual trust, valuing diversity and developing a commitment to equality, inclusion and social justice, along with a commitment to ongoing professional 'reflective integrity' (see Chapter 10), should be at the core of your work with parents and caregivers.

What Policies and Legislation Guide Our Work with Parents and Caregivers?

You will have been exposed to the policies and legislation that guide our work with parents and caregivers. The inclusion of parents and caregivers in early education settings in the UK has evolved over time and historically, prior to the Second World War, the home and school were seen as totally separate entities, with little or no involvement of parents (Turner et. al., 2014).

In the UK, the Plowden Report (Department of Education and Science 1967) was one of the early policy initiatives supporting the development of Parent Teacher Associations and greater communication between the home and school. However, it wasn't until the introduction of the National Curriculum through the Education Reform Act of 1988 (Legislation.gov.uk, 1988) and the Children Act 1989 (Legislation.gov.uk, 1989) that parents were recognised as having a role to play in their child's education. The Children Act 1989 declared that 'parents should be encouraged to work in partnership with agencies, participating in the processes of decisions relating to their child' (Wilson, 2015 53).

Policy development generally sits within each society's socio-cultural and political norms and values and is shaped by the political agenda of prevailing political parties. Social policy change often happens in response to social incidents that become a catalyst for change. In the UK, the lack of coordination of safeguarding practices to protect children resulted in the Every Child Matters Green Paper in 2003 and the subsequent passing of legislation, such as the Children Act 2004 (Legislation.gov.uk, 2004), which identified parents and caregivers as essential partners in multi-agency collaboration (Davies, Brotherton and McGillivray, 2010). In England and Wales, the Childcare Act 2006 (Legislation.gov.uk, 2006) established the legal framework for the Early Years Foundation Stage (EYFS) (DCSF, 2008) and the involvement of parents and caregivers in children's early education and care (Wilson, 2015).

The importance of parent collaboration was further consolidated in the revised Early Years Foundation Stage statutory framework (EYFS) in 2014 (Department for Education, 2014d) in response to a report by Dame Clare Tickell, who recommended more widespread and consistent involvement of parents and caregivers and greater recognition of the importance of parent–practitioner partnerships (Tickell, 2011). The EYFS mandates that a key person is assigned to each child and requires practitioners to support the child's learning and development at home through collaboration with parents and caregivers (Department for Education, 2021). The key person approach has been found to increase parents' trust and confidence in the professionals working with their child as well as resulting in greater staff satisfaction (Elfer, 2012).

However, while policies provide a framework to guide our work with parents and caregivers, it is important for practitioners to evaluate government policies with a critical eye to ensure that they are inclusive and respect the diversity of the families we work with. How do we ensure that we are applying a critical eye to policies that guide our work with parents and caregivers? Moss (2017) suggests that we question the 'dominant discourses', that is, the policies that govern what we do in practice and that shape how we see the world, by actively engaging to interrogate and interpret policies that guide Early Childhood professional practice.

How do the policies that guide our work as Early Childhood professionals frame the parents and caregivers we work with? As stated earlier, parents are not one homogeneous group, but rather consist of single parents, foster and adopted parents, same-sex parents, grandparents, extended family members, ethnic and culturally diverse parents and neurodiverse parents. Furthermore, we must ensure that the policies that shape our practice with parents and caregivers are not presenting parents through a deficit lens, identifying them as 'problem parents' or 'disadvantaged', 'needy' or 'vulnerable'? Cottle and Alexander (2014) caution against blindly accepting policies that perpetuate a system that stigmatises parents and caregivers and oversimplifies the complexity of the families we work with.

> ### Reflection Point
>
> What do you think about the policies in the EYFS that address parent and caregiver collaboration? Do you think they are adequate? If not, what would you change? How do you feel about your role as an 'agent of change'? Do you see this as your responsibility as an Early Childhood practitioner?

What are Some of the Challenges and Barriers to Good Parent–Practitioner Collaboration?

We see that there have been government initiatives to support parent collaboration, yet research suggests that there is a wide gap between the rhetoric promoting parent–practitioner partnerships and what actually occurs in practice (Hornby and Blackwell, 2018). Hornby and Lafaele (2011) propose a model identifying factors that can interfere with effective parent and caregiver involvement (Figure 8.1). Greater parent and caregiver involvement is said to be hindered:

- by issues relating to parents and families themselves, such as the parent/family's perceptions about their role in their child's education
- by factors that impact the child directly, such as SEND and emotional behavioural challenges
- by issues relating specifically to the practitioner/teacher and by political and economic macro issues.

Individual parent and family factors	Child factors
• Parents' beliefs about parent involvement • Parents' perceptions of invitations for parent involvement • Current life contexts • Class, ethnicity and gender	• Age • Learning difficulties and disabilities • Gifts and talents • Behaviour problems
Parent–teacher factors • Differing goals and agendas • Differing attitudes • Differing language used	**Societal factors** • Historical and demographic • Political • Economic

Figure 8.1   Factors impacting parent involvement (Hornby and Lafaele, 2011)

A useful way for you to examine the many and diverse factors that can hinder the development of parent–practitioner partnerships is to look at this through the lens of the ecological systems perspective (Bronfenbrenner, 1979). Your ECS programme will have introduced you to this model as an approach to help you to understand the many dynamics that impact children and families. Using an eco-map will help you to look at and organise the myriad of potential barriers to forming parent partnership across the four ecological systems (Swick and Williams, 2006).

On a *micro level*, you can think about what issues that are related to the individual child, parent or practitioner may be derailing the parent–practitioner relationship. For example, this may be the child's developmental challenges or the practitioner's anxiety or lack of confidence or possibly the parent's individual difficulties due to language challenges. On a *meso level*, the interaction between the school and the parents may be poor, with a lack of communication between home and the setting. On an *exo level*, issues that impact the parents, such as work-related stress, may affect their ability to work closely

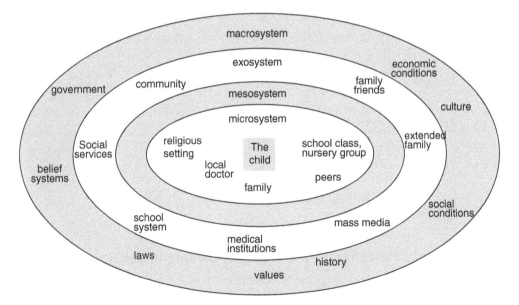

Figure 8.2   Bronfenbrenner's Ecological Systems model (Bronfenbrenner, 1979)

with the setting. Finally, on a *macro level*, cultural, political, social and legislative issues can influence the parent–practitioner partnership.

Reflection Point

Identify the factors on each of the micro, meso, exo and macro levels of the ecological system and see how many factors you can think of that may hinder your ability to develop partnerships with parent and caregivers.

The Importance of Effective Communication

One area that can seriously affect the development of parent partnerships is poor communication between parents and practitioners (Hughes and Read, 2012). But what exactly are we referring to when we talk about effective communication? Communication in practice is more than sharing information with parents, and it is more than being a good listener. Successful two-way, purposeful communication takes place within an affective (emotional) relationship and rests on your ability to effectively 'tune-in' to your communicative partner (Hughes and Read, 2012). When you are attuned to the parents you are working with, you will be able to read their body language, such as their posture, gestures, facial expressions and their tone of voice. This can very often provide great insight into the feelings behind what they are saying to you. Your reflexive practice is critical to developing your communication skills with parents and caregivers. Along with tuning-in to the parents' non-verbal communication, you have to be attuned to your own, internal emotional state and this is dependent on a high degree of self-awareness and self-reflection.

Another identified barrier to developing successful parent partnerships is inadequate resources and training (Ozmen et al., 2016). However, your ECS programme is designed to help you to develop the reflective capacities that you need to be an effective communicator. This relies on more than the development of communication skills; it rests on your commitment to developing and nurturing your reflexive practice throughout your education and continuing this throughout your professional practice. The next case study is one student's reflection on her work with parents in a school setting.

Case Study

A student's reflection of working with parents in a school setting

During placements I have completed throughout my degree I have worked alongside parents and caregivers on a daily basis. This involved communicating with parents by writing in children's planners regarding their progress and next steps for their reading and comprehension.

Also, my interaction with parents and caregivers involved speaking to them in the morning and after school at drop off and pick up, and answering any questions or worries they may have. I also engaged with parents and caregivers during handover at the end of the day to inform them of any difficulties their child experienced throughout the day.

Recently, I have begun working at a local nursery where I am a cover staff member. Transitioning from placement to full employment makes me feel extremely nervous as being a Level 3 practitioner I am expected to engage in daily interactions with parents and caregivers. Although I have had placement experience, it felt terrifying to speak to parents as a practitioner, particularly having to discuss difficult situations involving their child. My fears evolved around how the parent/caregiver would perceive me being a young and newly qualified practitioner and how they may feel that I am not experienced or mature enough to engage them in discussions about their child.

While my education and training on the Early Childhood Studies programme has given me the knowledge and skills to pursue a career in early education, I do not feel that I have acquired the skills or confidence to undertake work directly with parents and caregivers. I will be pursuing further education on a Primary PGCE programme, and I hope that this will better prepare me for working with parents and caregivers. However, I do feel that I will remain quite anxious collaborating with parents and caregivers when beginning my career as a qualified teacher.

Summary

Setting-based care for young children has increased in the UK and research and policy initiatives clearly underscore the importance of parent–practitioner collaboration (Cottle and Alexander, 2014; Department for Education, 2021; Department for Education and Skills (DfES), 2002, 2007; Sylva et al., 2004; Ward, 2018). The 'triangle of care' between the child, practitioner and parent is the accepted best practice and is associated with greater developmental and learning outcomes for young children (Brooker, 2010). Research has shown that provision that supports parent–practitioner collaboration is particularly impactful with working-class families and children living in poverty (Heckman, 2006; Van Laere and Vandenbroeck, 2014). However, parental involvement should not be viewed through a deficit or problem-focused lens, where parents and caregivers are seen as 'spectators of their alleged problems' (Van Laere, Van Houtte and Vandenbroeck, 2018: 189).

Engaging in ongoing reflexive practice will ensure that you are working *with* parents and caregivers in what Tronto (2013) calls 'a caring democracy', where all parties have an equal voice in the relationship. Your work with parents will be constructed within the constraints of your practice setting and the broader socio-political context, but as a reflexive practitioner you can challenge practices that perpetuate unequal power dynamics in the parent–practitioner relationship and place parents at the core of your practice.

Key Points

This chapter has explored some key areas for you to consider in your work with parents and caregivers. It has covered:

- Working with parents within a deficit or problem-focused framework
- Dealing with parent/caregiver expectations from relationships
- The implicit power dynamics within relationships with parents
- Inclusive practice and the diversity of parents and caregivers.

Further Reading

Hryniewicz, L. and Luff, P. (Eds) (2020) *Partnership with parents in Early Childhood settings: Insights from five European countries.* London: Routledge.

This book draws on research across Europe to explore how political, social and cultural contexts impact the relationship between practitioners and parents and families.

Tutwiler, S. J. W. (2017) *Teachers as collaborative partners: Working with diverse families and communities.* London: Taylor & Francis.

This is a good resource for practitioners to understand the dynamics of school and family relationships to support with work diverse families.

Online resources

The Professional Association for Childcare and Early Years: www.pacey.org.uk

This a professional association dedicated to supporting everyone working in childcare and Early Years. It is an excellent resource for both practitioners and parents.

The Anna Freud Centre: www.annafreud.org

This Centre has an array of information and resources to support your work with parents and caregivers. The Centre focuses on the mental health and wellbeing of infants, children and families.

The Interdisciplinary Council for Learning and Development (ICDL): https://icdl.com

This organisation provides online training, education and support for working with parents and children with developmental disabilities.

Chapter 9

COLLABORATING WITH OTHERS

Helen Perkins

Chapter Aims

This chapter will support your knowledge and understanding of how to create effective working relationships. By the end of the chapter, you will have had opportunities to reflect upon and extend your understanding of how to:

- evidence knowledge about the importance of creating successful, respectful professional relationships with colleagues and other professionals in and outside the setting (Graduate Competencies 8.1)
- apply collaborative skills in practice, including effective listening and working as a member of a team and in multi-professional contexts (Graduate Competencies 8.2)
- demonstrate an understanding of the barriers to working with others and how to address these in practice (Graduate Competencies 8.3)

Introduction

This chapter focuses on the importance of creating successful and respectful professional relationships with colleagues and other professionals. It will consider how graduate-level practitioners can develop their knowledge, skills and strategies to establish harmonious working relationships. This chapter will offer theoretical concepts and students' perspectives to help you to reflect on your practice.

What Do We Mean by Professional Relationships?

Professional relationships are those we engage in with workplace or placement colleagues, as well as those that extend beyond the workplace to other professionals, such as health visitors, speech and language therapists and social workers. Relationships with parents and children are addressed elsewhere in this book (see Chapters 2 and 8).

Relationships with colleagues

Good relationships between colleagues are important for the wellbeing of the staff team and for the children. When a team works well together and communication is effective, it is more likely to create a positive and productive working environment. There is a wealth of studies in the field of psychology that assert that positive work relationships, 'produce positive emotions which increase self-efficacy and task performance' (Geue, 2017: 275).

Developing relationships, whether it is with your placement or work colleagues, takes time and commitment. Starting your first placement can be daunting, particularly if you have not had any previous experience working with children. In the following case study, Early Childhood Graduate Practitioner Abbie Martin reflects on her experience of starting her first placement in a day care setting and offers some supportive advice for students embarking on their placement journey.

Case Study

Abbie Martin's reflection on starting a new placement

In reflection of my experience in Competency 8, it would be dishonest to omit the impact that being a student in placement had. I found that students were consistently treated differently to employed staff. This may seem obvious, but it is unfortunate how much of an effect it had on me. When you're in a placement to learn about being a practitioner, it doesn't help if you aren't treated like one. This is a difficult challenge to overcome and makes meeting this Competency more difficult. It can mean you have gaps in your experience, as you may not be trusted enough to do important tasks that you will be expected to do once employed. It also meant I received an excess of experience in less important tasks (i.e., washing up). As a result of this, I often felt that the setting staff believed me to be incompetent, or a burden, and I was frustrated at not being trusted to gain the experience I needed.

Eventually, I found that the best way to overcome being seen as 'the student' by staff is to throw yourself into both work and relationships. Even if you are usually a shy or introverted person, taking the initiative is so important. Setting staff may not always be so friendly to address you first, and it is up to you to make up the difference, as it is you who it will benefit. It is not always enough to simply do work when asked, you should also take the initiative and ask for the work. Showing not only that you are willing, but you are eager, can quickly result in a stronger relationship between you and members of staff, and they will soon see your value as a member of the team. Of course, relationships can also be built over time, but the sooner you are trusted, the sooner you can experience the full potential that your setting has to offer.

Commentary on Abbie's reflection

Abbie's reflection highlights the value of reflection. In particular, it shows how she used her understanding of the importance of developing a professional working relationship with colleagues. By taking the initiative, and moving out of her comfort zone, she was able to expedite the process and settle into her role as part of the team. Abbie makes the important point that relationships are rooted in trust, your willingness to trust someone else and your own trustworthiness. Abbie recognised that, as the new person, she needed to demonstrate her trustworthiness through her professional behaviour before this could be reciprocated. By being proactive and attending to her relationship with the team, Abbie began to flourish. With more meaningful work to do, her performance improved. She developed positive feelings about her work, became fully engaged with the team and experienced meaningfulness in her activities.

In their research into positive practices in the workplace, Cameron et al. (2011) suggest that positive relationships are based on six conditions:

- **Respect**: trusting and having confidence in one another
- **Care**: showing interest in and responding to one another
- **Support**: honouring and supporting one another in their endeavours, building strong relationships and helping those who are struggling
- **Inspiration**: sharing enthusiasm and inspiring one another
- **Meaning**: being motivated, renewed and elevated when they see purpose in their work
- **Forgiveness**: not blaming one another for errors but forgiving one another's mistakes

Reflection Point

Reflect on your working relationships with colleagues. How would you describe your relationships with your colleagues?

Do you agree with Cameron et al.'s (2011) conditions?

What would you add or take away, and why?

Relationships with other professionals

'Other professionals' is an umbrella term for the multifarious and interchangeable vocabulary that is used to describe working with people from other disciplines (Lumsden, 2018). Each country will have its own definitions. In England, multi-professional working is enshrined in *Working Together to Safeguard Children* (Department for Education, 2018) (see Chapters 6 and 8 for more discussion of this document).

Multi-professional working environments include:

- **Multi-agency working**: more than one agency working with a child and family, not necessarily jointly, but concurrently or sequentially with joint planning
- **Integrated working**: agencies working together within a single organisational structure
- **Inter-agency working**: more than one agency, working together in a formal way, either strategically or operationally
- **Collaboration**: agencies working together to achieve a common goal while still pursuing their own organisational goals
- **Multi-professional working**: staff with different professional backgrounds and training working together.

These terms are used interchangeably and often change when there is a new policy. However, they can all be considered as *partnership working*.

The concept of partnership working is not new. In the mid-nineteenth century, social care and health services worked together to reduce poverty in England. The foundations for multi-agency working were laid in the 1980s, with The Children Act 1989 and the 2004 amendment (Legislation. gov.uk, 1989, 2004) establishing the legal duty for joint working in relation to children and families. Working within a multi-agency context is essential as children's needs cannot be compartmentalised into Early Years, health, social care or education; rather, they should be considered holistically.

For Early Childhood Graduate Practitioners working in all aspects of the children's workforce, engaging with outside agencies has many benefits. Research suggests that professionals believe that multi-agency cooperation encourages a more child-centred approach (Owens, 2010). As a graduate practitioner you will be working with other professionals from a variety of agencies, disciplines and backgrounds when collaborating to meet the needs of children with special educational needs and disabilities (SEND), children in public care (looked-after children (LAC)) and vulnerable children whose welfare is at risk (safeguarding is covered in depth in Chapter 6 and inclusion in Chapter 7).

Multi-agency cooperation brings together people with a range of skills, expertise and experience from health, social care and education, who work collaboratively to respond effectively to prevent problems arising or escalating for children and families. The range of expertise and experience should be valued, respected and acknowledged. Multi-professional working affords the opportunity for graduate practitioners to demonstrate their unique knowledge of the child and child development as well as extend their knowledge and skills.

Below, Early Childhood Graduate Practitioner Amelia describes her experience of working alongside the speech therapist to support a child in her nursery who has Childhood Apraxia of Speech (CAS). Children with CAS have problems saying sounds, syllables and words. Amelia shared the positive impact on her own professional development through this experience:

> The speech therapist suggested recording my sessions so that she could see how X was progressing. I've only had three sessions so far, watching the videos with her, but I have noticed a difference. She comments on how well I've developed as well as X, so it's not just

about the child. The child has made progress and I have too … and it's good because I've learned a new theory and how to develop the child's speech … (Perkins, 2017: 101)

Amelia goes on to explain how she applies what she has learned from the sessions with the speech therapist to support other children's language development, demonstrating her developing self-efficacy and ability to transfer knowledge and skills to other situations (Rogoff, 2003).

Conversely, the protected professional identities of health, social work and education professionals can create barriers for Early Childhood Graduate Practitioners. The variations of their perceived rank and status, according to ontological and epistemological understanding of professionalism, hierarchy, status and influence, has been shown to subjugate the knowledge and expertise of the Early Years practitioners (Rose, 2011 Urrieta 2007). Early Childhood Graduate Practitioners have the potential to bridge this divide, as they have a different relationship with the children and families; they are an 'untapped resource' (Lumsden, 2018: 23).

In their research with Early Years Professionals (EYPs), Payler and Georgeson (2013) found that where EYPs proposed moving beyond the established practice, they were able to 'create and negotiate new connections with outside agencies, forming new relationships and developing new understandings', leading to 'change, not simply 'participation in the reproduction of the current state of affairs' but 'contributing to change it.' The extent to which Early Childhood Graduate Practitioners are competent and confident to use their agency has a complex relationship with status and power. The extended and broad practice-based experiences of Early Childhood Graduate Practitioners provide the opportunity to develop confidence when working with others. They have the potential to break down barriers and facilitate the development of respectful, reciprocal working relationships between Early Childhood practitioners and other professionals.

Reflection Point

Reflect on your experience of engaging with other professionals. What are your experiences of working other professionals?
How can you contribute to developing relationships with external professionals to support the children in your care?
What are your development needs for multi-professional working?

In summary, professional working relationships require trust, listening and understanding, being heard and having your contributions considered and valued. Developing a relationship requires time and emotional investment. It requires you to move beyond developing a rapport; it becomes a relationship when 'you cross the threshold, from getting on, into a trust-building relationship' (White, 2017: 8). We have looked at the importance of creating successful, respectful professional relationships with colleagues and other professionals. In the next section we bring these aspects together in exploring effective teamwork theory and practice.

Exploring Teamwork: Theory and Practice

Whichever area of the children's workforce we choose to work in, it is likely we will be required to work as part of a team. Understanding team dynamics and processes will be a valuable skill in your future employment. The theories offered in this section contribute to our understanding of potential conflicts and successes in effective teamwork. Teamwork is the foundation of children's services, whether referring to the team in the setting or other professionals. It is important to understand that building, leading and working in a team is a complex, ongoing process. In this section, we will consider Tuckman's team development model (Tuckman and Jensen, 1977) and, in the section on communication below, Luft and Ingham's Johari window (1955) provides a useful approach for learning how to improve our collaboration skills.

Effective teams support the achievement of common goals for improving the quality of care and education - and service provision. Individuals within a team do not have to think the same way, but they do need to respect each other's values, skills and experiences. Respecting diverse viewpoints enriches the team by bringing together different perspectives and ideas.

Theories of team development

Tuckman's team development model offers a way of reflecting on your place within the team as well as providing a framework with which to evaluate the progress and effectiveness of a team (Tuckman and Jensen, 1977). As an Early Childhood Graduate Practitioner, you may be in a leadership position. This might be as a social worker, family support worker, child advocate or leading pedagogy. Understanding the team dynamics and processes will help you to build an effective team.

Tuckman's original model had four stages: forming, storming, norming and performing. A fifth stage, adjourning, was added in a later revision of the model to explore the importance of closure at the end of a team relationship or project. You might think about the end of your degree, and how graduation acts as both a celebration of your achievement and the end of the group you have studied with (Tuckman and Jensen, 1977).

- **The Forming stage**: The team is a collection of individuals. There is little sense of being a cohesive team. Members may be wary of each other and what is expected of them. People may keep quiet rather than speak out at this stage, until they are sure of their role and position in the team. The team will seek a clear direction at this stage.
- **The Storming stage**: Here the team members are beginning to seek individual roles and space. Conflict can arise as people jostle for position and search for compatible roles within the team. Issues of power and control emerge. Conflict and divergence of attitudes can appear.

Sometimes this is about taking the lead, or questioning the norms of the team, challenging the priorities and process.

- **The Norming stage**: At this point, leadership is established and the basic rules, behaviour and order of the group are established. Conflicts from the storming phase have been resolved (this may or may not include people leaving the group). As the group norms are firmly established, there will be a feeling of cohesiveness; people become comfortable in their roles. The group begins to be important to the members, relationships matter and an emotional trust in 'our group' develops. Part of this process is the development of 'norms', which become accepted as 'our ways of doing things'.

- **The Performing stage**: Performing is the point at which the group becomes a largely self-sufficient resource, using all the skills and potential of the members to achieve its aims and solve problems. It is likely to have an enabling structure and a high level of cohesion and trust. At this point the group becomes autonomous. Everyone acts in a supportive way to enhance the possibility of group success.

- **The Adjourning stage**: This is about completion and disengagement, both from the tasks and the group members. Individuals will be proud of having achieved their goals and glad to have been part of the group. They need to recognise what they've done, and consciously move on. Some authors describe this stage as 'Mourning', recognising the sense of loss felt by group members as the group disbands.

Tuckman's model focuses on the interplay between interpersonal relationships and task activity (Bonebright, 2010). Similarly, in her writing about teamwork in Early Childhood settings, Rodd (2006) suggests that effective teams are underpinned by the concepts of working towards a common philosophy, and common ideals and values. A successful team is committed to working through conflict and takes shared responsibility for the team's successes and failures. Rodd goes on to assert the importance of open and honest communication and the importance of a support network. Tuckman's and Rodd's models help us to reflect on our experiences and evaluate our participation and impact on the team.

Barriers to effective teamwork

Tuckman tells us that a 'performing' team knows the task at hand, and individuals know their roles and are supportive of each other. In the following case study from first-year student Saba's journal, we see the impact of not attending to team development. Saba began her placement in a nursery but was experiencing difficulties as staff assumed that she knew the children's routine. Saba's experience is not uncommon. There can be an assumption that, as a graduate, you have had previous experience.

Case Study

Saba's experience of difficulties within the team and how they were rectified

I was feeling stressed about missing things such as activities, assessments and log updates. I worry about how this had a negative impact not only on my confidence and self-esteem, but also on the children and their parents. When they picked up their children at the end of the session, some parents would question me on their child's progression as they could not see it on their online log because it was not updated. They just kept telling me to get on with it, to do whatever I thought best. I just want to leave; they think I'm useless.

Commentary on Saba's reflection

Saba's commentary in her journal prompted a discussion about joining a new team. Together, we considered Tuckman's model. Saba identified that while the team was in the 'performing stage', she was in the 'forming stage', trying to understand the rules, the organisation and what was expected of her. We discussed possible ways forward. It became clear that Saba was expecting to be inducted into her placement, which was a reasonable assumption. However, this had not happened. She was therefore going to have to take the initiative and ask for clarity on her role and to share her needs as a student. Together, we made notes on the key points and rehearsed the conversation. By scaffolding the next steps, goals and responsibilities were established and Saba began to develop a relationship with the team.

Team cohesion is hindered when members:

- Feel inadequate and are unable to express themselves
- Believe they will be ridiculed
- Feel hostile towards members of the team
- Feel left out of the team's communication.

Reflection Point

A key aspect of teamwork is the extent to which all those involved in the team have shared, values and beliefs. What do you understand by the term 'team'?
What are your values, attitudes and beliefs relating to how children learn and develop?
Are your values, attitudes and beliefs congruent with those you work with?

The theories discussed above highlight that effective communication is crucial in building teams and relationships (Rodd, 2006). In the next section, we will explore communication.

Communication

When working in a demanding environment, it is important to communicate with others effectively. This is particularly important if you are sharing information that affects a child's wellbeing. In my own research, I asked newly qualified practitioners about the importance of communication skills for Early Childhood practitioners (Perkins, 2017*)*. One practitioner summed it up succinctly:

> … because [you have to] communicate with the children, children's parents, people in your
> room, other staff, other agencies. And if you are not going to communicate, nothing's
> going to get done, you're not going to get along with anyone. (Perkins, 2017: 102)

This practitioner is acknowledging her understanding of the wider role of the practitioner beyond the interaction with the children. Having appreciated how good communication is essential to successful and effective teamwork, we turn next to the key aspects and theories of communication, how individuals may interpret the same experience differently, and potential barriers to communication.

The communication cycle

A communication cycle begins with the formation and transmission of a message from one person (the sender) to another person (the receiver), through various means of communication, to elicit an appropriate response or feedback from the receiver. As a graduate practitioner, you will need to consider what form of communication is appropriate to the context and nature of your communication.

Argyle (1972) proposed a more detailed, six-stage communication cycle (Figure 9.1), involving:

1 The idea stage, when the thought arises.
2 The encoding stage, when the message is formed.
3 The signals stage, by which the message is transmitted using a channel of communication.
   [is this a correct interpretation of this stage?]
4 The decoding stage, when the recipient receives and interprets the message.
5 The meaning stage, by which the recipient understands the message.
6 The feedback stage, at which the recipient acts on or replies to the message.

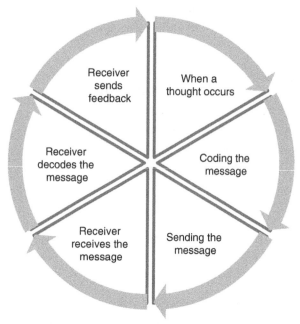

Figure 9.1 Argyle's cycle of communication (Argyle, 1972).

Examples of communication channels are:

- verbal communication – including face-to-face communication, videoconference, telephone or voicemail, sign language, Makaton and assistive technology
- written communication – including email, letter, social media.

How we communicate depends on the nature of the communication, for example:

- What is the purpose of the communication?
- How urgent or important is it?
- Does it concern a complex issue, such as safeguarding?
- Is further action, discussion or consultation required?

These factors should be taken into consideration when communicating with colleagues and other professionals. The nature of the communication will inform the channel you use and your approach, whether you are passing on a message about a child's absence or reporting at a family case conference.

When communicating with colleagues and other professionals, Early Childhood Graduate Practitioners should take account of their verbal, spoken and written communication, as well as non-verbal communication cues, such as facial expressions, eye or body movements and gestures. As these are familiar concepts, we should also consider paraverbal communication. Paraverbal communication is the pitch, cadence and tone of our voice. For example, do we seem happy, despondent, angry or confused? When we are angry, we tend to speak more rapidly and at a higher pitch. If we feel someone is being aggressive or offensive, we tend to respond in short, abrupt sentences (Valentzas and Broni, 2014).

Paraverbal and non-verbal signals can be misread, which can lead to a breakdown in communication. For example, regional or culturally-influenced accents can confuse our reading of the communication. Similarly, non-native English speakers may find paraverbal cues difficult to interpret, thus creating a barrier to communication. There is a solution: ask! Let people know that you are aware that cultural differences may create a communication barrier and that you will not be offended if they point out any issues, and that you are open to learn.

Communication can be synchronous, meaning it happens at the same time, or asynchronous. Asynchronous communication refers to communication that is not immediate and occurs over longer periods of time, such as in letters, email, or even text messages. Without the benefit of non-verbal and paraverbal cues, asynchronous communication can be open to misinterpretation as there is no opportunity to adjust your message in real time, in response to feedback or to clarify the content as you would in face-to-face communication (Valentzas and Broni, 2014). When using asynchronous methods of communication, it is imperative to proofread your message and to check for the following:

- Have you used an appropriate tone for the recipient (formal or informal)?
- Have you used the correct tone for your purpose?
- Have you used jargon? It is better to avoid jargon, unless you know your recipient is familiar with the terms you have used.
- Is your message clear?
- Is your message concise? It is important to get your point across quickly and efficiently.
- Is your message courteous and polite?
- Have you used grammar and punctuation correctly?

Clear messages help to build trust and integrity between the sender and the receiver. Being aware of these nuances can have a positive impact on our communication, not only in how we send messages, but also in how we receive and interpret them.

The Johari window

It is helpful to use the Johari window technique (Luft and Ingham, 1955) to explore how our communication can impact how we develop relationships. The Johari window model is a useful tool for illustrating and improving self-awareness and mutual understanding between individuals within a team. It comprises four quadrants representing what is known and unknown about an individual (the self) and the other members of a team.

The four Johari window quadrants represent the information, feelings, motivation and values known about an individual and the others in the group, in terms of whether the information is known or unknown by the individual, and whether the information is known or unknown by others in the group. The four quadrants in the grid are the open area, blind area, hidden area and unknown area (see Figure 9.2), and they can change in size to reflect the relevant proportions of each type of 'knowledge' about an individual.

	Known to self	Not known to self
Known to others	Open area	Blind area
Not known to others	Hidden area	Unknown area

Figure 9.2 The Johari window (Luft and Ingham, 1955)

The **open area** is for what you know about yourself and are happy to share with others. For example, you might be happy to tell someone about the strengths that you bring to your role, or some of the experiences you have had working with children and families. We can expand the open area by asking colleagues for feedback.

The **blind area** is what other people know about you, but that you are not aware of. For example, you may not know that your supervisor finds you supportive, thinks you are very good at identifying children with additional needs, or that you have a habit of invading people's personal space. These may be identified by having regular supervision sessions with your mentor. Asking and acting upon feedback can help reduce the blind area.

The **hidden area** contains things you know about yourself but do not wish to share with colleagues. This could include opinions on managing children's behaviour, your politics, or any weaknesses that you feel you have, perhaps due to a lack of confidence. A larger unknown area would be expected in younger people and people who lack experience or self-belief.

The **unknown area** represents information that is unknown to you and to others. This might include talents, capabilities, feelings and qualities. We can reduce the size of the unknown area through self-discovery, for example, intentionally doing things you have not done before or, with the help of others, sharing a discovery through other people's observations or interventions.

The information transfers from one quadrant to another as the result of growing mutual trust, which is achieved through familiarity and the feedback received from other members of the group. The size of each quadrant changes as we gain awareness of how others see us and as we develop our confidence within the team, maximising the open area and reducing the others (Luft and Ingham, 1955).

In addition to being a useful tool for improving self-awareness and mutual understanding between individuals within the team, it may also be used to improve a team's relationship with others, for example, when working with external agencies, in avoiding some of the barriers to multi-agency working discussed earlier in the chapter. The Johari Window model is especially relevant in the Early Childhood workforce, with its emphasis on, and influence of, 'soft' skills, behaviour, empathy, cooperation, and inter-agency and interpersonal development. Established members in the team logically tend to have larger open areas as they have developed relationships over time. New team members start with small open areas because relatively little knowledge about the new team member is shared. The size of the open area can be expanded into the blind space by seeking and actively listening to, and acting on, feedback, as described in the next case study from Early Childhood Graduate Practitioner, Jenny Stanley.

Jenny reflects on her first placement experience at the beginning of her Early Childhood Studies degree. She had no previous experience of working in an Early Childhood education setting. She describes her experience of receiving feedback.

Case Study

....

Jenny Stanley's experience of receiving feedback

Upon starting placement, I had no experience of working with children. For me, this caused me to feel incredibly nervous around practitioners in the setting, meaning I never asked for help for fear of looking silly. A turning point came when I had an awful tutorial with my mentor, who (in lengthier terms) said that I did not look like I cared about being there.

If I think about this incident in terms of Gibbs' Reflective Cycle (Gibbs, 1988), I first had to overcome the huge amount of embarrassment and anger I felt. It was not that I did not care, I just lacked in confidence. However, when I evaluated the incident, I realised that there was no way that my mentor would have known that I was nervous, because I had not effectively communicated with her how I felt. Although horrible, this tutorial allowed me to talk to my mentor about my role in the setting and gave me a starting point to build upon when trying to improve.

Analysing the incident, I came up with three different areas where I needed to improve: communicating more with staff, taking a more active role in lessons, and using my initiative to get on with tasks. I created an action plan that related to these development targets and pushed myself to behave as though I was a proper part of the Early Years Team. I am now employed as a teacher alongside the mentor who told me I did not care. If I had not reflected upon what she said, the relationship I had with my now colleagues would never have got past the initial awkwardness and developed into the professional (and friendly) working relationship that we have today.

Commentary on Jenny's reflection

Communicating with other professionals is something students and newly qualified practition-ers find challenging (Sylva et. Al., 2010; Perkins, 2017). Jenny's reflection highlights the poten-tial of using models of reflection to improve her practice. In particular, it shows the challenges that new team members face when joining an established team. She was unprepared for the feedback. If we apply the communication cycle here, there is clear evidence of a breakdown in the cycle between the message sent and the message received.

Jenny shares how using a structured approach to reflection enabled her to identify her own part in the miscommunication. Engaging in regular reflection is potentially empowering and can help students and graduate practitioners to navigate future professional contexts. The process enabled Jenny to take control and be proactive in addressing the issue. Rather than passively accepting the feedback, she can respond more dynamically and with more understanding.

This case study also shows that effective self-reflection on the development of communication skills involves more than just knowing about different theories and models of communication and team working. Sharing her discussion of how she responded and what it felt like may offer support to others in helping them to recognise that feedback is not personal criticism, but a means of developing knowledge skills and practice. Giving and receiving feedback is key to good teamwork. This is something to consider embedding further in the students' learning experience, challenging them to probe deeper into how exactly they put the theory into practice. For example, how exactly does the student demonstrate commitment to team working? What exactly does this look like?

Reflection Point

Thinking about Jenny's experiences and the reflections of the Case Study above, how does this link to your experiences in placement when communicating with colleagues or external agencies?

Reflect on a time when you have been involved in a misunderstanding in communication (either as the sender or receiver). Think about what happened and how you would do things differently now.

Task

This task is about linking theory and practice, but it positions practice first and theory as the tool to facilitate deep reflection, as opposed to using theory as the starting point for practice.

Capture a five-minute visual interaction between yourself and another team member, either by recording it yourself or better still by asking another colleague to do the recording for you. Look closely at how you are interacting and how they respond – what they say and what their body language is communicating. How does this relate to the theories of team working and communication discussed in this chapter?

Summary

This chapter has discussed the key team working and communication models and theories that we use to develop effective working relationships with colleagues and other professionals. It is therefore important for you, as an Early Childhood Graduate Practitioner, to understand what effective 'teamwork' might look like in practice, and to consider how working with colleagues and other professionals is influenced by your underpinning values and beliefs. As an Early Childhood Graduate Practitioner, the challenge is understanding not only the theoretical concepts, but also the value and impact that effective working relationships have on practice.

Like any theory, teamwork and communication models are just that — a theory. They are dependent on the individuals involved and the context. The daily experience of children in Early Years settings and the overall quality of provision depend on all practitioners having appropriate skills and knowledge and a clear understanding of their roles and responsibilities. Teamwork can have a positive impact on quality.

Key Points

This chapter has explored many aspects of collaborating with others to promote effective working relationships. It has looked at:

- Theories of communication and teamwork
- How communication can foster and obstruct the development of good working relationships
- The concept of multi-agency working and the inherent challenges for Early Childhood practitioners when engaging in partnership working
- Students' lived experiences, and considered how these can be used to support your own practice.

Further Reading

The texts and resources below have been chosen to enable you to explore further the tools of participation and to understand specific approaches to effective team working and communication.

Belbin, R. (1993) *Team roles at work*. Oxford: Butterworth-Heinemann.

Belbin's model can give you a greater understanding of your strengths, which can support your participation and communication within the team.

Covey, S. (2013) *7 habits of highly effective people*. Carlsbad: Hay House.

This book puts forward a principle-centred approach to both personal and interpersonal effectiveness.

Lumsden, E. (2018) *Child protection in the Early Years: A practical guide*. London: Jessica Kingsley.

The book highlights the importance of effective communication with children, parents, colleagues and other professionals. The author emphasises the importance of non-judgemental reflective practice in a way that enables readers to understand the importance of their role in working with young children.

Chapter 10

PROFESSIONAL DEVELOPMENT AND PROFESSIONAL IDENTITY

Sigrid Brogaard-Clausen and Michelle Cottle

Chapter Aims

This chapter will address Competency 9 entitled 'Professional Development'. Ongoing professional development ensures that we, as Early Childhood professionals, continually reflect on and develop our knowledge, understanding and practice in a variety of capacities, often in collaboration with other practitioners. The chapter presents research, theory and examples from practice attending to:

- critical reflective practice to enhance continuing professional development in Early Childhood (Competency 9.3), debating democratic and inclusive practice with attention to social and emotional encounters, as an underpinning value and foundation of the Early Childhood Graduate Practitioner Competencies (ECGPC) (Competency 9.4). The importance of professional dialogue and communication and its challenges are emphasised throughout these discussions (Competency 9.5)
- self-awareness and knowledge of anti-discriminatory practice, promoting social justice and the importance of valuing difference (Competency 9.1). As a part of this, we draw on examples of how students work to enable the voice of young children to be heard (Competency 9.2) and include reflections on self-awareness of the emotional work in Early Childhood
- democratic, distributed and advocacy leadership (Competency 9.4), which is linked to the consideration of Early Childhood professional identity

Introduction

Professional development can take many different forms depending on roles and responsibilities, but it usually includes the development of knowledge, skills and leadership related to different aspects of policy and practice. However, opportunities and support for professional development varies, often depending on the commitment of policymakers and employers (Oberhuemer, 2013). Therefore, we place *professional reflection* at the heart of this chapter, as this is a form of professional development in which practitioners can and should always engage. Drawing on a workshop discussion with ECGPC students, this chapter emphasises the importance of continually examining our professional experience, values and professional identity, focusing on democratic living and leadership as part of a reflective, dialogic process. It is important to keep the focus on collaborative reflection and decision-making with the aim of empowering both children and adults within the Early Childhood community.

Democratic Living and Inclusive Practice

Together with advocacy and participation, democracy forms the interlinked context for ECGPC practice, knowledge and skills development, and as such, it is a key part of continuing professional development (CPD), as is displayed in Figure 10.1.

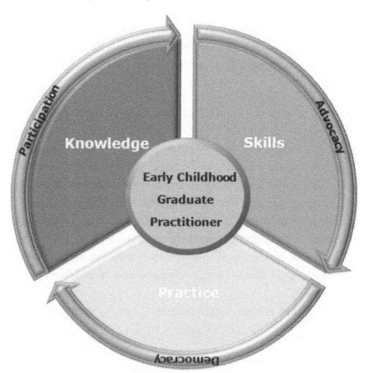

Figure 10.1 Continuing professional development of the Early Childhood Graduate Practitioner

The notion of democratic living complements the more often discussed representational democracy, which includes voting, democratic rule and governing. Ahrenkiel and Warring (2016) propose a distinction between democracy as governing and as a way of life, both forming part of a democratic practice:

- as governing, it is related into gaining influence through voting, conversations and acting in relation to representation of interests and/or
- as a way of life, democracy is perceived as a part of processes that continuously take place in everyday situations, interactions and relations.

Democratic practice is a way of enabling democratic living within an Early Childhood community. Democratic living attends to respecting differences while creating unity. Creating an inclusive environment through democratic living, requires us to take and hold social responsibility together. This responsibility materialises when we ethically and sensitively observe, respond, negotiate and co-decide with children, families and colleagues. In facilitating acceptance, belonging, respect and trust, we support social responsibility and citizenship for all children and adults (see Brogaard-Clausen et al., 2022, for further exploration of democratic living). Having a willingness to contribute to community life and common goals means engaging in critical dialogue and reflexive practice and, as in the above, being open to experiment and the unknown (Moss, 2020). However, this is not an easy process. In our first case study from the student discussions, Jayde, Florence and Rose reflect on what democratic practice can look like in a nursery and their roles and responsibilities as well as the challenges involved. All students involved in the discussions below were studying at either Level 5 or Level 6.

Case Study

Student voices 1: Jayde, Florence and Rose reflect on democratic practice

Jayde: 'I was at a nursery school and they had a swing which was really popular. All the children wanted to go on there so they would have a timer where children would line up and wait for their turn [...]'

Following from this, Florence reflects on how practitioners may 'observe, respond … negotiate and co-decide with the children, because they have decided with the children to queue up and wait for their turn and not to push for the swing.'

But questions arise about who decides rules and how.

Jayde: 'When the practitioners saw how popular the swing was, they put the rule into place so all children could have a go and, when I first went to the Nursery, my mentor explained the rule to me, which helped me when I had children wanting to go on the swing. There were a few children who would argue 'it's my turn now' or children who would not get off the swing so, using the timer, I would explain that their turn was over and they could have a go later. They would normally accept the rule even if sometimes they were not happy with it and some did not want to go on the swing then. I think that as the rule had been implemented for some time, they understood that it was a rule they had to follow.'

Rose extends this consideration of rules with an example of conflict in the outdoor playground, where she is asked by the children to help enforce a rule: 'Usually I will go to the place with them and discuss it with them, [...] and then try to find a solution with them.'

The academic tutor then comments on her own experience of the lack of time for such negotiations and this is confirmed as problematic by Rose.

The students in the case study demonstrate the complexity of enforcing the rules, while observing different responses from the children and trying to co-create or negotiate the rules with the children.

Reflection Point

Consider two or three rules in the setting that you have been in. Who decided the rules (and why)?

How did children respond to the rules?

How did you act on their responses?

What kind of opportunities were there for children to negotiate rules and consider the needs of others?

Critical Reflective Practice and Dialogue

Why democratic practice is not easy

Democratic practice prioritises attention to children's initiatives, interests, inquiries, interactions, engagement and relationships. Our role as adults is to attend to these: to interpret the children's intentions and actions, and to assist when the self-regulating and co-regulated processes with peers are too difficult by offering support and guidance (Ahrenkiel and Warring, 2016). This means that we need to continually reflect on the understanding gained through these experiences, as in the case study of the children's experience of rules and rule-making. However, it is not easy to acknowledge and attend to the uniqueness of each child within diverse groups of children. We need to consider what a rule means to an individual child, the group of children and the adults simultaneously. Above, Jayde demonstrates some of the challenges inherent in this process when she notes that there were some children who 'disengaged' and did not try the swing.

Negotiating rules means being open to unpredictable outcomes and encounters. Such encounters may include collisions and conflicts that put demands on the social and emotional resources of each member of the community. Nevertheless, such encounters are part of democratic living. As Rose explains, in negotiating rules with the children we are all listening to others, which requires us to respect and appreciate diversity and difference. Therefore, in problem-solving and negotiation, we enable and promote children's rights and critical voices, encouraging experimentation and resistance to social injustice (Brogaard-Clausen et al., 2022).

However, there may be barriers to this, and it is important to identify these and develop new ways of working where possible. For example, there may be little time for the democratic process of negotiation, as the students acknowledged in discussion of Rose's example above, and this may be a constant struggle. Also, there can sometimes be insufficient acknowledgement of the importance of negotiation itself and how this contributes to children's development, learning and wellbeing. Another barrier occurs when there is a focus on maintaining rules rather than why and how we make these work inclusively for all children and adults. Depending on how external pressures are influencing the ethos of the setting, there may even be a culture of blame and a focus on who is 'right' or 'wrong' (Penn, 2019). Recognising and questioning the above aspects and factors is part of the purpose and value of the critical reflection. Collaborative professional dialogue is an essential part of this process, as the students demonstrate in the next case study. In this example, they are reflecting on their experience of conflict, conflict resolution and social justice as well as the challenges of being an inclusive practitioner.

Case Study

Student voices 2: Annie, Rose, Sara and Florence reflect on conflict, conflict resolution and social justice

Contrary to the example of 'the swing rule' in the case study 'Student voices 1', Annie found that the children would not follow the rules in settings she had worked in, that they would 'throw tantrums or run away'. She noted how this could be linked to what she termed 'favouritism' in the setting, which connected with other student experiences. Although unsure about how some children became 'favourites', we reflected on whether 'conforming to rules' played a part in this. However, this notion of 'favouritism' highlighted the emotional and social complexity and challenge of encounters with children. Annie's critical discussion ensued with Rose recognising that some children are 'more interesting to me, although I have not acted in a non-inclusive way, and I try to be the same towards them all in an inclusive way'. She reflected further on how there is always meaning behind a child's behaviour, such as when children do not follow rules.

Annie picks up on this: 'that is really interesting what you brought up Rose, but I also think that it is quite challenging to try and be inclusive equally to all children'. Explaining how she had made a special effort to connect with a child who did not speak English, Annie said: 'I will hold my

(Continued)

hand up and say that […] I found it was difficult to equally give my energy to all children, and not prioritise this individual boy'.

This prompted Sara to discuss how she noticed that some children would come up to her more than others. She gave the example of a child with a disability, which she understood deeply due to her own family experiences, and how this enabled a different connection between her and the boy.

Following this example, Annie reflected further on how she felt that the child who did not speak English 'deserved someone to put an effort in' and 'I just wanted to try and include his background and where he came from as much as possible and this probably was why I gravitated more towards him, and why it made it even more challenging…'.

Florence then discussed an example related to the context of the Covid-19 handwashing rules. She was asked to help a boy who did not like to have his hands washed and although she explained the situation and the different strategies she tried, she ended by saying, 'He continued to resist and I didn't find any way to make him more comfortable'.

Rose focused on the dilemmas that situations like these present, how practitioners can follow class rules and at the same time pay close attention to the needs of the individual child. She noted 'the conflict there can be in this' and also 'the unpredictable nature of this, and not being able to prepare for the unpredictable'.

The students in both case studies demonstrate the complexity of enforcing the rules, while observing different responses from the children and trying to co-create or negotiate the rules with the children. In situations like these, the role of the Early Childhood professional is to observe and lead, establishing rules deemed to benefit most or all children and enabling an inclusive environment. Nevertheless, the negotiation and operation of these rules is an ongoing, collaborative process.

Self- and other awareness in social and emotional encounters

Developing self-awareness by articulating what we find difficult is an important part of professional development. The case studies above evidence students' self-awareness and the key role of dialogue and collaborative critical reflection in enabling this type of professional development. Each student presents a difficult example; they respond to each other, sometimes affirming and sometimes challenging, but always engaging critically and respectfully. Their examples from practice demonstrate the struggles inherent in social and emotional encounters and that these are not (always) easily solved. They acknowledge the messiness of democratic practice which involves conflict and ongoing negotiation.

By taking part in professional reflection together and sharing examples in this way, we can debate and come up with different strategies to support children. Another strength of this process is the opportunity it presents to acknowledge and articulate the emotional nature of the encounters together (Elfer, 2012). As evidenced in the case study 'Student voices 2', this may be in terms of building stronger bonds with specific children or reflecting together on a situation that we cannot solve or that continues to upset a child or even one that upsets us. Such critical reflections are crucial in helping us to examine and articulate our principles and the ways we put them into practice.

Creating a trusting, open and tolerant dialogue in which we can share examples like this enables us to learn from each other (Freire, 1998). This is challenging in itself and we, as Early Childhood professionals, can feel very vulnerable when sharing emotional and situational challenges, particularly because this requires us to acknowledge our own limitations and uncertainty (Elfer, 2012). However, we need these conversations to help us cope with complex emotional encounters and to share and develop expectations. It requires considerable emotional and cognitive resources to acknowledge the voice and needs of the individual child and therefore the diversity of the group of children and families (and colleagues), and to find ways to balance needs and wishes with social rules, setting rules and external expectations. It is essential to reflect on our own differences and identify potential barriers and biases as part of this process in order to offer equal opportunities for all children.

Critical Reflection and Social Justice

Critical reflection acknowledges the challenges involved in democratic practice, as already discussed. Engaging in critical dialogue does not mean criticising and finding fault, but constructively evaluating evidence and opinions, although it is important to challenge these where necessary. As demonstrated in the case studies above and proposed in the Reflection Point, this can be in examining how rules are agreed and implemented, and giving priority to the voice of all children to develop an inclusive environment. The role of the Early Childhood professional is therefore to apply critical pedagogies, to question and challenge power relationships and to seek changes where inequality and social injustice are present (Luff et al., 2019).

Continuing professional development through critical reflective practice therefore involves:

- reflection on one's own practice and that of others
- comparing similar and different pedagogical approaches
- working together to cultivate a supportive collegial culture
- addressing and resisting inequalities.

As Annie discusses in the case study 'Student voice 2', we need to make a special effort for all children, especially when they are at risk of being excluded due to having a different language or culture or having a disability or another 'protected characteristic' (Equality Act 2010, legislation.gov.uk, 2010). Sharing examples of the ways that we address and resist inequalities can help us to develop a collective pedagogy. Equally, developing further knowledge from research on inequalities and discrimination is helpful in widening knowledge and understanding to aid reflection and practice.

Task

Read Nutbrown's (2018) introduction and overview into continuing and historical inequality in relation to disability, gender and race, or view the following video: Equality and Human Rights Commission (2010) *Protected Characteristics*. Available at: https://youtu.be/VXLtKlmtrvM (accessed 26 January 2021).

Think of an example where you have observed or experienced a sense of struggle. Has the struggle been related to meeting children's needs or listening to their voices? Or has it been a struggle to have your own voice heard?

How did you respond? How could you have addressed it differently?

Advocacy, emotional work and strengthened self-awareness

In the case study 'Student voice 2' and the case study below, the students refer to emotional encounters and how to prepare for the unknown. Early Childhood professionals facilitate to enable children's involvement and engagement. This includes their expression and experience of wellbeing, and how we can enable engagement to develop into persistence and resilience. In so doing, adults can help children to feel confident and at ease by providing environments that respond to children's need for tenderness and affection, relaxation, inner peace, enjoyment, openness, safety, clarity and social recognition (Laevers, 2006). In their collaborative reflections on young children's voice (see also Chapter 2 on holistic understanding of 'voice' and the 100 languages of Competency 1), the students drew on the nature of their relationship with the children, reflecting on elements such as trust, safety, affection and tenderness. The reflections in the next case study evidence the interlinked nature of democratic living and wellbeing.

Case Study

Student voice 3: Jayde and Layla reflect on emotional work

Following on from the 'Student voices 2' case study, Jayde agrees that it is important to treat children equally, also acknowledging that some children come up to her more than others. 'It is the sense that they trust you and can rely on you during the day'. This led Layla to reflect on a child who was new in the nursery and got very upset when his mum would leave. She expresses her empathy with the child's feelings and actions, reflecting that he would often come to her when unhappy. 'I think this could have been because I wasn't involved when the other practitioners would get him to come away from the door or away from his mum so she could leave'

In this case study and the ones above, the students advocate for helping children to actively make choices in their relationships. They are continually developing self-awareness of their complex professional role in offering and recognising the children's choice of comfort and affection. They recognise that attention to individual children and making yourself available and accessible is key, noting that the children came to them because they felt safe and recognised. As professionals, they are attuned with the children and can then share this practice with parents and colleagues in order to recognise children's and adults' agency, their ideas, their autonomy, their interests, their curiosity – their explorative drive (Laevers, 2006). For example, Sara enables the boy to be comforted and find trust in the professional relationship, and Annie and Sara make special efforts to include children experiencing language and disability barriers. This attunement acknowledges the children's autonomy and relational interests or preferences. Also in the example of 'hand washing' in 'Student voices 2' case study, Florence makes us aware that the anxiety reflected in the boy's behaviour needed more attention, not only in the specific situation, but also generally for both the individual child and the whole group of children. Children pick on up general anxiety in a society, noticing how it changes habits, rules and routines. In the very difficult context of COVID-19, human relationships, including touch, holding and cuddles, have become charged with uncertainty (Working Group of the All-Party Parliamentary Group on a Fit and Healthy Childhood, 2020). Therefore, continued critical reflections with colleagues form an essential part of Early Childhood practice in tackling these ongoing challenges.

Task

Reflect on examples where you have and have not had the time to engage with children who are struggling, who express anxieties or concerns and need further reassurance. Talk to colleagues, fellow students or tutors about this, so that it becomes shared reflective practice rather than an individual problem and responsibility.

Anti-discriminatory practice and critical reflection leading to transformative praxis

Critically reflective practice means trying not to take things at face value, but asking questions of your observations and daily practices and being committed to lifelong professional learning. The notion of 'praxis' takes this further, exploring the relationship between theory and practice. Freire (1993 [1972]: 33) defines 'praxis' as theoretically informed reflection which leads to 'action upon the world in order to transform it'. The aim is thus to actively challenge inequalities and to promote and maintain a focus on social justice and anti-discriminatory practice. Informed by theory, research and collegial dialogue, we can further our critically reflective praxis and open up space for transformational possibilities and increasing opportunities for democratic and inclusive practices. In this we need to acknowledge our unconscious bias and be open to and talk about our 'ignorance' (Freire, 1998), otherwise we restrict these opportunities.

Our pedagogies are informed by the way that we understand young children's holistic development and learning as Early Childhood professionals/practitioners, particularly when it is interlinked with young children's wellbeing and participation. Articulating and sharing such examples can lead to transformative practice, influencing how we organise time, space, activities and daily routine to reflect the individual child and all children's diverse development, needs, participation, wellbeing and learning.

Critical Reflection on Leadership in Early Childhood Contexts

We asked the students to reflect on leadership as part of our discussions, specifically their own leadership role in practice. Initially they found this difficult, as Florence put it, 'I guess I've never really seen myself as a leader'. Leader-follower theories have a powerful legacy (Northouse, 2019) and it can be quite common for Early Childhood professionals resist being positioned as a leader or lack confidence if leadership is perceived as 'being in charge' (McDowall Clark, 2012). However, there has been an increasing focus on leadership specific to Early Childhood contexts and deliberation on the aspects of the sector that make Early Childhood leadership distinctive, particularly its multi-disciplinary nature. Several key themes from this research can be linked to the students' practical experiences and critical reflections in the case studies in this chapter. This research offers a foothold for critical analysis so that we, as Early Childhood professionals can develop our own democratic leadership stories and theories, and articulate the transformative potential of our work to develop a sense of confidence and competence both individually and collectively (Murray and Clark, 2013). Leadership experiences must be contextualised as part of this reflection process, acknowledging the challenges that externally-developed policies may present to democratic approaches and the ways that Early Childhood professionals are positioned by others. It is therefore important that professionals are well-informed about necessarily political nature of their work and prepared to take on advocacy roles as needed.

Leading, managing and pedagogical leadership

Competency 9 establishes the importance of drawing on research demonstrating knowledge of 'leadership and management' and its application in pedagogical leadership. In research, leadership and management are sometimes seen as separate but overlapping roles or categories. For example, 'leadership' may include a focus on a particular vision that influences direction leading to change, while 'management' can be associated with the administration of that which has already been established, for example organising resources, including staff, or coordinating efforts (Lindon et al., 2016). In practice, although it can be helpful to distinguish between these different skill sets, leadership and management responsibilities are frequently distributed across a team.

Leadership and management can relate to setting, room, year group or specific areas of knowledge and expertise, such as safeguarding, nurturing care, outdoor learning and play, and so forth (Davis and

Ryder, 2016). Thus, practitioners can share out the responsibility for planning, enacting, monitoring and assessing pedagogical practices within their teams. They work towards collectively agreed goals as key workers with their group of children or within the parameters of their particular area. This is a form of *pedagogical leadership* (Heikka et al., 2019). However, pedagogical leadership is more than leading according to planned intentions; it encompasses the notions of praxis discussed above. Rather than assuming that there is a 'right' way to act, it is a set of actions 'imbued with theoretical substance' and a 'quest' for understanding learners and their experiences within the community (Male and Palaiologou, 2015: 220). There is a commitment to collective meaning making and problem-solving which requires a constant focus on relationship and interaction. The foundation of pedagogical leadership is therefore the practitioner's principled approach, their aim to work for the benefit of their learning community and their willingness to embrace complexity and unpredictability in this regard. This may involve taking risks with the curriculum, particularly where curriculum is viewed as a prescriptive framework. Rather, it is an approach that acknowledges learning as an inherently creative and social process (Dewey, 1998).

The discussions in the next case study follow on from Florence's comment, 'I guess I've never really seen myself as a leader', demonstrating a growing recognition of the leadership dimensions of their professional role. Their discussion highlights different leadership abilities, influences and skills, as well as the importance of professional development through collaborative, critical reflection, which enables Early Childhood professionals to cultivate a sense of themselves as leaders.

Case Study

Student voices 4: Rose, Florence, Jayde and Sara reflect on leadership

Rose: 'I agree with Florence, I don't think I see myself as a leader, but I do sometimes feel that I take initiative in my actions. So instead of asking for help, I slowly have the confidence to take initiative in the actions I do based on experience I have previously had. [...] It is not being a leader but more being a part of a team and working with each other and be able to take initiative.

Jayde: '[...] I was quite new, and I didn't feel like I was in a place to be a leader when I was still learning, not only about the setting but the children too.'

Florence: 'I know that I lead activities, it's normally with another member of staff. I agree with Rose about being part of a team and working together to support children. I feel that I struggle to take initiative when there is a lull in the day and will let someone else lead.'

Jayde: 'I think I have played important roles throughout my placement, and I have had the practitioners telling me I've done a great job, or I've really done well with a certain child who hasn't had the bond with other practitioners. It's rewarding hearing that I've made an impact on their lives or even their day. [Florence agrees] [...] I feel I was really supported by the staff; they were really great, and I felt I had been accepted and I was sort of seen as part of the staff there even though it was placement.'

Florence: 'That is how I felt when I first started the placement where I felt I could go to any member of the staff.'

Sara: 'My confidence is not that great but when developing a relationship with my mentor I felt comfortable.'

The students' dialogue in this case study relates to the thinking and understanding of leadership, and Northouse's (2019) six dimensions can be used to consider how they perceive leadership generally:

(1) 'Leadership is a trait', (2) 'Leadership is an ability', (3) 'Leadership is a skill',
(4) 'Leadership is a behaviour', (5) 'Leadership is a relationship', (6) 'Leadership
is an influence process'. (Northouse, 2019: 1–7)

The students refer to support and being supported and accepted, to developing responsibility and to being met with openness but with staff being available for their questions and concerns. This shows how they recognise the relational aspects of leadership, and how they themselves lead in their work and feel recognised and rewarded by leaders, mentors and colleagues when doing so. Although they position themselves as novices, discussing a lack of confidence or experience and their uncertainties, they also acknowledge 'their own individual ability to make a difference' (McDowall Clark and Murray, 2012: 33). They recognise their capacity to enhance children's learning and development and to advocate for change wherever necessary (Davis and Ryder, 2016). We can continue to develop these skills through academic work alongside practical experience and professional development, making a significant contribution to ongoing debates about the nature of leadership in Early Childhood through sharing understandings with academics and colleagues in settings.

Reflection Point

How do you see yourself as a leader now and in the future?
How do your self-perceptions relate to the student discussions and the theory that underpins them?

Distributed leadership and democratic leadership

Distributed leadership and democratic leadership are two key concepts in the literature, and it can be useful to reflect on these when considering how we can develop collectively as a team or organisation. Although it has proved difficult to define, *distributed leadership* tends to emphasise practical strategies that enable teams to develop shared vision, power and responsibility (Heikka, Waniganayake and Hujala, 2013). Professionals working in teams bring different skills, values, principles and experiences to Early Childhood settings so finding a balance can be difficult when deciding who is taking the lead, on what and how. Power dynamics can add further complications. For example, although leadership may be distributed, this does not necessarily imply an absence of hierarchy. This is evident from the fact that distributed leadership may comprise teams, informal work groups, committees and so on, operating within a hierarchical organisation (Woods, 2004: 6). Thus, it is the organisational culture that is key, requiring both validation of expertise as well as empowerment (Heikka et al., 2013). It is therefore vital to keep the democratic principles we have discussed throughout this chapter constantly in mind.

Democratic leadership is discussed separately from distributed leadership in the literature focusing on processes. It includes both collaborative decision-making and shared reflection and, again, the aim is to empower both children and adults within the Early Childhood community. It 'implies interdependency rather than dependency' (Aubrey, 2011: 170) and acknowledges that capabilities and expertise are distributed across the organisation. Where there is trust and respect, this can lead to concerted action. The student discussions in the case studies indicate that they were engaging in these processes and felt empowered and supported by colleagues, although they did not see this as leadership until there was space for professional reflection and discussion. Florence expresses a feeling of not being good enough at initiating activities. However, democratic pedagogy in the Danish context emphasises the importance of how set activities can get in the way of attention to the children's play, their enquiries and the learning opportunities driven by the children (Greve, 2015, cited in Ahrenkiel and Warring 2016). Therefore, being alert to when you are making yourself available and attentive to the children's actions and interests, rather than focusing mainly on initiating activities, can be seen as a form of democratic leadership in practice.

Advocacy leadership

Advocacy leadership is another useful lens for examining our collective practice. It focuses on the ways that professionals actively promote Early Childhood values and learning within and through their team as well as beyond the local setting, involving parents and the wider community (Fenech, Salamon and Stratigos, 2019). When professionals are constantly looking for multiple and diverse ways of engaging with their particular community, they can promote inclusive relationships and shared values. Within this conception, the professionals are again positioned as 'change agents' where the 'change comes about through the recognition of new possibilities rather than being enforced from above' (McDowell Clark, 2012: 398). A focus on advocacy leadership also stresses the moral dimensions of leadership – the social responsibility. Leaders influence the lives of others, and they must therefore be particularly sensitive to the ways their leadership can affect the wellbeing of the people with whom they work – children and adults in the case of Early Childhood services – and regularly assess their values and ethical stance (Northouse, 2012, 2019).

The political nature of Early Childhood (Cameron and Moss, 2020) means that Early Childhood leaders need to have strong commitments to inclusion and equality of opportunity. They need to proactively change and challenge practices and policies that exclude and do not provide equal opportunities for children, families and practitioners with protected characteristics (Equality Act, legislation.gov.uk, 2010), and where other personal, family or societal aspects/characteristics do not enable equal opportunities.

Critical Reflection on Professional Identity

Drawing together our reflections on professional development and the leadership dimensions involved, it is important that we consider professionalism and professional identity within the context of the political nature of Early Childhood. Linked to democratic practice and critically reflective dialogue, Oberheumer's (2005) distinction between the 'democratic professional' and the 'technical expert' is helpful in understanding our own and shared professional identity.

> Early Years pedagogues need to be able to reflect openly on their personal and professional beliefs, relating these to the expectations arising from the documented principles. They need to be encouraged to see themselves as interpreters and not as mere implementers of curricular frameworks. Such an individual and collective repositioning can be best achieved in a collaborative culture, in a spirit of what some researchers have called democratic professionalism. (Oberheumer, 2005: 12)

The case studies in this chapter demonstrate this movement 'towards the critically reflective emotional professional' (Osgood, 2010). However, the process Oberheumer describes, and the students exemplified, can be challenging. It may also be emotionally risky not only for the reasons already discussed, but also because of the lack of attention given to emotion in Early Years policy (Elfer, 2015) and the external expectation of a 'technical expert' approach.

External expectations are present in the policy framework and are part of how we are positioned as professionals by others. As contemporary Early Childhood policies, both nationally and internationally, tend to focus on standardised, measurable outcomes, Early Childhood services are increasingly (risking) being viewed from the lens of 'market-based competition', based on notions of parental choice. More settings operate through business models and on a profit-making basis (Cottle and Alexander, 2012), positioning parents as consumers and other settings as competitors (Penn, 2019: 104). Leaders in settings are held accountable to externally prescribed, centralised targets (Palaiologou and Male, 2019), and these performative, standardised, individual targets become goals both for the individual child and the setting (Brogaard-Clausen, 2015). Although initially enforced through coercive strategies (e.g., Ofsted inspections), this performativity eventually becomes 'naturalized, part of the taken-for granted, part of the language' (Blackmore, 2004: 455) and can start to shape how the self is practised (Ball, 2003; Cottle, 2019). This may result in the dominance of Oberheumer's 'technical expert' perspective and what Osgood (2010) writes about as the contextual barriers in Early Childhood professionalism, drawing attention to the clash between affectivity, altruism, self-sacrifice and conscientiousness and 'accountability, transparency and measurability' (2010:123) within the boundaries of a 'regulatory' 2010:(122) regime.

However, we can understand identity as something multifaceted, something we individually and collectively create and negotiate as a *narrative* of who we are through continued interactions with others and the world around us (Giddens, 1991, cited in Brogaard-Clausen and Ringsmose, 2017). Professional identity is constantly under reconstruction (Dalli and Urban, 2008: 132). It is formed through our relationships with others and is informed by our knowledge, education and training, skills and competences, values, ethics, autonomy, status, power and reward, as perceived by the individual, by Early Years professionals as a collective group and by society more widely (Brock, 2006). There are likely to be tensions between striving towards a political ideal of the professional as rational and detached and the emotional labour and ethical commitment actually required of the role (Taggart,2011). However, our professional reflections with colleagues (and any discomforts attached to these) are necessary parts of being a critically reflective emotional professional (Osgood, 2010). Through such collaborative critical dialogue, we can focus on articulating and sharing vital components of Early Childhood professionalism, also recognising when it is in opposition to how we are positioned by policies and societal structures. Dalli (2008) suggests attention to the following:

- Pedagogical strategies and style: a focus on building warm, respectful, caring relationships
- Professional knowledge and practice: including being knowledgeable about children and the 'theory of Early Childhood', qualifications and professional development, content knowledge and reflective practice
- Collaborative relationships as the basis of practice: with children, families, colleagues and agencies outside the Early Childhood setting.

The role of both collegial reflection and mentoring, both formal and informal, is also key to this process of negotiating professional identity and developing critically reflective professional development practices. Hargreaves 2000) developed four ages of professionalism, which relates to the 'democratic professional' quotation by *Oberhuemer referred to earlier*. Hargreaves (2000) conceptualised the development of teacher professionalism as passing through four historical phases, which he termed the pre-professional, the autonomous professional, the collegial professional, and the post-professional. Hargreaves (2000) argued that the individual autonomy which teachers have had (autonomous professional) since the 1960s has become unsustainable, so they have moved into the new age of the collegial professional. This collegial professional or mentor works towards developing trust and confidence in each other's different but equally important experiences, competences and knowledge. Equally important is to note how these formations are locally embedded as 'processes that constitute professional identities [which] are not only diverse, but also closely connected to the cultural, historical and social contexts in which they take place' (Arndt et al., 2018: 351).

Informed by research by Gregoriadis, Papandreou and Birbili (2018) and Rekalidou and Panitsides (2015), we can therefore evaluate both initial and ongoing professional development and professional reflection in the context of whether they allow for:

- Meaningful cooperation for all parties, empowering professionals and practice
- Interdependence, supporting self-confidence and self-efficacy
- Building community and belonging, on a one-to-one basis, in small groups, within settings and across settings and communities, creating flexible learning/reflecting communities
- Open and reflective way of thinking (self-assessment)
- Situated experiences, collective analysis of situational practice
- Recognitions of the social, emotional, environmental, local, national and cultural context, and the complexity of policy, traditions, cultural norms, etc.

Also, in the context of continuing professional development (CPD) and mentoring, we need to advocate practices where social, intellectual and practical involvement are viewed as co-existing and co-dependent (Day, 2004), and are integrated into the Early Childhood Education and Care (ECEC) centre's practice. In both the ECEC setting and university, a full engagement with and encouragement of community dialogue and debate is needed to create and recognise different kinds of valuable knowledge, including tacit knowledge, knowledge in action and reflection in action (Jensen, 2015: 157). This practical wisdom – emotional (and social) capital – that we continually use in our everyday practice with young children and their families is a strength: the everyday ability to manage your own responses (conflicts and upsets) can, in dialogue and reflection, be turned into how we together can learn to empower and support each other as an Early Childhood community (Andrew, 2015: 361).

Task

··

How do you see yourself as a continually developing Early Childhood professional?

As a 'technician', who is willing to comply and unquestioningly deliver prescribed practice and meet externally set occupational standards and curricula?

As a democratic professional, who is willing to reflect openly with colleagues about your personal and professional beliefs, including critical evaluation of the emotional labour and ethical commitment required of the role?

As something in between? Or as neither one nor the other?

Summary

In this chapter, we have addressed Competency 9, advocating for and recognising the interconnected nature of democratic values, social justice, reflection and leadership underpinned by research. The Graduate Practitioner Competencies position the ethical and moral values of the Early Childhood professional as a commitment to 'reflective integrity' (McDowall Clark and Murray, 2012: 36), where critical reflection happens in a democratic forum of emotional encounters, celebrating diversity and principled leadership, while acknowledging our own uncertainties, and developing trust and learning from each other.

Knowing that there is evidence from research to support our practice, knowledge, experiences and values can become a part of developing confidence in professional identity, practice and advocacy. Equally, knowing a wide range of research enables us to see situations from different perspectives and know that differing perspective and evidence are present both to support and challenge our beliefs and knowledge.

In this chapter, we have argued that democratic values, a social justice orientation and collaborative, critical reflection are vital to our professional development and identities As Early Childhood professionals.

Key Points

In our critical pedagogies we question and challenge, and seek changes where inequality and social injustice are present. To do this, we need depth of knowledge of individual, social and societal factors and contexts. Therefore, the Graduate Practitioner Competencies seek to continually develop professional and personal skills and confidence in the following:

- Taking a critical stance, *you need to* … be informed by both research and your own and other's experience; *you need to* … listen to the diverse voices of both children and adults, colleagues and parents.
- Cultivating a sense of freedom, *you need to* … know what the limits are and provide opportunities for freedom …; *you need to* … know the social and historical context and policy framework of young children's lives; *you need to* … know the individual child's life circumstances and the specific and diverse group of children that you work with.
- Resisting inequalities, *you need to* … know about historical and systemic inequalities in society and act on that knowledge to challenge and prevent inequalities for groups and individuals.
- Effecting social change in the process of promoting democracy, *you need to* … know and articulate your values and what arguments and evidence these are based on and act on this knowledge (bullet point extension of Luff et al., 2019).

Further Reading

Fenech, M., Salamon, A. and Stratigos, T. (2019) Building parents' understandings of quality Early Childhood Education and Care and early learning and development: Changing constructions to change conversations. *European Early Childhood Education Research Journal*, 27(5), 706–721.

This article explores five case studies within an Australian context with a focus on advocacy leadership: the moral dimensions of leadership, responsibility and sensitivity as well as values and ethical stance.

Luff, P., Kanyal, M., Shehu, M. and Brewis, N. (2016) Educating the youngest citizens – possibilities for Early Childhood Education and Care in England. *Journal for Critical Education Policy Studies* (JCEPS), 14(3)3, 197–219.

This article explored social justice and critical pedagogies as a part of continued professional reflection/development.

Nutbrown, C. (2018) Inclusion and diversity in early childhood education and care. In C. Nutbrown, *Early childhood educational research: International perspectives* (Chapter 8). London: Sage.

This chapter provides a good introduction and overview into continuing and historical inequality in relation to disability, gender and race.

Palaiologou, I. and Male, T. (2019) Leadership in Early Childhood education: The case for pedagogical praxis. *Contemporary Issues in Early Childhood*, 201, 23–34. doi: 10.1177/1463949118819100

This article focuses on graduate leadership as pedagogical praxis, in the context of performative threats. It is a conceptual article, which lends itself better to Level 6 and Level 7 reading.

Chapter 11

MOVING FORWARD

Carolyn Silberfeld

Chapter Aims

This final chapter will explore the future development of the Early Childhood Graduate Practitioner Competencies following on from Chapter 10, which focuses on professionalism and professional identity. Integral to this is how the future development is perceived by my colleagues and the graduate practitioners, as well as my own hopes and wishes. Therefore, the aims of this chapter are primarily to:

- discuss how the influence of the Competencies and graduate practitioners can gain further recognition by policymakers, employers and practitioners
- highlight the importance of mentorship by analysing what underpins mentorship and how this can influence both the quality of the experience for students and practitioners
- consider appropriate continuing professional development for the graduate practitioners
- further explore the development of the Competencies both nationally and internationally

Introduction

In Chapter 1, Eunice Lumsden interviewed herself and Helen Perkins (see case studies). One of the questions she posed is 'What now?'. I will explore their responses in this chapter as well as communications (both in conversation and written text) that I have had with Helen Haygarth, one of the first graduates from the University of Sunderland's Early Childhood Studies Degree undergraduate programme. I am extremely grateful for her very valuable contribution.

There are certain questions I posed to myself before starting to write this chapter. How do we move forward with the Competencies themselves? Can they be suitably adapted for anything other than an Early Childhood Studies (ECS) degree? Can they be adapted by international Early Childhood practitioners? Will recognition of the Competencies help to raise the status of Early Childhood graduates and those who work with young children? How can we improve the experiences of the students, graduates and practitioners? How do we support the continuing professional development of graduate practitioners?

Recognition by Policymakers, Employers and Practitioners

As Eunice states in her introduction, it will take time for Early Childhood Graduate Practitioners to become part of the recognised workforce in the UK because it will need many more practitioners to gain this qualification as part of an Early Childhood Studies degree. Although the workforce is encouraged to look at young children holistically, these Competencies are unique in the way that they draw on interdisciplinary knowledge in a multi-professional context at graduate level and are relevant for children from birth to eight years. Recent recognition of ECS degrees with Early Childhood Graduate Practitioner Competencies (ECGPC) by the Department for Education (2019) will help in the process. It is hoped that employers from health and social care will recognise the value of a graduate who has gained the Competencies alongside their degree. Acknowledgement by the Department for Education demonstrates the importance of the higher-level knowledge and skills required to work with young children and their families and encourages practitioners and employers to understand the benefits of this qualification to support young children's learning and development. It is hoped that employers will support practitioners in their settings to gain graduate Competency status and will be encouraged to employ new graduate practitioners.

However, unlike many of our European colleagues, the UK does not universally subsidise childcare, which means that additional costs fall to employers and parents, who find themselves having to pay more to cover the shortfall of government funding. The funding systems are confusing for parents, who are faced with a 'complexity of multiple entitlements with different eligibility criteria' (Archer and Oppenheim, 2021: 17). Recognition by government and policymakers may also be more challenging because of the cost implications associated with graduate practitioners, despite the fact that investment during early childhood is known to generate long-lasting, cumulative benefits (First 1001 Days Movement, 2021), which reduce long-term costs to society and the economy much more effectively than later, more costly, interventions. Recent research (Bonetti and Blanden, 2020) has highlighted the lack of key policies to improve workforce qualifications and the impact of this 'missed opportunity', and has identified how policies to improve workforce qualifications can be made more effective. One of the report's recommendations is for the government to review the quality and content of Early Childhood Studies degrees and their equivalent, with a view to some form of standardisation. This links to another recent study (Campbell-Barr et al., 2020) which identified the huge variation in Early Years degrees. As well as being confusing for employers and graduates themselves, these differences do not help to strengthen the degrees as graduate qualifications.

Recognition of Early Childhood Studies Degrees

Although all degrees are validated using the Early Childhood Studies Subject Benchmark Statements (Quality Assurance Agency for Higher Education (QAA 2022), which define the nature of the study and academic standards expected of graduates in the Early Childhood programmes, each Higher Education institution can develop their own version of the degree programme, which has created this variation in what is offered. However, it has never been the intention of the Early Childhood Studies Degree Network (ECSDN), nor the ECS community to create some form of standardisation because of the holistic nature of Early Childhood Studies. Fundamentally, ECS is an academic interdisciplinary subject which provides the foundation for 'professional education and training for new professional roles' (QAA, 2019: 4). If a national review of ECS degrees was carried out, care would have to be taken because of the academic and holistic nature of ECS degrees. Of the many Early Childhood degree programmes, those which offer assessed practice as part of the course retain not only the holistic dimensions, but also the academic and practical credibility. The Graduate Practitioner Competencies, by their very nature, promote this holistic approach as they cover all aspects of children's development, learning, health and welfare while retaining the academic credibility of the subject area. As Helen so aptly stated when she was asked what would support the Competencies to continue to develop in this holistic way:

> So many of the Competencies intersect that this [*holistic*] approach should be a natural
> process and avoid a tick-box approach. It's almost impossible to work through each
> competency in isolation. Children and students/practitioners all have differing learning
> styles so utilising a whole approach fits with the Competency agenda. This again
> strengthens the natural intersectionality of the Competencies when compiling a portfolio
> of evidence. You just have to be 'smart' about it.

Although Helen is aware that, in general, Early Childhood-related topics are usually 'low on the government agenda', she has also found that 'awareness of the ECGPC within local networks has been disappointing, despite marketing on social media, etc.'. Helen suggests that this:

> needs to be revisited to raise awareness again and perhaps target Further Education so
> awareness begins earlier in students' academic journeys. Expectations and standards need to
> be high within this sector so emphasising the professional status is key. As much as it pains
> me to say this, ECGPC link so closely to Ofsted inspection requirements so perhaps
> settings could be sold on this? It would be lovely to see this qualification begin to appear
> on Job Person Specifications as a 'desirable'.

This is quite a controversial statement because of the holistic nature of the Practitioner Competencies, and no one would want it to become narrowed by an inspection system. However, Helen is making the point about the importance of the recognition of the Competencies within settings and within the systems under which settings work. National recognition will not develop widely unless it is seen as a sought-after qualification by the settings and employers.

Successful Advocacy and Changing Perceptions

Closely linked to the wider understanding of the Graduate Competencies is the recognition of Early Childhood Studies degrees and Early Childhood Graduate Practitioners in the Standard Occupational

Classification (SOC) used in England. Until September 2020 (Office for National Statistics, 2020), the majority of staff in the Early Childhood workforce were in Major Group 6 (Caring, Leisure and Other Service Occupations). The ECSDN has campaigned for many years to have greater recognition for the Early Childhood workforce, which included ECS degrees with assessed practice, and, more recently, the graduates with Level 6 Practitioner Competencies. In the 2020 SOC, these Early Childhood Studies graduates have been recognised as being Associate Professionals in Major Group 3 – an enormous leap from Major Group 6, mainly thanks to the lobbying of the ECSDN. These changes mean that both the ECS degrees and those with Graduate Competencies strengthen the position of the graduates and the Competencies themselves. This is not only important for the graduates, but also for the Higher Education institutions, which are facing challenges with funding and course viability. Programmes which are seen to promote employment prospects have more chance of survival than those which do not. Improved employment prospects will also influence the policymakers as governments encourage more people to work in the Early Childhood private, voluntary and independent (PVI) sector, which is largely ungoverned insofar as terms and conditions.

It has long been acknowledged in previous studies that well-qualified practitioners providing good quality education and care can make a difference to young children's learning and development (Pascal, Bertram and Cole-Albäck, 2020; Sylva et al., 2014), particularly more disadvantaged children. However, the cost of having highly qualified staff has been seen, by both policymakers and employers, as a barrier to raising the status of Early Childhood practitioners and the professionalisation of the Early Childhood workforce. It seems so illogical in view of the consistent findings that there is insufficient investment in the Early Childhood workforce. Pascal et al. (2020) urge the government to acknowledge the importance of this investment in children's futures. Knowing there is such a variation in Early Childhood qualifications, Bonetti and Blanden's (2020) key recommendation from their research findings is that the government undertakes research into the impact of the Early Childhood workforce on children's learning and development, particularly noting the impact of the more highly qualified practitioners. ECSDN would support this as it would help to recognise the contribution of practitioners with Graduate Competencies and hopefully improve their professional standing.

The Importance of Mentorship

Mentorship seems to be a key factor in the development and competence of graduate practitioners. The role of the mentor is of crucial importance to help the student develop their pedagogy confidently and competently. Mentors are perceived to be experts in their field, who are willing to pass on their knowledge and expertise to the next generation of practitioners. Mentoring is a 'facilitated process where two or more people hold a mutual interest in professional learning and development' (Bonnett and Ly, 2017: 29). However, in practice this has not often been as mutually beneficial as it could have been. Of importance is that mentorship is perceived to be a two-way process and that there is a shared and mutual understanding between the mentor and mentee of what this process involves, so that it can facilitate learning of both mentor and mentee. Both mentor and mentee need to agree what needs to be accomplished in the time available to them. Although both need to be willing to put time and effort into the process, it is not usually possible to set aside long periods for discussion and reflection. It is more productive to set aside a mutually convenient regular time during the day or week for such interactions. It is also essential that both mentor and mentee come to any meeting with a prepared plan. In their study, Bonnett and Ly (2017) found that mentoring relationships were beneficial to both novices and 'seasoned' practitioners, enhancing expertise, knowledge, confidence and leadership skills in both mentor and mentee. However, the challenges identified in the study included a lack of time to commit to the process and unclear expectations.

Evaluation of Pilot Programmes

In reality, mentors for graduate practitioner students are often selected according to who is available and who has the appropriate qualifications, rather than on who would best support the student. Although all Higher Education institutions have the responsibility to make appropriate provision, the mentor may not have much knowledge and understanding about the Competencies themselves. In an evaluation I carried out in the eight pilot institutions, in 2020, mentorship varied tremendously. Although all eight pilot institutions had provided some form of mentor training, it was not necessarily taken up by the mentors. Where mentor training was not undertaken, the mentors had to rely on the documentation, which varied in quantity and quality from institution to institution. Most of the mentors did not have sufficient in-depth knowledge and understanding of how to support the practitioners to achieve the Competencies at the appropriate level – they were much more used to Level 3 Further Education students and Teacher Training students, with the accompanying narrowness of the intended outcomes. Without sufficient knowledge and understanding, the Competencies may be seen in a similar way – as a tick-box exercise rather than a holistic approach to children and childhood. Although there was the possibility for students to change mentor if there was a personality clash or inappropriate mentorship, in reality, it was not often possible in practice. In addition, the relationship always has a power dimension, which can mean that even broaching the subject of mentorship expectations may be difficult and sometimes impossible for some students.

Helen Haygarth was an extremely able student who worked well independently. This was essential as her mentor did not have sufficient time and availability to support her as much as she would have liked in practice. Helen found it challenging to be part of such a small pilot undertaking a brand new programme. She did not have peers with whom to discuss any issues which arose:

> It was a learning process for all. I perhaps felt isolated at times. I did meet with another student, which helped, but we both worked so differently it was difficult to visualise how the portfolios should and could look. In the end, I merely did what made sense to me at the time.

Helen would have appreciated peer support and suggests that, with increasing numbers of students, institutions should facilitate more regular meetings and drop-in sessions for peer-to-peer discussions.

Not all students would have flourished as Helen did. One of the reasons she was able to do this was because she was already an experienced practitioner. This is not always the case, as many have found to their detriment. Although Helen enjoyed the 'freedom' she had due to her prior knowledge and understanding, she was acutely aware that not all students would necessarily know what to do, or how to find the required documentation, yet would not feel able to discuss this with their mentor because of the power dimensions.

> I wonder how easy this will be for students who would not normally have responsibility for things like safeguarding (even though it is everyone's responsibility). I remember being a student and knowing my place – hence the importance of the relationship with mentor/mentee.

Helen sees mentorship as an integral part of the process of learning and development as a graduate practitioner:

> I see mentoring as I see my role as a practitioner or child's key worker – there to support children in becoming and flourishing, always mindful that we facilitate learning and development but also encouraging a sense of self-esteem, confidence and wellbeing. The Graduate Competencies are there to provide a framework to evidence and reflect on best practice, thus supporting a practitioner's development and experience. Mentorship allows all to be familiar with this framework with regular meetings, and conversations to give a greater understanding of the Competencies. However, these meetings need to be meaningful with clear agendas, aims and goals set to be reviewed. Without this accountability, they risk being tokenistic.

What is clear to me is that mentorship training needs to be at the forefront of any Higher Education institution which has validated an Early Childhood Graduate Practitioner programme. Despite all the pilot institutions I visited having well-established mentorship training, the uptake was poor. In order to find out why this was the case, I telephoned a Key Stage 1 coordinator at a local primary school who had been invited to attend mentorship training by the university. He would very much have liked to participate in the training, but he did not have the time, nor the cover, to attend. This was disappointing for the university as they had scheduled their mentorship programme to be held outside school/nursery hours so that it did not impinge on the working day. This teacher would have liked the mentorship training to have taken place in their setting. Although this would have been convenient for the one setting, it would not have been beneficial for others, nor cost-effective. In some institutions, I know that mentorship training takes place in one setting, at which others locally can attend. Helen, whose mentor was unable to attend any mentorship training, offers her thoughts on these issues:

I wonder if formal sessions for mentors could be delivered on university premises to validate the qualification with potential mentors and to ensure the information is shared and a sense of accountability is given. I handed my mentor a printed mentor handbook and emailed her an e-copy – I never saw her with them once.

Although I can appreciate that teachers and practitioners have heavy workloads, this demonstrates, to me, the lack of value placed on such programmes by the practitioners themselves. Somehow this needs to be addressed by those who deliver and also participate in mentorship training. It also highlights the need for practitioners to have the opportunity and access to a broad spectrum of continuing professional development, including online training, and to understand why this is so important.

Professional Development for Graduate Practitioners

Although Early Childhood Graduate Practitioners are a recent addition to the workforce, their professional development requirements are similar to any other practitioner. On graduation, regardless of employment route undertaken, they need appropriate induction and professional development plans. Some professions, such as social work and teaching, unlike the Early Childhood workforce, have additional funding available for the newly qualified periods and nurses also have a budget for training. As they will be the mentors of the future, they need to have appropriate mentorship training, rather then basing their mentorship on their own experiences. Unfortunately, in our present climate, professional development which is not statutory is often not accessible to many practitioners. Although the term 'continuing professional development' (CPD) is familiar to practitioners and professionals, it is not always easy to define, or to identify, as you will have learned in Chapter 10 in relation to professional identity. Most commonly, CPD is concerned with practice for employees' development beyond that derived from any training which has taken place, and it can be both formal and informal (Collin et al., 2012). It can be seen as lifelong learning and links well to the Organisation for Economic Co-operation and Development's (OECD) (2000: 403) definition, which has been universally recognised for the past two decades:

education and training activities in which people take part in order to obtain knowledge and/or learn new skills for a current or a future job, to increase earning and to improve job and/or career opportunities in current or other fields.

These activities can be both formal and organised and informal, daily relational opportunities between practitioners. Oberhuemer's (2013) review of continuing professional development research from six countries found that although there was a common understanding of CPD, the commitment and support from policymakers and employers, and opportunities for appropriate ongoing professional development, varied considerably. As well as the cost of CPD, it was often dependent on how CPD was defined by different stakeholders, the entitlement of practitioners to CPD as well as access to CPD, and the way in which CPD made a contribution to career development. Three clear themes emerged from Oberhuemer's study, which would seem to remain pertinent nearly a decade later:

- CPD needs to be seen as an entitlement for all those working in Early Childhood Education and Care, with the necessary funding support for both providers of and practitioners in Early Childhood settings to make sure it becomes a reality
- Professional development approaches that support active engagement and
- critical reflection, in the Early Childhood setting context, are more likely to encourage ongoing critical reflection, and thus lead to improvement of practices.
- CPD needs to be viewed from a system-wide perspective which takes into account the sometimes varying goals and needs of policymakers and setting providers and practitioners. (Oberheumer, 2013: 105)

Although statutory CPD usually takes place formally in a central setting, traditionally CPD in the Early Childhood sector has taken place within individual settings. Since the outbreak of the Covid-19 pandemic, there has been a dearth of face-to-face CPD, with any training and development work taking place using online tools such as Zoom or Microsoft Teams. A flurry of CPD support material has also been made available online. Although this has been expedient in such extraordinary times, it is not ideal. Much of the benefit of CPD is in the interaction between the participants, through discussion and dissemination. Even informal CPD within settings has been curbed with changing work practices associated with the pandemic. It has also had a knock-on effect for the students who are undertaking the Graduate Competencies, and for graduates in their informal development of practices. I would suggest that the whole issue of CPD needs to be re-examined in light of recent events. There needs to be a specific continuous development framework for those who choose to move into the Early Childhood sector, akin to other professional areas in health and social care. More importantly, in this way, the new Early Childhood Graduate Practitioners will be in a good position to contribute to any new research which takes place. However, this will need central funding by government and training and professional organisations.

Further Development of the Competencies

Further development of the Early Childhood Graduate Practitioner Competencies is essential if they are to be recognised nationally by policymakers, employers and practitioners. At present, they should only be undertaken by Higher Education institutions that deliver Early Childhood Studies degrees and who are members of the ECSDN. This is clearly stipulated in the documentation that has received validation from the Quality Assurance Agency for Higher Education (QAA), as part of the Early Childhood Studies Benchmark Statements. The documentation had also been recognised by the Department for Education in the statement on their website (Department for Education, 2019). However, in order for further development to take place they need to be accessible for a wider audience. The reason they can only be undertaken as part of an ECS degree is because they reflect the holistic nature of these degree programmes. Other allied degree programmes, the institutions of which are also members of the ECSDN, such as Childhood Studies, Early Childhood Education, Childhood and Youth, Early Years, and those that combine Early Childhood Studies with other subjects, do not have this holistic and comprehensive focus on Early Childhood. Without this holistic focus, it would be extremely difficult for what is required for the Competencies to be achieved.

Nevertheless, there has been a truly phenomenal uptake of the Graduate Competencies by the majority of universities which deliver ECS degrees, and this interest has also boosted the membership of the ECSDN. It is expected that numbers of programmes and students will continue to grow, which should increase the number of graduate practitioners in Early Childhood settings. Recognition by the Department for Education, the QAA and the Office for National Statistics will help them reach a critical mass within the Early Childhood workforce.

However, in order to continue to grow and develop in a sustainable manner, the Graduate Competencies need to become accessible to others. In turn, many of the allied programmes will need to develop more holistic programmes and interdisciplinary teams, if they wish to embed the Competencies, to make sure that holistic practice with young children is supported appropriately. As the only recognised Early Childhood Competencies at Level 6, they could be used as the benchmark framework for other practitioner practice at this level in similar contexts. Within the Early Childhood Graduate Practitioner Competencies documentation, there is a separate section for external examiners. As the number of programmes increase in more universities, it is essential that the pool of external examiners for these embedded programmes have experiences of the Competencies themselves. It is a quality issue of appropriate knowledge and understanding as much as an external validation of the quality of the programme delivered. Unless the external examiners are competent in their knowledge and understanding of the Early Childhood Graduate Practitioner Competencies, they will be unable to externally examine the programme adequately.

However, until there is a sufficient critical mass of academics in Higher Education who are sufficiently skilled in their knowledge and understanding of the Competencies, there will need to be specific professional development offered to them. This could be by the institutions themselves or by institutions buying in this support from the ECSDN. In many ways, this has already been established by the ECSDN in the workshops, facilitated by Tanya Richardson (University of Northampton) and Sigrid Brogaard-Clausen (University of Roehampton), the Vice-Chairs for Workforce Development and Professional Issues, for institutions that have embedded, or are thinking of embedding, the Competencies in their Early Childhood programmes. They are continuing to develop an online tool-box for members, which is gaining momentum and providing even more work for Tanya and Sigrid! They continue to encourage the collegiate sharing of materials between ECSDN members as the Graduate Competencies develop in more institutions.

Until now, this kind of support has been included in membership of the ECSDN. It is now time for Higher Education institutions to financially support additional CPD for practitioners and external examiners.

International Interest in the Early Childhood Graduate Practitioner Competencies

There has been international interest in the Early Childhood Graduate Practitioner Competencies from the time they were first published. Although there is a reticence to develop the Competencies internationally until they are further developed nationally, this needs to be taken into consideration with any further development and initiatives. There is a general anxiety that the Competencies will not be embedded appropriately into Early Childhood programmes, and their equivalent, if they are made more widely available to all institutions which deliver Level 6 programmes. One of the innovations already taking place is with ECSDN members which offer Master's ECS programmes. Although it is important that Master's students have sufficient knowledge of Early Childhood practice, the Competencies can be embedded into MA ECS programmes. This will provide another avenue for recognition and development of the Competencies. Internationally, it is more common for Early Childhood undergraduate programmes to have practice embedded into the academic programme. We need to work together with our international colleagues to recognise similar pressures and challenges faced by us all in relation to the narrow parameters of practice and the emphasis on schoolification, getting young children ready for school by exposing them to the culture of primary schooling whilst they are still in pre-school settings (OECD, 2017). Compulsory schooling usually begins later in many other countries than it does in the UK, with children not starting compulsory schooling until the age of six or seven years. This may be advantageous to the embedding of the Competencies internationally, as they are relevant for children up to eight years of age. Before it could become a reality, there will need to be more in-depth research and development associated with the Competencies, to see how they can be embedded in different Early Childhood programmes internationally, which may be tied down by particular curricular parameters. However, if learning and development for children is to be transformational, context and interpretation is more important than the application of universal standards and should be uppermost in our deliberations and discussions (Cameron and Moss, 2020). Professional and practitioner colleagues in different countries and contexts can learn from, and support, each other to develop this kind of global graduate workforce with interdisciplinary knowledge, who can work effectively, respectfully and sensitively with children, families and communities.

Research, Development and Professional Identity

Research relating to the influence of the Early Childhood Graduate Practitioner Competencies is already being undertaken by members of the ECSDN, funded by the ECSDN in 2020. One of the projects, is being undertaken by academics from different universities who have been involved in the pilot programmes. It is exploring practitioner, academic and student perspectives of the ways in which the competencies can help to build professional identities and relationships. The second research project is focused on the Early Childhood Education and Care sectors' perspective on the ECS graduates and the Practitioner Competencies. I am sure that these two projects are just the start of the robust research required to convince policymakers and employers, and Higher Education institutions, about the long-term benefits of having such skilled practitioners in the Early Childhood workforce. Sigrid Brogaard-Clausen and Michelle Cottle have eloquently made the case for professional identity linked to democratic practice and critically reflective dialogue in Chapter 10. This can only be achieved by a common understanding of these concepts by those who are writing, validating and delivering the ECS programmes with embedded competencies, and those who enrol on the programmes. A holistic Early Childhood pedagogy needs to be encouraged so that the students and graduates can develop their own pedagogies steeped in democratic practice and critically reflective dialogue.

I, like Sigrid and Michelle (the authors of Chapter 10), consider professionalism and professional identity to be bound up in the politics of Early Childhood. I can remember having discussions with colleagues who considered Early Childhood to be apolitical and wanted politics left out of the discussion. However, this is counterproductive to any advancement within the Early Childhood field. One of the books that I found to be very influential in my thinking, as long ago as 1987, when I was a health visitor in the community, was entitled *The Politics of Childhood* (Hoyles, 1987). For me, it demonstrated how children have agency during childhood; that they could make choices and influence their daily lives. This was in contrast to the commonly held perspective that viewed childhood as the nurturing process for adulthood. During the late twentieth and early twenty-first centuries, academics began to write about the politics of Early Childhood, most notably James, Jenks and Prout (1998) and Peter Moss (2007) in the UK and Gunhilla Dahlberg in Sweden. Moss (2007: 12) urged Early Childhood institutions to become places of democratic (and political) practice which offer 'opportunities for everyone, younger and old, to participate, children or parents, practitioners or politicians, or indeed any other local citizen'. This was at a time when Early Childhood Care and Education was high on the Labour government's agenda, when there was a growth of policy interest in Early Childhood education and increased spending on Early Years education, childcare and Sure Start. Subsequent research in later years demonstrate that these investments in Early Childhood had long-lasting benefits (Stewart, 2013).

The Future Political Landscape

Most recently, there has been renewed political interest in the Early Childhood sector through the formation of the Early Years Commission – a cross-party initiative that was formed in 2021 and is chaired by two Members of Parliament on opposite sides of the House: Sharon Hodgson (Labour) and Edward Timpson (Conservative). Both have held responsibility for young children in previous governments and have campaigned for young children for many years. The have worked with many organisations and individuals who share similar interests to draw up *A Cross-Party Manifesto* (Early Years Commission, 2021). The Covid-19 pandemic of 2020–2022 has highlighted previous issues relating to health, education, care and the wellbeing of children which have been neglected for many years, particularly for children living in poverty, of which there are 4.3 million in the UK (Francis-Devine, 2021). The *Cross-Party Manifesto* puts forward both short-term (by 2024) and long-term strategies (by 2030) and recommendations. One of these relates to the Early Childhood workforce. In the short term, the Commission recommends raising the skills of practitioners by investing in continuing professional development, and in the long term, to change the funding structure so that it prioritises young children more effectively. Graduates with graduate-level competencies, who can draw on their holistic and interdisciplinary understanding of young children and child development, fit well into both these strategies. It is hoped that the *Manifesto* will follow through with the appropriate actions its intentions advocate. Although the agenda of the Early Years Commission remains neoliberal in its approach, with its positioning of children as investments for the economic future, there is an emphasis on the quality of the learning, development and wellbeing opportunities for children. It is yet another reason why the development of the Early Childhood Graduate Practitioner Competencies is so timely. Having graduate-level competencies will enable highly skilled ECS graduates to be distinctive when applying for employment opportunities. Their breadth and depth of knowledge and understanding will certainly contribute to making children's lives better. Several of my wonderful colleagues in the ECSDN have said over the years that we need an Institute of Early Childhood – now is the time to promote this as well.

Summary

This chapter has explored different aspects of the contemporary Early Childhood sector and has outlined how the Early Childhood Graduate Practitioner Competencies can be further developed. It has highlighted the many challenges faced by students, graduates and practitioners to have their appropriate status and professional identity recognised by policymakers and employers, and the place for the Early Childhood Graduate Practitioner Competencies in this process. It raises questions about the standardisation of Early Childhood programmes and the challenges that transferability of the Competencies poses. The importance of appropriate mentorship and mentorship programmes cannot be underestimated; neither can the need for continuing professional development.

Key Points

This chapter looks towards the future development of the Early Childhood programmes and the Graduate Practitioner Competencies for Early Childhood graduates, students and practitioners. It has explored:

- The challenges for the further development of the Early Childhood Graduate Practitioner Competencies
- Their adaptation for other programmes, both nationally and internationally
- The political landscape and the status of Early Childhood graduates and those who work with young children
- Improving the experiences of the students, graduates and practitioners
- The importance of appropriate mentorship and mentorship programmes
- Supporting the continuous professional development of graduate practitioners.

Final Thoughts

In Chapter 1, Helen Perkins suggested that the Early Childhood Graduate Practitioners become known simply as Graduate Practitioners. Interestingly, I found myself more frequently referring to them as graduate practitioners as I wrote this chapter.

We hope that you benefit from (and enjoy reading) this text, and that you gain more knowledge and understanding about working with young children and each other. When in conversation with Helen Haygarth, I asked her what she would want to pass on to all those who have been, and will be, involved with the Early Childhood Graduate Practitioner Competencies. Here are her very wise responses!

To new students

'If you are unsure, ask! No question is ever too silly. Learn from peers around you; that itself is priceless.'

To new graduates

'Make the difference – use your knowledge to reflect and transform your practice.'

To new practitioners

'Always be the advocate for the child. If something does not feel right for the child, it usually is not. Please have the confidence in your own skills to challenge/question yourself or colleagues. Reflect … reflect … reflect!'

To mentors

'Support, scaffold, communicate and remember how it was when you learnt. Be honest but be kind.'

To academics

'See the perspective of the practitioner. It is so easy to forget when absorbed in the academia of it all. Support the links from theory.'

Finally, my grateful thanks to Helen for helping me to make this chapter more meaningful and for all her other contributions to this book.

PROFESSIONAL ROLES FOR EARLY CHILDHOOD GRADUATES

EMPLOYMENT AND FURTHER CAREER PROSPECTS

Carolyn Silberfeld

Employment following an Early Childhood Studies degree (and its equivalent) can be variable when you graduate. You need to make sure you also have generic employability skills, which can be transferable as well as your degree. 'Prospects' is a useful website to find out more information about jobs and employability when graduating with an Early Childhood Studies degree. Here is the direct link: www. prospects.ac.uk/careers-advice/what-can-i-do-with-my-degree/early-childhood-studies

'Prospects', and other employment and careers websites, highlight essential generic skills as including teamwork, problem-solving, communication, time management, IT skills and numeracy. I would like to emphasise the importance of good communication and interpersonal skills, plus the need to be critically reflective, confident and flexible. Employment opportunities in practice often depend on the graduate's previous practical experience, whether or not they have a Level 3 practice qualification. This does not seem to be so important in non-practice employment, such as research or some local authority roles.

Studies (e.g., Silberfeld and Mitchell, 2021) have shown that Early Childhood Studies graduates either could not find employment within the Early Childhood sector or chose not to work with young children, even if they would have liked to. Many of these graduates were put off by the attitude of employers and the salary of those who work with children. Even though they would have liked to work with children, their degree was not recognised by employers unless they had a practice qualification, and the salary was less than they could earn in retail. Unsurprisingly, though disappointingly, the majority of graduates in the study worked in retail. Although the degrees were highly rated by the graduates, they were not always understood by employers and careers advisors. In addition, opportunities for relevant and sufficient practice during the degree programmes were considered to be essential by the graduates, not all of whom were offered sufficient opportunity. This was also highlighted in an early study (Woods, Thurtle and Silberfeld, 1999) which looked at employment outcomes among the first cohort of graduates (Woods et al., 1999). However, Woods et al. (1999) found that all the graduates gained relevant employment in practice or research. One of the major differences between the studies by Woods et al. (1999) and Silberfeld and Mitchell (2021) was the small number of Early Childhood studies graduates looking for employment in 1996 (15) and very large cohorts of graduates in 2021 (approximately 2500/year). In addition, the first cohort either already held professional qualifications or did post-graduate courses. The later graduates (Silberfeld and Mitchell, 2021) found achieving employment in the sector was much more of a challenge. These research studies and the employability statistics of Early Childhood Studies graduates were some of the influences and catalysts for the need to develop the Early Childhood Graduate Practitioner Competencies.

At the time of writing this chapter, there is a wide diversity of graduate employment, which can include working in education, health care and voluntary or charity organisations, in nurseries and preschools, in state and independent schools, in local authorities, and in local and national charities and health authorities (www.prospects.ac.uk).

According to 'Prospects' (www.prospects.ac.uk), roles may include the following:

Education mental health practitioner
Family support worker
Health play specialist
Learning mentor
Play therapist
Primary school teacher
Special educational needs coordinator (SENCO)
Special educational needs teacher
Social worker
Teaching assistant
Youth worker

There are employment opportunities in other roles, such as researchers, particularly in Early Childhood/childhood contexts, or for research focusing on early childhood/children. In addition, there have been some interesting roles within the charities sector, in voluntary organisations and local authorities. It is important to look at employment opportunities in health and social care as well as education and childcare.

Having Early Childhood Graduate Practitioner Competencies will hopefully improve the employment prospects for graduates, particularly those who do not already hold a practice qualification. It is also hoped that leadership roles will be offered to graduates who have achieved the Early Childhood Graduate Competencies.

To be employed in the following professions, it is necessary to undertake a post-registration professional course:

Teaching – Qualfied Teacher Status(QTS); Early Years Teacher (EYT)

Child psychotherapy

Children's nursing

Midwifery

Community development work

Counselling

Educational psychology

Speech and language therapy

A good Early Childhood Studies degree, plus the abovementioned generic skills, will help you get on to these professional programmes, if this is what you wish to do.

As the Early Childhood Graduate Practitioner Competencies become more familiar to employers, employment opportunities should increase. Having the Department for Education recognise the Competencies in their framework has also given them the necessary credibility.

GLOSSARY

Active learning 'Learning which engages and challenges children's thinking using real-life and imaginary situations. It takes full advantage of the opportunities for learning presented by spontaneous play; planned, purposeful play; investigating and exploring events and life experiences; focused learning and teaching; supported when necessary, through sensitive intervention to support or extend learning' (Education Scotland, 2007: 5).

Adverse childhood experiences (ACEs) This critiqued term, emerged from research in North America and embraces a range of factors, such as abuse and living in families where there is drug and alcohol abuse and domestic violence.

Agency Children's capacity to choose, act and influence matters in their everyday lives (Houen et al., 2016).

Bronfenbrenner's Ecological Systems theory (1977) A theory that views child development as a complex system of relationships affected by multiple levels of the surrounding environment, from immediate settings of family and school to broad cultural values, laws and customs (Bronfenbrenner, 1977).

Child abuse/maltreatment These terms embrace the different types of abuse to which children can be subjected, including physical, emotional and sexual abuse, and neglect.

Child development A holistic concept which ensures that each child is seen as an individual and all different skills and areas of development are intertwined (Lindon and Brodie, 2016).

Child protection A term that embraces the legislative and policy frameworks to protect children.

Civicness Children's ability to 'act with and on behalf of their community (be civic) through both verbal and nonverbal actions' (Payne, 2020).

Early Childhood A specific period of childhood development, from conception usually ending at the age of eight (Murray, Swadener and Smith, 2020). In some societies and cultures this is different and the transition to middle childhood ranges from five to eight years (Berk, 2012).

Early Childhood development 'A multifaceted concept from an ecological framework that focuses on the child's outcomes (development), which depends on characteristics of the child and the context, such as health, nutrition, protection, care and/or education' (Britto, Engle and Super, 2013: 4).

Early Childhood Education and Care (ECEC) 'Growth, development and learning – including health, nutrition and hygiene, and cognitive, social, physical and emotional development – from birth to entry to primary school in formal, informal and non-formal settings' (UNESCO, 2009: 3).

Early Childhood Care and Education (ECCE) UNESCO states that this 'is more than preparation for primary school. It aims at the holistic development of a child's social, emotional, cognitive and physical needs in order to build a solid and broad foundation for lifelong learning and wellbeing. ECCE has the possibility to nurture caring, capable and responsible future citizens' (UNESCO, 2021: lines 7–11).

Early Childhood services   Services in health, social care and education, which include general and specialist services.

Early Years   A generic term in common usage in education, health and social care. However, there is no definition of the term as there is with Early Childhood.

Inclusion   Children of all abilities have equal access to and can participate meaningfully in all activities and experiences, 'maximising participation in, and minimising exclusion from, Early Years settings, schools and society' (Nutbrown and Clough, 2009: 194).

Inclusive pedagogy   The belief that all children have potential to progress and succeed, and none should be excluded from opportunities based upon individual capabilities.

Inclusive practice   Practice which recognises the differences between children and uses this to ensure that all students can access educational content and participate fully in their learning. It understands that no two children are the same and ensures that experiences and activities accommodate this.

Inter-agency   Interaction that '… only involves *two* professionals from different agencies' (Walker, 2018: 8).

Legislation   Legislation is the process of making or enacting laws and is a fundamental aspect of society. Laws may be static or amended over time through subsequent legislation, e.g. The Children Act 1989, 2004, 2006; Childcare Act 2002, 2006, 2016; Children and Families Act, 2014.

Mosaic approach   A creative framework for listening to young children's perspectives through talking, walking, making and reviewing together (Clark and Moss, 2011).

Multi-agency   Interaction that '… involves three or more professionals from different agencies' (Walker, 2018: 8).

Multi-disciplinary   Interaction that '… *may* involve the collaboration of workers' from different disciplines who work within the same agency' (Walker, 2018: 8). For example, in a school there may be a teacher, nursery assistant and speech and language therapist.

Partnership with parents   A term defined as 'multiple ways of establishing connections and reflecting a desire to identify common goals for the learning environment and joint decision making at all levels' (Palaiologou and Male, 2017: 14).

Pedagogue   This term has been taken from the Danish social pedagogues, who are the main workers in nurseries and other childcare settings in Denmark. Their training typically involves a three- or four-year degree, with courses covering behavioural sciences, working with conflict, promoting teamwork and subjects aimed at building self-esteem.

Policy   Policy emerges from legislation (the law). Health, education and social care, for example, all have legislation relevant to their specific area, and policy and procedures that stem from it.

Professional development   Advancement of the knowledge, skills, dispositions and practices of Early Childhood practitioners and professionals, and the promotion of a culture for ongoing professional growth in individuals and systems (Sheridan et al., 2009).

Professional identity   results from 'connections made and interactions between societal and personal philosophies as well as professional training and practice.[…] 'It is enmeshed in a broader societal discourse that is underpinned by values, personal qualities, ideology, relationships, status, training, and qualifications' (Moloney, 2010: 172).

Risk assessment   A systematic review of the potential dangers in an activity or undertaking and an evaluation of the consequences (Perry, 2016).

Safeguarding   An umbrella term that embraces promoting health, wellbeing and safety of all children.

Twin-track nature of education   A term that refers to actions or processes, including funding, resources, training and curriculum development, which all need to occur together and simultaneously.

United Nations Convention for the Rights of the Child (1989)   Comprising 54 articles, a convention that covers all aspects of a child's life and sets out the civil, political, economic, social and cultural rights to which all children everywhere are entitled. It also explains how adults and governments must work together to make sure all children can enjoy all their rights. The Convention has been ratified by 196 countries. Only the USA has not ratified it (UNICEF, 2005).

REFERENCES

1001 Critical Days (2019) *The 1001 critical days: The importance of the conception to age two period.* London: 1001 Critical Days.

Ahrenkiel, A. and Warring, N. (2016). Demokrati i hverdagen in 'paedagogisk. In B. Elle, L. Togsverd and T. Ellegaard (Eds), *Tema: Demokrati I Børnehøjde – En Truet Livsform?* (pp. 16–23). Odder, Denmark: Narayana Press

Ainsworth, M. D. S., Bell, S. M. and Stayton, D. J. (1971) Individual differences in strange situation behavior of one-year-olds. In H. R. Shaffer (Ed.), *The origins of human social relations* (pp. 17–57). London and New York: Academic Press.

Ainsworth, M. D. S., Blehar, M. C., Waters, E. and Wall, S. (1978) *Patterns of attachment: A psychological study of the strange situation.* Hillsdale, NJ: Erlbaum.

Andrew, Y. (2015) What we feel and what we do: Emotional capital in early childhood work. *Early Years*, 35(4), 351–365. doi: 10.1080/09575146.2015.1077206

Archer, N and Oppenheim, C. (2021) *The role of early childhood education and care in shaping life chances: The changing face of early childhood in the UK.* London: Nuffield Foundation.

Argyle, M. (1972) Non-verbal communication in human social interaction. In R.A. Hinde (Ed.), *Non-verbal communication.* Cambridge: Cambridge University Press.

Arndt, S., Urban, M., Murray, C., Smith, K., Swadener, B. and Ellegaard, T. (2018) Contesting early childhood professional identities: A cross-national discussion. *Contemporary Issues in Early Childhood*, 19(2), 97–116. doi:10.1177/1463949118768356

Athey, C. (2007) *Extending thought in young children* (2nd edition). London: PCP.

Atkinson, H., Bardgett, S., Budd, A., Finn, M., Kissane, C., Qureshi, S. … and Sivasundaram, S. (2018) *Race, ethnicity & equality in UK history: A report and resource for change.* London: The Royal Historical Society.

Aubrey, C. (2011) *Leading and managing in the Early Years* (2nd edition). London: Sage.

Baldock, P., Fitzgerald, D. and Kay, J. (2013) *Understanding Early Years policy* (3rd edition). London: Sage.

Ball, C. (1994) *Start right: The importance of early learning.* London: RSA

Ball, S. J. (2003) The teacher's soul and the terrors of performativity. *Journal of Education Policy*, 18(2), 215–228. doi: 10.1080/0268093022000043065.

Ball, S.J. (2017). *The education debate.* (3rd edition) Bristol University: Policy Press

Bauer, A., Parsonage, M., Knapp, M., Iemmi, V. and Adelaja, B. (2014) *The costs of perinatal mental health problems.* London: Centre for Mental Health.

Belsky, J., Melhuish, E. C. and Barnes, J. (Eds) (2007) *The national evaluation of Sure Start: Does area-based early intervention work?* Bristol, UK: Policy Press.

Berk, L. E. (2012). *Child development: International edition.* Boston, MA: Pearson Education

Berk, L.E (2019). *Child development.* Boston, MA: Pearson Education

Bernard, C. and Harris, P. (2016) Concluding remarks. In C. Bernard and P. Harris (Eds), *Safeguarding Black children: Good practice in child protection* (pp. 271–273). London: Jessica Kingsley.

Blackmore, J. (2004) Leading as emotional management work in high-risk times: The counterintuitive impulses of performativity and passion. *School Leadership and Management*, 24(4), 439–459.

Bolton, G. (2014) *Reflective practice writing and professional development* (4th edition). London: Sage.

Bonebright, D. A. (2010) 40 years of storming: A historical review of Tuckman's model of small team development. *Human Resource Development International*, 13(1), 111–120.

Bonetti, S. and Blanden, J. (2020) *Early years workforce qualifications and children's outcomes*. London: Education Policy Institute.

Bonnett, T. and Ly, K. (2017) Leading the way in Early Childhood Education and Care through a mentor/protégé program. *Journal of Childhood Studies*, 42(1), 23–31.

Bornstein, M. H., and Putnick, D. L. (2012). Cognitive and socioemotional caregiving in developing countries. *Child Development*. 83(1), 46–61

Bottrill, G. (2018) *Can I go play now? Rethinking the Early Years*. London: Sage.

Bowlby, J. (1969) *Attachment and loss* (Vol. 1). New York: Basic Books.

Bowlby J. (1973) *Separation*. New York: Basic Books.

Bowlby J. (1980) *Loss*. New York: Basic Books.

Bowlby J. (1982) *Attachment* (2nd edition). New York: Basic Books.

Bradbury, A. (2020) A critical race theory framework for education policy analysis: The case of bilingual learners and assessment policy in England. *Race Ethnicity and Education*, 23(2), 241–260.

Britto, P. R., Engle, P. L., & Super, C. M. (Eds.). (2013). *Handbook of early childhood development research and its impact on global policy*. Oxford University Press. https://doi.org/10.1093/acprof:oso/9780199922994.001.0001

Brock, A. (2006) *Dimensions of Early Years professionalism: Attitudes versus competences?* Leeds: Metropolitan University.

Brodie, K. (2015) *The power of schematic play*. Available at: www.kathybrodie.com/articles/schematic-play/ (accessed 19 January 2021).

Brogaard-Clausen, S. (2015) Schoolification or Early Years democracy? A cross curricular perspective from Denmark and England. *Contemporary Issues in Early Childhood*, 16(4), 355–373. https://doi.org/10.1177/1463949115616327

Brogaard-Clausen, S., Guimaraes, S., Tang, F. and Rubiano C. (2022) Wellbeing and democratic living in early childhood curricula in China, Colombia, Denmark, England and Portugal. *Early Years. An International Research Journal*. Published on-line 05.01.22. https://doi.org/10.1080/09575146.2021.2010663

Brogaard-Clausen, S. and Ringmose, C. (2017) The professional identity, power and control of the Danish pedagogue. In G. Kragh-Müller and C. Ringsmose (Eds), *The Nordic social pedagogical approach to Early Years learning*. London: Springer.

Bronfenbrenner, U. (1977) Toward an experimental ecology of human development. *American Psychologist*, 32(7), 513–531.

Bronfenbrenner, U. (1979) *The ecology of human development: Experiments by nature and design.* Cambridge, MA: Harvard University Press.

Bronfenbrenner, U. (2005) *Making human beings human: Bioecological perspectives on human development.* London: Sage

Brooker, L (2010). Constructing the triangle of care: power and professionalism in practitioner/parent relationships. *British Journal of Educational Studies* 58(2): 181–196.

Brookfield, S. (2017) *Becoming a critically reflective teacher* (2nd edition). San Fransisco, CA: Jossey-Bass.

Brotman, L. M., Calzada, E., Huang, K. Y., Kingston, S., Dawson–McClure, S., Kamboukos, D. … and Petkova, E. (2011) Promoting effective parenting practices and preventing child behavior problems in school among ethnically diverse families from underserved, urban communities. *Child Development*, 82(1), 258–276.

Bruner, J. S. (1986) *Actual minds, possible worlds.* Cambridge, MA, and London: Harvard University Press.

Burman, E. (2008) *Deconstructing developmental psychology* (2nd edition). London: Routledge.

Calder, P.A. (1999). The development of early childhood studies degrees in Britain: Future prospects. *European Early Childhood Education Research Journal* Vol. 7 1, 45–68

Calder, P.A. (2019) Historical view: Is childcare working? *Nursery World* 7th May.

Cameron, C. and Moss, P. (2020) *Transforming early childhood in England: Towards a democratic education.* London: UCL Press.

Cameron, K., Mora, C., Leutscher, T. and Calarco, M. (2011) Effects of positive practices on organizational effectiveness. *Journal of Applied Behavior Sciences*, 47, 266–308.

Campbell-Barr, V. (2015) The research policy and practice triangle in early childhood education and care. In R. Parker-Rees and C. Leeson (Eds), *Early childhood studies* (4th edition, Chapter 16). London: Sage.

Campbell-Barr, V., Bonetti, S., Bunting, F. and Gulliver, K. (2020) *A systematic review of Early Years degrees and employment pathways.* Plymouth/London: Institute of Education/University of Plymouth/Education Policy Institute.

Carr, M. (2001) *Assessment in Early Childhood settings: Learning stories.* London: Paul Chapman.

Carr, M., May, H. and Podmore, V. N. with Cubey, P., Hatherly, A. and Macartney, B. (2000) *Learning and teaching stories: Action research on evaluation in early childhood.* Wellington, New Zealand: Council for Educational Research and Ministry of Education. ERIC 447930.

Carr, M., Smith, A. B., Duncan, J., Jones, C., Lee, W. and Marshall, K. (2010) *Learning in the making: Disposition and design in early education.* Rotterdam: Sense Publishers.

Cheater, S. (2019) Sure Start children's centres. *International Journal of Health Promotion and Education*, 57(5), 297–299, doi:10.1080/14635240.2019.1643592

Chilvers, D. (2020) Observation, assessment and the Development Map. Interview by K. Brodie for *Early Years TV Masterclass*, 28 August. Available at: kathy@kathybrodie.com (accessed 28 August 2020).

Chitty, C. (2004) *Education policy in Britain (Contemporary political studies).* London: Palgrave Macmillan

Clark, A. (2017) *Listening to young children: A guide to understanding and using the Mosaic Approach* (Expanded 3rd edition). London: National Children's Bureau UK.

Clark, A. and Moss, P. (2001) *Listening to young children: The mosaic approach.* London. National Children's Bureau for the Joseph Rowntree Foundation.

Clark, A. and Moss, P. (2011) *Listening to young children: The mosaic approach* (2nd edition). London: National Children's Bureau for the Joseph Rowntree Foundation.

Collin, K., Van der Heijden, B. and Lewis, P. (2012) Continuing professional development. *International Journal of Training and Development*, 16(3), 155–163.

Corby, B., Shemmings, D. and Wilkins, D. (2012) *Child abuse: An evidence base for confident practice* (4th edition). Maidenhead: Open University Press.

Cottle, M. (2019) *Enacting 'creativity' in a neoliberal policy context: A case study of English primary school teachers' experiences.* Doctoral dissertation, University of Roehampton. Available at: https://pure. roehampton.ac.uk/portal/en/persons/michelle-cottle/studentTheses/

Cottle, M. and Alexander, E. (2012) Quality in Early Years settings: Government, research and practitioners' perspectives. *British Educational Research Journal*, 38(4), 635–654. doi:10.1080/ 01411926.2011.571661.

Cottle, M. and Alexander, E. (2014) Parent partnership and 'quality' Early Years services: Practitioners' perspectives. *European Early Childhood Education Research Journal* [online], 22(5), 637–659.

Coventry Local Safeguarding Children Board (2013) *Serious Case Review. RE: Daniel Pelka. Coventry: Coventry Local Safeguarding Children Board.* Available at: https://edemocracy.coventry.gov.uk/ documents/s13235/Daniel%20Pelka%20Serious%20Case%20Review%20SCR.pdf (accessed 12 October 2013).

Crosse, K. (2007) *Introducing English as an additional language to young children.* London: Sage.

Crul, M., Schneider, J., Keskiner, E. and Lelie, F. (2017) The multiplier effect: How the accumulation of cultural and social capital explains steep upward social mobility of children of low-educated immigrants. *Ethnic and Racial Studies*, 40(2), 321–338.

Cullen, M. A., Cullen, S. and Bailey, T. (2020) *Evaluation of pilot delivery of ParentChild+ in England, 2018–2020.* Final report, July.

Cunningham, H. (2006) *The invention of childhood.* London: BBC Books.

Dalli, C. (2008) Pedagogy, knowledge and collaboration: Towards a ground–up perspective on professionalism. *European Early Childhood Education Research Journal*, 16(2), 171–185.

Davies, H., Brotherton, G. and McGillivray, G. (2010) *Working with children, young people and families.* London: Sage.

Davis, G. and Ryder, G. (2016) *Leading in early childhood.* London: Sage.

Day, C. (2004). *A passion for teaching.* London: Routledge.

Department for Children, Schools and Families (DfES) (2008). *Statutory framework for the early years foundation stage.* Nottingham: DCSFPublications

Department for Education. (2012). *The Nutbrown review: Foundations for quality: The independent review of early education and childcare qualifications. DFE-00068-2012.* London:DfE

Department for Education (2014a) *The Equality Act 2010 and schools: Departmental advice for school leaders, school staff, governing bodies and local authorities.* Reference: DFE-00296-2013. London: DfE.

Department for Education (2014b) *Early Years under 5s Foundation Stage framework.* London: DfE. Available at: www.gov.uk/government/publications/early-years-foundation-stage-framework–2 (accessed 2 March 2016).

Department for Education (2014c) *Listening to and involving children and young people.* Reference: DFE-00011-2014. London: DfE.

Department for Education. (2014d). *Statutory framework for the Early Years Foundation Stage.* London: HMSO.

Department for Education (2015) *Special educational needs and disability code of practice: 0 to 25 years: Statutory guidance for organisations which work with and support children and young people who have special educational needs or disabilities.* Reference: DFE-00205-2013. London: DfE.

Department for Education (2017) *Early Years Foundation Stage framework.* London: HMSO.

Department for Education (2018) *Working together to safeguard children: A guide to inter-agency working to safeguard and promote the welfare of children.* London: HMSO. Available from: www.gov.uk/government/publications/working-together-to-safeguard-children–2 (accessed 30 April 2021).

Department for Education (2019) *Check Early Years qualifications guidance.* London: HMSO. Available at: www.gov.uk/guidance/early-years-qualifications-finder#overview (accessed 30 April 2020).

Department for Education (2020a) *Development matters: Non-statutory curriculum guidance for the Early Years Foundation Stage.* London: HMSO. Available at: https://assets.publishing.service.gov.uk/government/uploads/system/uploads/attachment_data/file/988004/Development_Matters.pdf (accessed 30 April 2020).

Department for Education (2020b) *Keeping children safe in education.* London: HMSO. Available at: www.gov.uk/government/publications/keeping-children-safe-in-education–2 (accessed 30 April 2020).

Department for Education (DfE) (2021) *Statutory framework for the Early Years Foundation Stage.* London: HMSO. Available at: www.gov.uk/government/publications/early-years-foundation-stage-framework–2 (accessed 30 April 2020).

Department for Education and Skills (DfES) (2002) *Birth to three matters.* London: DfES/Sure Start Unit.

Department for Education and Skills (2003) *Every child matters: Agenda for change.* Nottingham: DfES Publications

Department for Education and Skills (DfES) (2004) *Every child matters: Next steps.* Nottingham: DfES.

Department for Education and Skills (DfES) (2007) *Every parent matters.* Nottingham: DfES.

Department of Children, Schools and Families (DCSF) (2008) *The Early Years Foundation Stage: Setting the standards for learning, development and care for children from birth to five.* Nottingham: DCFS Publications

Department of Education and Science (1967) *Children and their primary schools. A report of the Central Advisory Council for Education (England) (The Plowden Report).* London: HMSO

Dewey, J. (1998) *Experience and education* (60th anniversary edition). West Lafayette, IN: Kappa Delta Pi.

Doherty, J. and Hughes, M. (2009) *Child development: Theory and practice 0–11*. Harlow, UK: Pearson Education.

Drummond, M. J. (2003) *Assessing young children's learning* (2nd edition). London: David Fulton.

Drummond, M. J. (2012) *Assessing children's learning* (Classic edition). London: David Fulton.

Early Childhood Studies Degrees Network (ECSDN) (2019) *Early childhood graduate practitioner competencies*. London: Early Childhood Studies Degree Network.

Early Education (2012) *Development matters in the Early Years Foundation Stage (EYFS)*. London: Early Education.

Early Years Coalition Partners (2020) *Birth to 5 matters: Guidance by the sector, for the sector*. Available at: www.birthto5matters.org.uk/ (accessed 4 February 2021).

Early Years Commission (2021) *A cross-party manifesto*. London: Centre for Social Justice/Fabian Society.

Education Scotland (2007) *A curriculum for excellence: Building the curriculum 2*. Edinburgh: Education Scotland. Available at: www.education.gov.scot/Documents/btc2.pdf (accessed 4 February 2021).

Eisenstadt, N. (2011) *Providing a sure start: How government discovered early childhood*. Bristol, UK: Policy Press.

Eisner, E. (2002) *The arts and the creation of mind*. New Haven, CT: Yale University Press.

Elarousy, W. and Abed, S. (2019) Barriers that inhibit reporting suspected cases of child abuse and neglect among nurses in a public hospital. *East Mediterranean Health Journal*, 25(6).

Elfer, P. (2012) Emotion in nursery work: Work discussion as a model of critical professional reflection. *Early Years*, 32(2), 129–141. doi: 10.1080/09575146.2012.697877

Elfer, P. (2015). Emotional aspects of nursery policy and practice – progress and prospect. *European Early Childhood Education Research Journal*. 23(4), 497–511

Facebook (2004) *About us*. Available at: www.facebook.com/facebook (accessed 7 December 2020).

Feldman, D. H. (2012). Cognitive development in childhood. In R. M. Lerner, M. A. Easterbrooks, & J. Mistry (Eds.), *Handbook of psychology: Developmental psychology*. (2nd edition).6, 195–210.

Felitti, V. J., Anda, R. F., Nordenberg, D., Williamson, D. F., Spitz, A.M., Edwards, V., Koss, M. P., and Marks, J. S. (1998). Relationship of childhood abuse and household dysfunction to many of the leading causes of death in adults. The Adverse Childhood Experiences (ACE) Study. *American Journal of Preventive Medicine*. 14(4), 245–58

Fenech, M., Salamon, A. and Stratigos, T. (2019) Building parents' understandings of quality Early Childhood Education and Care and early learning and development: Changing constructions to change conversations. *European Early Childhood Education Research Journal*, 27(5), 706–721.

Fenton, C. (2021) What are we playing at? In K. Owen (Ed.), *Play in the Early Years*. London: Sage.

Ferlazzo, L. (2013) The differences between parent involvement and parent engagement. *Library Media Connection*, 31(5), 28.

First 1001 Day Movement (2021). *The First 1001 Days: An age of opportunity.* London: Parent Infant Foundation

Fisher, R. (2004) What is creativity? In R. Fisher and M. Williams (Eds), *Unlocking literacy: A guide for teachers.* London: Routledge.

Fitzgerald, D. and Maconochie, H. (2020) Introduction. In D. Fitzgerald and H. Maconochie (Eds), *Early Childhood studies: A student's guide* (pp. xxxiv–xxxv). London: Sage.

Florez, I. R. (2011) Developing children's self-regulation through everyday experiences. *Young Children,* 66(4), 46–51. Washington, DC: National Association for the Education of Young Children (NAEYC).

Fonagy, P., Gergely, G., Jurist, E. and Target, M. (2002) *Affect regulation, mentalization, and the development of the self.* New York: Other Press.

Food Standards Agency (2015) *Safer food, better business for caterers.* London: Food Standards Agency. Available at: food.gov.uk/sites/default/files/media/document/sfbb-caterers-pack-fixed-pdf (accessed 3 January 2021)

Food Standards Agency (2020) *Safer food, better business for childminders.* London: Food Standards Agency. Available at: food.gov.uk/business-guidance/safer-food-better-business-for-childminders (accessed 3 January 2021).

Francis-Devine, F. (2021) *Poverty in the UK: Statistics.* Briefing Paper Number 7096, 31 March. London: House of Commons Library.

Freire, P. (1993 [1972]) *Pedagogy of the oppressed.* Translated by M. Bergman Ramos. London: Penguin.

Freire, P. (1998) *Pedagogy of freedom: Ethics, democracy, and civic courage.* Oxford: Rowman and Littlefield.

Gallahue, D. L. and Ozmun, J. C. (1998) *Understanding motor development: Infants, children, adolescents, adults.* Dubuque, IA: McGraw-Hill.

Geue, P. E. (2017) Positive practices in the workplace: Impact on team climate, work engagement, and task performance. *Journal of Applied Behavioral Science,* 54(3), 272–301.

Giardiello, P. (2013. *Pioneers in Early Childhood Education: The roots and legacies of Rachel and Margaret McMillan, Maria Montessori and Susan Isaacs.* London: Routledge

Gibbs, G. (1988). *Learning by doing: A guide to teaching and learning methods.* Further Education Unit, Oxford Brookes University, Oxford.

Giddens, A. (1991) *Modernity and self-identity: Self and society in the late modern age.* Stanford, CA: Stanford University Press

Gifford S. (2015) Early Years mathematics: How to create a nation of mathematics lovers? In *NRICH.* Available at: https://nrich.maths.org/11441 (accessed 4 December 2020).

Glazzard, J., Potter, M. and Stones, S. (2019) *Meeting the mental health needs of young children 0-5 years.* St Albans, UK: Critical Publishing.

Goodall, J., & Montgomery, C. (2014). Parental involvement to parental engagement: A continuum. *Educational Review,* 66(4), 399–410.

Gregoriadis, A., Papandreou, M. and Birbili, M. (2018) Continuing professional development in the Greek early childhood education system. *Early Years*, 38(3), 271–285. doi: 10.1080/09575146.2016.1265486

Hall, J., Sammons, P., Smees, R., Sylva, K., Evangelou, M., Goff, J., Smith, T. and Smith, G. (2019) Relationships between families' use of Sure Start children's centres, changes in home learning environments, and preschool behavioural disorders. *Oxford Review of Education*, 45(3), 367–389. doi: 10.1080/03054985.2018.1551195

Hanson, K. and Appleby, K. (2015) Reflective practice. In M. Reed and R. Walker (Eds), *A critical companion to early childhood*. London: Sage.

Hardyment, C. (2007) *Dream babies: Childcare advice from John Locke to Gina Ford*. London: Frances Lincoln.

Hargreaves, A (2000) Four ages of professionalism and professional learning. *Teachers and Teaching Theory and Practice* 6(2):151–182

Harrison, J. and Harris, D. (2020) *Topology of meaningful listening: The helping hand of participation*. Dissertation/report? Place (to be published).

Harts, R. (1992) Children's participation: From tokenism to citizenship. *Innocenti Essay 4*. New York: UNICEF

Hartshorne, J. K., Tenenbaum, J. B. and Pinker, S. (2018) A critical period for second language acquisition: Evidence from 2/3 million English speakers. *Cognition*, 177, 263–277. https://doi.org/10.1016/j.cognition.2018.04.007

Health and Safety Executive (2021) *Management of healthcare waste*. London: HSE. Available at: www/hse.gov.uk/healthservices/healthcare-waste.htm (accessed 2 January 2021).

Health and Safety Authority (HAS). (2016) *A guide to risk assessments and safety statements*. London: HAS. Available at: www.hsa.ie/eng/publications_and_forms/publications/safety_and_health_management/guide_to_risk_assessments_and_safety_statements.pdf

Health and Safety Executive (HSE) (2012) *Using work equipment safely*. London: HSE. Available at: https://www.hse.gov.uk/pubns/indg229.pdf

Health and Safety Executive (2009) *Health and safety law*. London: HSE Available at: Available at: www.hse.gov.uk/pubns/lawleaflet.pdf

Hearn, G., Iliff, A., Jones, I., Kirby, A., Ormiston, P., Parr, P., Rout, J. and Wardman, L. (1998) Postnatal depression in the community. *British Journal of General Practice*, 48(1), 1064–1066.

Heckman, J. J. (2006) Skill formation and the economics of investing in disadvantaged children. *Science*, 312(5782), 1900–1902. doi: 10.1126/science.1128898

Heikka, J., Pitkäniemi, H., Kettukangas, T. and Hyttinen, T. (2019) Distributed pedagogical leadership and teacher leadership in early childhood educational contexts. *International Journal of Leadership in Education: Theory and Practice*, 24(3), 333–348. https://doi.org/10.1080/13603124.2019.1623923

Heikka, J., Waniganayake, M. and Hujala, E. (2013) Contextualizing distributed leadership within early childhood education: Current understandings, research evidence and future challenges. *Educational Management Administration & Leadership*, 41(1), 30–44.

Henry-Allain, L. and Lloyd-Rose, M. (2021). *The tiney guide to becoming an inclusive, anti-racist early educator.* London: tiney

Hohmann, M., D. Weikart, and A. S. Epstein. (2008). *Educating young children.* 3rd ed. Ypsilanti, MI: HighScope Press

Hopkin, P. (2013) *Risk management.* London: Kogan Page.

hsa.ie/eng/Publications_and_Forms/Publications/Safety_and_Health_Management/Guide_to_Risk_Assesssments_and_Safety_Statements.html

Hornby, G. (2000) *Improving parental involvement.* London and New York: Cassell.

Hornby, G. (2011) *Parental involvement in childhood education: Building effective school–family partnerships.* New York: Springer.

Hornby, G. and Blackwell, I. (2018) Barriers to parental involvement in education: An update. *Educational Review,* 70(1), 109–119.

Hornby, G. and Lafaele, R. (2011) Barriers to parental involvement in education: An explanatory model. *Educational Review,* 63(1), 37–52. doi:10.1080/00131911.2010.488049

Horwath, J. and Morrison, T. (2007) Collaboration, integration and change in children's services: Critical issues and key ingredients. *Child Abuse & Neglect,* 31, 55–69. doi:10.1016/j.chiabu.2006.01.007.

Houen, S., Danby, S., Farrell, A. and Thorpe, K. (2016) Creating spaces for children's agency: 'I wonder …' formulations in teacher–child interactions. *International Journal of Early Childhood,* 48, 259–276.

Hoyles, M. (1987) *The politics of childhood.* London: Pluto Press.

Huffman, M. (2015). *Whoops! I forgot to achieve my potential: Create your very own personal change management strategy to get the fun, purpose, meaning and happiness back into your life!* Washington, DC: The Difference Press

Hughes, A. M. and Read, V. (2012) *Building positive relationships with parents of young children: A guide to effective communication.* London: Taylor & Francis.

Information Commissioner's Office (2018). *Guide to the general data protection regulation.* Wilmslow: ICO Available at: www.gov.uk/government/publications/guide-to-the-general-data-protection-regulation

Instagram (2010) *About us.* https://about.instagram.com/ (accessed 7 December 2020).

James, A., Jenks, C. and Prout, A. (1998) *Theorizing childhood.* London: Polity Press.

James, A. and Prout, J. (Eds) (1997) *Constructing and reconstructing childhood: Contemporary issues in the sociological study of childhood.* Abingdon, UK: RoutledgeFalmer.

Jensen, J. J. (2015) Placement supervision of pedagogue students in Denmark: The role of university colleges and early childhood centres, *Early Years,* 35(2), 154–167. doi: 10.1080/09575146.2015.1024616

Johnston, J. and Oates, R. (2018) Reflective practice. In J. Johnston, L. Nahmad-Williams, R. Oates and V. Wood (Eds), *Early Childhood Studies* (pp. 308–343). London: Routledge.

Jones, L., Powell, J. and Holmes, R. (2005) *Early childhood studies: A multiprofessional perspective.* Maidenhead: Open University Press.

Kolb, D.A. (1984). *Experiential learning*. New Jersey: Prentice Hall

Korczak, J. (1999) *A voice for the child* (Edited by S. Josephs). London: Thorsons.

Laevers, F. (Ed.) (1997) *Well-being and involvement in care settings: A process-orientated self-evaluation instrument research centre for experiential education*. Leuven, Belgium: Leuven University.

Laevers, F. (2000) Forward to basics! Deep–level–learning and the experiential approach. *Early Years*, 20(2), 20–29. doi: 10.1080/0957514000200203

Laevers, F. (2006). *Making care and education more effective through wellbeing and involvement. An introduction to experiential education*. Leuven, Belgium: Centre for Experiential Education, University of Belgium.

Laird, S. and Tedam, P. (2019) *Cultural diversity in child protection. Cultural competence in practice*. London: Red Globe Press.

Laming, Lord (2003) *The Victoria Climbié Inquiry*. London: HMSO. Available at: https://assets.publishing.service.gov.uk/government/uploads/system/uploads/attachment_data/file/273183/5730.pdf (accessed 7 April 2021).

Langston, A. (2014). *Facilitating children's learning in the EYFS (Supporting learning in the EYFS)*. Maidenhead: McGraw-Hill

Lawson, M. A. and Alameda-Lawson, T. (2012) A case study of school-linked, collective parent engagement. *American Educational Research Journal*, 49(4), 651–684.

Leer, J. and Lopez-Boo, F. (2019) Assessing the quality of home visit parenting programs in Latin America and the Caribbean. *Early Child Development and Care*, 189(13), 2183–2196. doi: 10.1080/03004430.2018.1443922

Legislation.gov.uk (1974) *Health and safety at work*. [Online]. Available at: www.legislation.gov.uk/ukpga/1974/37/section/37 (accessed 3 December 2020).

Legislation.gov.uk (1989) *The Children Act 1989*. [Online]. Available at: www.legislation.gov.uk/ukpga/1989/41/contents (accessed 3 December 2020).

Legislation.gov.uk (1992) *The Controlled Waste Regulations 1992*. [Online]. Available at: legislation.gov.uk/uksi/1992/588/made (accessed 3 January 2021).

Legislation.gov.uk (2002) *Adoption and Children Act 2002*. [Online]. Available at: www.legislation.gov.uk/ukpga/2002/38/contents (accessed 22 April 2021).

Legislation.gov.uk (2004) *Children Act 2004*. [Online]. Available at: www.legislation.gov.uk/ukpga/2004/31/contents (accessed 22 April 2021).

Legislation.gov.uk (2006) *Childcare Act 2006*. [Online]. Available at: www.legislation.gov.uk/ukpga/2006/21/contents (accessed 22 April 2021).

Legislation.gov.uk (2010) *Equality Act 2010*. [Online]. Available at: www.legislation.gov.uk/ukpga/2010/15/contents (accessed 18 March 2021).

Legislation.gov.uk (2014) *Children and Families Act 2014*. [Online]. Available at: www.legislation.gov.uk/ukpga/2014/6/contents/enacted (accessed 22 April 2021).

Legislation.gov.uk (2018). *The Data Protection Act*. [Online]. Available at: https://www.legislation.gov.uk/ukpga/2018/12/contents/enacted

Leijten, P., Gardner, F., Landau, S., Harris, V., Mann, J., Hutchings, J. ... and Scott, S. (2018) Research review: Harnessing the power of individual participant data in a meta–analysis of the benefits and harms of the Incredible Years parenting program. *Journal of Child Psychology and Psychiatry*, 59(2), 99–109.

Lewin, K. (1946) Behavior and development as a function of the total situation. In L. Carmichael (Ed.) *Manual of Child Psychology* (pp. 791–844). Hoboken, NJ: John Wiley and Sons.

Lewis, M. (2010) The emergence of consciousness and its role in human development. In W. Overton and R. Lerner (Eds), *Handbook of lifespan development* (2nd edition). New York: Wiley.

Liebovich, B. and Adler, S. (2009) Teacher advocacy in Early Years initial teacher education programmes. *Forum*, 31(1).

Lindon, J. and Brodie, K. (2016) *Understanding child development 0–8 years: Linking theory and practice* (4th edition). London: Hodder Education.

Lindon, J., Lindon, L. and Beckley, P. (2016) *Leadership in early years* (2nd edition). (Series: Linking theory and practice). London: Hodder Education.

Lindon, J. and Webb, J. (2016) *Safeguarding and child protection* (5th edition). London: Hodder Education.

Little, H. and Wyver, S. (2008) Outdoor play. *Australian Journal of Early Childhood*, 33(2), 33–40.

Luff, P., Kanyal, M., Shehu, M. and Brewis, N (2016) Educating the youngest citizens – possibilities for early childhood education and care, in England. *Journal for Critical Education Policy Studies*, 14(3), 197–219.

Luft, J. and Ingham, H. (1955) The Johari window: A graphic model of interpersonal awareness. *Proceedings of the Western Training Laboratory in Group Development*. Los Angeles, CA: University of California, Los Angeles.

Lumsden, E. (2018) *Child protection in the Early Years*. London: Jessica Kingsley.

Lumsden, E. (2020) The (in)visibility of infants and young children in child protection. In J. Murray, B. B. Swadener and K. Smith (Eds), *The Routledge international handbook of young children's rights* (pp. 107–119). London: Routledge.

Male, T. and Palaiologou, I. (2015) Pedagogical leadership in the 21st century: Evidence from the field. *Educational Management Administration & Leadership*, 43(2), 214–231.

Male, T., & Palaiologou, I. (2021). Historical developments in policy for early childhood education and care. In I. Palaiologou (Ed.), *The Early Years Foundation Stage*. London, UK: Sage.

Mapp, K., Lander, J. and Carver, I. (2017) *Powerful partnerships: A teacher's guide to engaging families for student success* [e-book]. New York: Scholastic.

Marmot, M. (2020) *Health equity in England: The Marmot review 10 years on*. London: Institute of Health Equity (IHE)

Mathivet, S. and Francis, T. (2007) *Listening together*. London: PLA.

McDowall Clark, R. (2012) 'I've never thought of myself as a leader but...': The Early Years professional and catalytic leadership. *European Early Childhood Education Research Journal*, 20(3), 391–401.

McDowell Clark, R. and Murray, J. (2012). *Reconceptualizing leadership in the early years.* Maidenhead: McGraw-Hill/Open University Press

McManis, L. D. and Gunnewig, S. B. (2012) Finding the education in educational technology with Early Learners. *Young Children,* 67(3), 14–24. Washington, DC: National Association for the Education of Young Children (NAEYC).

Mejia, A., Calam, R. and Sanders, M. R. (2012) A review of parenting programs in developing countries: Opportunities and challenges for preventing emotional and behavioral difficulties in children. *Clinical Child and Family Psychology Review,* 14, 163–175. doi: 10.1007/s10567-012-0116-9

Melhuish, E (2004) *A literature review of the impact of early years provision upon young children, with emphasis given to children from disadvantaged backgrounds: Report to the Comptroller and Auditor General. London.* London: National Audit Office.

Miller, L. and Hevey, D (2012). *Policy issues in the Early Years.* London: Sage

Ministry of Education (1996) *Te Whariki: He Whariki Matauranga mo nga Mokopuna o Aotearoa: Early Childhood Curriculum.* Wellington: Learning Media

Moloney, M. (2010) Professional identity in early childhood care and education: Perspectives of pre-school and infant teachers. *Irish Educational Studies,* 29(2), 167–187.

Moody, I. and Fernley, B. (2014) *Child protection: Safeguarding children against abuse.* New York: Routledge.

Moon, J. (2000) *Reflection in learning and professional development: Theory and practice.* London: Kogan Page

Moore, G., Cohn, J. and Campbell, S. (2001) Infant affective responses to mother's still face at 6 months differentially predict externalizing and internalizing behaviors at 18 months. *Developmental Psychology,* 37(1), 706–714.

Mosley, J. (2014) *Circle time for young children.* Abingdon, UK: Routledge.

Moss, P. (2006) Structures, understandings and discourses: Possibilities for re-envisioning the early childhood worker. *Contemporary Issues in Early Childhood.* 7(1), 30–41.

Moss, P. (2007) Bringing politics into the nursery: Early Childhood education as a democratic practice. *European Early Childhood Education Research Journal,* 15(1), 5–20.

Moss, P. (2013). Beyond the investment narrative. *Contemporary Issues in Early Childhood,* 14(4), 370–372. doi:10.2304/ciec.2013.14.4.370

Moss, P. (2016). Loris Malaguzzi and the schools of Reggio Emilia: Provocation and hope for a renewed public education. *Improving Schools,* 19(2), 167–176. doi:10.1177/1365480216651521

Moss, P. (2017) Power and resistance in early childhood education: From dominant discourses to democratic experimentation. *De Gruyter Open,* 8(1), 11–32.

Moss, P. (2020). Towards a unified and unifying ECEC system. In C. Cameron and P. Moss (Eds). *Transforming early childhood in England towards a democratic education.* (pp 54–66). London: UCL Press.

Moyles, J. (1989) *Just playing? The role and status of play in early childhood education.* Milton Keynes: Open University Press.

Moyles, J. (2005) *The excellence of play* (2nd edition). Maidenhead: Open University Press.

Mumsnet (2000) *About us*. Available at: www.mumsnet.com/info/about-us (accessed 7 December 2020).

Murray, J. (2020) Introduction to young children's rights to protection. In J. Murray, B. B. Swadener and K. Smith (Eds), *The Routledge international handbook of young children's rights* (pp. 79–84). London: Routledge.

Murray, J. and Clark, R. M. (2013) Reframing leadership as a participative pedagogy: The working theories of early years professionals. *Early Years*, 33(3), 289–301.

Murray, J., Swadener, B. B. and Smith, K. (Eds) (2020) *The Routledge international handbook of young children's rights*. London: Routledge

Musgrave, J. (2017) *Supporting children's health and wellbeing*. London: Sage.

Nahmad-Williams, L. and Oates, R. (2018). Reflective practice. In J. Johnston; L. Nahmad-Williams; R.Oates and V. Wood (Eds.). *Early childhood studies principles and practice*. (pp. 467–500). (2nd edition). London: Routledge

Netmums (2000) *About us*. Available at: www.netmums.com/info/about-us (accessed 7 December 2020).

New Zealand Government (2017) *The regulatory framework for early childhood education*. [Online]. Wellington: New Zealand Government. Available at: education.govt.nz

Newman, R. and Blackburn, S. (2002) *Interchange 78. Transitions in the lives of children and young people: Resilience factors*. Edinburgh: Scottish Executive Education Department.

Northouse, P. (2012) *Introduction to leadership: Concepts and practice*. Thousand Oaks, CA: Sage

Northouse, P. (2019) *Introduction to leadership* (5th edition). Thousand Oaks, CA: Sage. Available at: https://app.kortext.com/borrow/570459 (accessed 18 October 2020).

NSPCC (2021) *Disguised compliance: Learning from case reviews*. London: NSPCC. Available at: https://learning.nspcc.org.uk/research-resources/learning-from-case-reviews/disguised-compliance (accessed 7 April 2021).

Nutbrown, C. (2018) Inclusion and diversity in early childhood education and care. In C. Nutbrown, *Early childhood educational research: International perspectives* (Chapter 8). London: Sage.

Nutbrown C and Carter C (2010) 'The tools of assessment: watching and learning' in Pugh G and Duffy B (eds) *Contemporary issues in the Early Years*. 5th edition. (Chapter 8). London: Sage

Nutbrown, C. and Clough, P. (2009) Citizenship and inclusion in the early years: Understanding and responding to children's perspectives on belonging. *International Journal of Early Years Education*, 17(3), 191–206.

Nutbrown, C. and Page, J. (2008) *Working with babies and children from birth to three*. London: Sage.

Oberhuemer, P. (2005) Conceptualising the early childhood pedagogue: Policy approaches and issues of professionalism. *European Early Childhood Education Research Journal*, 13(1), 5–16.

Oberhuemer, P. (2011) The early childhood education workforce in europe between divergencies and emergencies. *International Journal of Child Care and Education Policy* 5, 55–63. https://doi.org/10.1007/2288-6729-5-1-55

Oberhuemer, P. (2013) Continuing professional development and the Early Years workforce. *Early Years*, 33(2), 103–105. doi: 10.1080/09575146.2013.793483

Office for National Statistics (2020) *SOC 2020 Volume 1: Structure and descriptions of unit groups.* London: ONS. [SOC – Standard Occupational Classification]. Available at: www.ons.gov.uk/methodology/classificationsandstandards/standardoccupationalclassificationsoc/soc2020/soc2020volume1structureanddescriptionsofunitgroups (accessed 2 April 2022).

Olusoga, Y. (2014) 'We don't play like that here': Social, cultural and gender perspectives on play. In A. Brock, P. Jarvis and Y. Olusoga (Eds), *Perspectives on play: Learning for life* (2nd edition). Abingdon, UK: Routledge.

Organisation for Economic Co-operation and Development (OECD) (2000) *Where are the resources for lifelong learning?* Paris: Organisation for Economic Co-operation and Development.

Organisation for Economic Co-operation and Development (OECD) (2017), *Starting strong key OECD indicators on early childhood education and care*, Starting Strong, Paris: OECD Publishing. https://doi.org/10.1787/9789264276116-en.

Osgood, J. (2010) Reconstructing professionalism in ECEC: The case for the 'critically reflective emotional professional'. *Early Years*, 30(2), 119–133.

Owens, S. (2010) *An introductory guide to the key terms in inter-agency initiatives in use in the children services' committees in Ireland.* Dublin: Centre for Effective Services.

Ozmen, F., Akuzum, C., Zincirli, M., and Selcuk, G. (2016). The communication barriers between teachers and parents in primary schools. *Eurasian Journal of Educational Research*, 66, 27–46.

Palaiologou, I. (2008) *Child observation.* London: Learning Matters/Sage.

Palaiologou, I. and Male, T. (2017) Partnerships with parents. In Z. Brown and S. Ward (Eds), *Contemporary issues in childhood: An ecological approach* (pp. 83–97). London: Routledge.

Palaiologou, I. and Male, T. (2019) Leadership in early childhood education: The case for pedagogical praxis. *Contemporary Issues in Early Childhood*, 201, 23–34. doi: 10.1177/1463949118819100.

Paley, V. G. (1991) *The boy who would be helicopter: The uses of storytelling in the classroom.* Cambridge, MA: Harvard University Press.

Parker-Rees, R. and Leeson, C. (Eds) (2015) *Early childhood studies* (4th edition). London: Sage.

Pascal, C., Bertram, T. and Cole-Albäck, A. (2020) *Early Years workforce review: Revisiting the Nutbrown Review – policy and impact.* London: The Sutton Trust.

Payler, K. J. and Georgeson, J. (2013) Personal action potency: Early Years practitioners participating in interprofessional practice in Early Years settings. *International Journal of Early Years Education*, 21(1), 39–55.

Payne, K. (2020) Starting with children's democratic imagination: A response to *That's My Voice!* Participation and citizenship in early childhood. *Democracy & Education*, 28(2), 1–6.

Peacock, A., & Pratt, N. (2011). How young people respond to learning spaces outside school: A sociocultural perspective. *Learning Environments Research*, 14, 11–24.

Pederson, S. (2016) The good, the bad and the 'good enough' mother on the UK parenting forum Mumsnet. *Women's Studies International Forum*, 59, 32–38.

Penn, H. (2005) *Unequal childhoods.* London: Routledge

Penn, H. (2019) Understanding the contexts of leadership debates. *Contemporary Issues in Early Childhood*, 20(1), 104–109. doi: 10.1177/1463949118800768

Perkins, H. (2017) *From training to qualification: The journey of Level 3 Early Years student-practitioners*. EdD thesis, University of Sheffield.

Perry, P. (2016) *Risk assessments: Questions and answers*. ICE Virtual Library, ICE Publishing. Available at: https://www.icevirtuallibrary.com/doi/pdf/10.1680/raqa.60760.fm

Pollard, A. et al. (2008) *Reflective teaching* (3rd edition). London: Continuum.

Porges, S. W. (2005). The role of social engagement in attachment and bonding: A phylogenetic perspective. In C. S. Carter, L. Ahnert, K. E. Grossmann, S. B. Hrdy, M. E. Lamb, S. W. Porges, & N. Sachser (Eds.), *Attachment and bonding: A new synthesis* (pp. 33–54). Boston Review.

Pritchard, C. L. (2015) *Risk management: Concepts and guidance* (5th edition). London: Taylor and Francis.

Public Health England (2020) *Childhood obesity: Applying all our health*. [Online]. Available at: www.gov.uk/government/publications/childhood-obesity-applying-all-our-health/childhood-obesity-applying-all-our-health (accessed 15 January 2021).

Quality Assurance Agency (QAA). (2019). *Subject Benchmark Statements Early Childhood Studies*. London QAA

Quality Assurance Agency (QAA). (2022). *Subject Benchmark Statements Early Childhood Studies*. 4th Edition London QAA https://www.qaa.ac.uk/quality-code/subject-benchmark-statements/early-childhood-studies

Reder, P., Duncan, S., and Gray, M. (1993). *Beyond blame: Child abuse tragedies revisited*. London: Routledge

Regnaut, O., Jeu-Steenhouwer, M., Manaouil, C. and Gignon, M. (2015) *Risk factors for child abuse: Levels of knowledge and difficulties in family medicine: A mixed method study, BMC Research Notes*. 8. 10.1186/s13104-015-1607-9.

Rekalidou, G. and Panitsides E. A. (2015) What does it take to be a 'successful teacher'? Universities' role in preparing the future early-years workforce. *Early Years*, 35(4), 333–350. doi: 10.1080/09575146.2015.1080231

Roberts-Holmes, G., & Moss, P. (2021). *Neoliberalism and early childhood education: Markets, imaginaries and governance* (1st ed.). London: Routledge.

Roberts, R. (2010) *Wellbeing from birth*. London: Sage.

Rodd, J. (2006) *Leadership in early childhood* (3rd edition). Maidenhead: Open University Press.

Rogoff, B. (2003) *The cultural nature of human development*. Oxford: Oxford University Press.

Rolfe, G. (2001) *Critical reflection for nursing and the helping professions: A user's guide*. London:

Ropeik, D. and Gray, G. (2002) *Risk: A practical guide for deciding what's really safe and what's really dangerous in the world around you*. Boston, MA: Mariner Books.

Rose, J. (2011) Dilemmas of inter-professional collaboration: Can they be resolved? School of education and lifelong learning. *Children & Society* 25(2), 151–163

Royal College of Midwives (RCM) (2020) *Position statement: Infant feeding*. London: RCM. Available at: www.rcm.org.uk/media/2289/infant-feeding.pdf (accessed 7 December 2020).

Sadler, L. S., Slade, A., Close, N., Webb, D. L., Simpson, T., Fennie, K. and Mayes, L. C. (2013) Minding the baby: Enhancing reflectiveness to improve early health and relationship outcomes in an interdisciplinary home–visiting program. *Infant Mental Health Journal*, 34(5), 391–405.

Saleeby, D. (2002) *Strengths perspective in social work practice. (3rd edition).* Boston: Allyn & Bacon

Santana, L., Rothstein, D., and Bain, A. (2016). *Partnering with parents to ask the right questions: A powerful strategy for strengthening school-family partnerships.* Alexandria, VA: ASCD

Schon, D. A. (1983). *The reflective practitioner: How professionals think in action.* Aldershot: Avery Publishing

Schön, D. A. (1991) *The reflective practitioner: How professionals think in action.* Farnham, UK: Ashgate Publishing.

Schore, A. N. (2017) Modern attachment theory. In S. N. Gold (Ed.), *APA handbook of trauma psychology: Foundations in knowledge* (pp. 389–406). Washington, DC: American Psychological Association. https://doi.org/10.1037/0000019-020

Schunk, D. and Mullen, C. (2013) Toward a conceptual model of mentoring research. *Educational Psychology Review*, 25, 361–389.

Seitz, H. and Bartholemew, C. (2008) Powerful portfolios for young children. *Early Childhood Education Journal*, 36(1), 63–68.

Share, M. and Kerrins, L. (2013) Supporting parental involvement in children's early learning: Lessons from community childcare centres in Dublin's Docklands. *Child Care in Practice*, 19(4), 355–374. doi: 10.1080/13575279.2013.799457

Sharma, A. and Cockerill, H. (2014) *Mary Sheridan's from birth to five years: Children's developmental progress* (4th edition). Abingdon, UK: Routledge.

Sheridan, S. M., Pope Edwards, C., Marvin, C. A. and Knoche, L. L. (2009) Professional development in early childhood programs: Process issues and research needs. *Early Education and Development*, 20(3), 377–401.

Sheridan, S. M., Knoche, L. L., Boise, C. E., Moen, A. L., Lester, H., Edwards, C. P., Schumacher, R., & Cheng, K. (2019). Supporting preschool children with developmental concerns: Effects of the Getting Ready intervention on school-based social competencies and relationships. *Early Childhood Research Quarterly*, 48, 303–316

Shier, H. (2001) Pathways to participation: Openings, opportunities and obligations. *Children and Society*, 15(2), 107–117.

Silberfeld, C.H. and Mitchell, H. (2018) Graduates' perspectives on their Early Childhood Studies programmes and employment opportunities. *Early Years: An International Research Journal*, 41(1), 5–22

Simmons, H. (2020) *Surveillance of modern motherhood: Experiences of universal parenting courses.* Basingstoke: Palgrave Macmillan.

Siraj-Blatchford, I., Sylva, K., Muttock, S., Gilden, R., & Bell, D. (2002). *Researching effective pedagogy in the early years, DfES research report 356.* London: DfES.

Slade, A. (2005) Parental reflective functioning: An introduction. *Attachment & Human Development*, 7(3), 269–281.

Smidt, S. (2015) *Observing young children* (2nd edition). Abingdon, UK: Routledge.

Social Work England (2021) *Professional standards.* London: Social Work England. Available at: www.socialworkengland.org.uk/standards/standards-guidance/professional-standards-guidance/ (accessed 23 April 2021).

Solly, K. (2017) Following in Froebel's footsteps. *Early Years Educator*, 19(8), 38–44. https://doi.org/ 10.12968/eyed.2017.19.8.38

Solomon, M. (2019) Becoming comfortable with chaos: Making collaborative multi-agency working work. *Emotional and Behavioural Difficulties*, 24(4), 391–404, doi: 10.1080/13632752.2019.1633743

Spelke, E. (2004) Core knowledge. In N. Kanwisher and J. Duncan (Eds), *Attention and performance* (Vol. 20). Oxford: Oxford University Press.

Stewart, K. (2013) *Labour's record on the under fives: Policy, spending and outcomes 1997–2000*. Social policy in a cold climate working – paper 4. London: Centre for Analysis of Social Exclusion/ London School of Economics.

Strong-Wilson, T. (2007). Children and place: Reggio Emilia's environment as third teacher. *Theory Into Practice* 46(1):40–47

Sutterby, J. A. (Ed.) (2016) *Family involvement in early education and child care* [e-book]. Bingley, UK: Emerald.

Swick, K. J. and Williams, R. D. (2006) An analysis of Bronfenbrenner's bio-ecological perspective for early childhood educators: Implications for working with families experiencing stress. *Early Childhood Education Journal*, 33(5).

Sylva, K., Goff, J., Hall, J., Eisenstadt, N., Smith, T., Evangelou, M. and Sammons, P. (2015) Evaluation of Children's Centres in England (ECCE). *Strand 3: The organisation, services and reach of children's centres in England (DFE-RR433)*. London: Department for Education.

Sylva, K., Melhuish, E., Sammons, P., Siraj, I. and Taggart, B. (2014) *The Effective Pre-school, Primary and Secondary Education (EPPSE 3–16+) project: Students' educational outcomes at age 16*. London: Department for Education.

Sylva, K., Melhuish, E., Sammons, P., Siraj-Blatchford, I., & Taggart, B. (2010). *Early childhood matters: Evidence from the Effective Pre-School and Primary Education project*. Oxford: Routledge.

Sylva, K. Melhuish, E., Sammons, P., Siraj-Blatchford, I. and Taggart, B. (2004) *The Effective Provision of Pre-school Education (EPPE) project: Findings from Pre-School to end of Key Stage 1*. Nottingham: Department for Education.

Sylva, K., Melhuish, E., Sammons, P., Siraj-Blatchford, I., Taggart, B. and Elliot, K. (2003) *The Effective Provision of Pre-school Education (EPPE) project: Findings from the pre-school period*. London: Department for Education.

Taggart, G. (2011) Don't we care? The ethics and emotional labour of Early Years professionalism. *Early Years*, 31(1), 85–95.

Taylor, J., Woods, M. and Bond, E. (2013) *Early Childhood Studies: A multidisciplinary and holistic introduction* (3rd edition). London: Hodder.

Tedam, P. (2021) *Anti-oppressive social work practice*. London: Learning Matters/Sage.

Thompson, N. (2021a) *Anti-discriminatory practice* (7th edition). London: Red Globe Press.

Thompson, N. (2021b) *People skills* (5th edition). London: Red Globe Press.

Tickell, C. (2011) *The Early Years: Foundations for life, health and learning: An independent report on the Early Years Foundation Stage to Her Majesty's Government*. Nottingham: Department for Education.

Tuckman, B. W. and Jensen, M. A. (1977) Stages of small-team development revisited. *Team and organization studies*, 2(4), 419–427.

Tronto, J. C. (2013). *Caring democracy: Markets, equality, and justice.* New York: New York University Press

Twigg, E. (2021) The safeguarding practitioner. In R. Oates (Ed.), *The student practitioner in early childhood studies* (2nd edition, pp. 70–86). London: Routledge.

Turner, I., Reynolds, K. J., Lee, E., Subasic, E., and Bromhead, D. (2014). Well-being, school climate, and the social identity process: a latent growth model study of bullying perpetration and peer victimization. *School Psychology Quarterly.* 29, 320–335

UN General Assembly (1989) *Convention on the Rights of the Child.* United Nations Treaty Series. Vol. 1577, p. 3. New York: United Nations.

UNESCO. (United Nations Educational and Scientific and Cultural Organisation) (2006). *Cross-National compilation of national ECCE profiles.* Geneva: UNESCO International Bureau of Education

UNESCO (United Nations Educational and Scientific and Cultural Organisation) (2009) *General conference draft resolution with definition of ECCE.* Paris: UNESCO.

UNESCO (United Nations Educational and Scientific and Cultural Organisation) (2021) *Early childhood care and education.* Paris: UNESCO. Available at: https://en.unesco.org/themes/early-childhood-care-and-education lines 4-7

UNICEF (2005) *United Nations Convention on the Rights of the Child* (UNCRC). New York: UNICEF. Available at: https://downloads.unicef.org.uk/wp-content/uploads/2010/05/UNCRC_united_nations_convention_on_the_rights_of_the_child.pdf (accessed 30 April 2021).

UNICEF (2010) *The State of the World's Children 2010: Special edition.* New York: UNICEF.

UNICEF (2015) *The State of the World's Children 2015: Reimagine the future.* New York: UNICEF.

UNICEF. (2020). *Global Annual Results Report 2020: Goal Area 2.* New York: UNICEF

United Nations (2008) *Report on the Committee on the Rights of the Child.* New York: United Nations. Available at: www.iom.int/jahia/webdav/shared/shared/mainsite/policy_and_research/un/63/A_63_41.pdf (accessed 30 April 2021).

United Nations (2015) *The sustainable development goals.* New York: United Nations. Available at: https://sdgs.un.org/goals (accessed 21 April 2021).

Urban, Mathias & Dalli, Carmen. (2008). Special issue: Professionalism in early childhood education and care. *European Early Childhood Education Research Journal.* 16. 131–133.

Urrieta Jr, L. (2007) Figured worlds and education: An introduction to the special issue. *The Urban Review*, 39(2), 107–116.

Valchanov, B. L., Parry, D. C., Glover, T. D. and Mulcahy, C. M. (2015) 'A whole new world': Mothers' technologically mediated leisure. *Leisure Sciences*, 38(1), 50–67, DOI: 10.1080/01490400.2015.1043414

Valentzas, J. and Broni, G. (2014) *Communication cycle: Definition, process, models and examples.* Greece: Technological Institute of Western Macedonia. Available at: http://wseas.us/e-library/conferences/2014/Istanbul17.pdf

Van Laere, K. and Vandenbroeck, M. (2014) 100 jaar leerplicht in België: en nu de kleuters? [100 years of compulsory education: And now toddlers?] *Pedagogiek*, 34(3), 191–208. doi: 10.5117/PED2014.3.LAER

Van Laere, K., Van Houtte, M. and Vandenbroeck, M. (2018) Would it really matter? The democratic and caring deficit in 'parental involvement'. *European Early Childhood Education Research Journal*, 26(2), 187–200. doi: 10.1080/1350293X.2018.1441999

Vygotsky, L. (1978) *Mind in society: The development of higher psychological processes*. Cambridge, MA, and London: Harvard University Press.

Walker, G. (2018) *Working together for children: A critical introduction to multi-agency working* (2nd edition). London: Bloomsbury Academic.

Ward, U. (2018) How do early childhood practitioners define professionalism in their interactions with parents? *European Early Childhood Education Research Journal*, 26(2), 274–284. doi: 10.1080/1350293X.2018.1442043

White, N. (2017) How do stakeholders from multiple hierarchical levels of a large provincial health system define engagement? A qualitative study. *Implementation Science*, 12(1), 98

Willan, J. (2017) *Early childhood studies. A multidisciplinary approach*. London: Palgrave.

Williams, B., Williams, J. and Ullman, A. (2002) *Parental involvement in education*. Research Report 332. London: Department for Education and Skills.

Wilson, T. (2015) *Working with parents, carers and families in the early years: The essential guide*. Abingdon, UK: Routledge.

Winstone, R. (2020) The emergence of early childhood studies: An historic overview. In D. Fitzgerald and H. Maconochie (Eds), *Early childhood studies: A student's guide* (pp. 3–16). London: Sage.

Wood, E. (2008) Listening to young children: Multiple voices, meanings and understandings. In A. Paige-Smith and A. Craft (Eds), *Developing reflective practice in the Early Years*. Maidenhead: McGraw Hill/Open University Press.

Wood, E. and H. Hedges (2016) Curriculum in early childhood education: Critical questions about content, coherence, and control. *The Curriculum Journal*, 27(3), 387–405. doi:10. 1080/09585176.2015.1129981.

Woodhead, M. (2016). *Early childhood development in the SDGs young lives policy brief 28*. January 2016. Oxford: Young Lives

Woods, M., Thurtle, V. and Silberfeld, C. (1999) A report on the post-course destination, reflections and career aspirations of the Early Childhood Studies students who graduated from University College Suffolk in 1996. *Journal of Further and Higher Education*, 23(1), 17–30.

Woods, P. A. (2010). Democratic leadership: drawing distinctions with distributed leadership. *Theory and Practice*. 7(1), 3–26

Working Group of the All-Party Parliamentary Group on a Fit and Healthy Childhood (2020) *Wellbeing and nurture: Physical and emotional security in childhood*. Chair: S. McCabe. London. Available at: https://fhcappg.org.uk/ (accessed 2 April 2021).

World Bank (2020) *Primary school starting age (years)*. Washington, DC: World Bank. Available at: https://data.worldbank.org/indicator/se.prm.ages?view=map (accessed 10 April 2021).

World Health Organisation (WHO) (1948) *Complementary feeding: Family foods for breastfed children*. Geneva: WHO. Available at: www.who.int/health-topics/complementary-feeding#tab=tab_2 (accessed 7 December 2020).

World Health Organisation (WHO) (2016) *Inspire: Seven strategies for ending violence against children*. Geneva: WHO. Available at: www.who.int/publications/i/item/inspire-seven-strategies-for-ending-violence-against-children (accessed 30 April 2021).

Yates, E. (2021 The critically reflective and creative practitioner. In R. Oates (Ed.), *The student practitioner in early childhood studies* (2nd edition pp 108–122). Abingdon, UK: Routledge.

Yates, E., Twigg, E., Wall, S. and Appleby, M. (2021) The emerging practitioner. In R. Oates (Ed.), *The student practitioner in early childhood studies* (2nd edition pp 19–33). Abingdon, UK: Routledge.

INDEX

Page numbers in *italic* indicate figures and in **bold** indicate tables.